Words in Ads

Dedication
to H.A.P. Myers and Pat Myers

Words in Ads

Greg Myers

**Department of Linguistics & Modern English Language
University of Lancaster**

Edward Arnold
A member of the Hodder Headline Group
LONDON   MELBOURNE   AUCKLAND

First published in Great Britain 1994

Distributed in the USA by Routledge, Chapman and Hall, Inc.
29 West 35th Street, New York, NY 10001

British Library Cataloguing in Publication Data

Available on request

ISBN 0-340-61444-7

Produced by GreenGate Publishing Services, Tonbridge, Kent
Printed in Great Britain for Edward Arnold,
a division of Hodder Headline plc,
338 Euston Road, London NW1 3BH,
by St Edmundsbury Press, Bury St Edmunds, Suffolk.
Bound by Hartnolls Ltd, Bodmin, Cornwall

Contents

Illustrations

Preface

New! Improved!! Not Tested on Animals!!!

It is only fair that a book on advertising state its sales brief up front: my aim is to lure unsuspecting students of media, popular culture, and communication into studying further how language works in society. I could have done this by looking at the language of radio, or newspapers, or school children, or scientists, or poetry, all of which have been the subjects of intensive linguistic study. But I am focusing on ads here because of their complexity, their ubiquity, and their importance in any model of how we communicate and of what we take for granted about society. Besides, I enjoy ads.

I should say here that I have no expertise in copy writing or marketing; what I know about is analysing texts. A marketing textbook would tell you how to analyse society and copy in order to sell things, but I analyse sales pitches in order to find out about language and communication in society. I start with the most basic units – sounds and letters. Then I go on to the words, and the associations they have and ways they are interpreted. I look at different types and structures of sentences, and at advertisers' uses of varieties of English. I go on to the way texts are interpreted in context – how we interpret implied meanings, and non-literal meanings, and how our interpretation of words relates them to pictures. Finally I apply these analyses to three issues of social concern: advertising on the environment, on AIDS, and on smoking.

The examples of ads that I have chosen are not all prize winners, and are not offered as a representative sample; they are what was handy at the time to make the point (with something of a bias towards ads I enjoyed). I have tried to include a range of products, from a range of countries, just so that it would be clear that the clever ads were not restricted to, say, beer ads in Britain. I have included descriptions of some broadcast ads, even though they can hardly have their full effect on the page; perhaps my efforts at description will make readers realise just how complex these effects are. Actually, both broadcast and print ads lose a great deal, and I will have to beg forgiveness from the creative teams for what reproduction or description does to their work. But one of the advantages of advertising as material for discussing language is that unless the readers happen to be climbing in the Himalayas or orbiting the earth in a space capsule, they should have no trouble finding examples of their own – on the nearest radio, television, bus stop, or T-shirt. I can thus restrict myself to a few examples for each topic.

I have avoided breaking up the text with what would have to be thick forests of references. Instead, I follow each chapter with a rather opinionated guide to further reading; readers who do not have access to a full university library (or who find the books they want have already been checked out) may find these selective comments more useful in determining what to look for than a longer bibliography would be. Because I am trying to include a wide range of topics, I will sometimes just mention issues that have been discussed at much greater length, and with more sophistication, elsewhere. If my book gets readers to go on to find these more detailed and demanding studies, it will have served its purpose.

I teach in a linguistics department where there is an excellent group of critical linguists; but there is more to language studies than linguistics. Those who have already read some studies of the language of advertising will recognise my debts throughout to such non-linguists as Roland Barthes, Judith Williamson, Gillian Dyer, Kathy Myers, Robert Goldman, and Roland Marchand, as well as to such linguists as Geoffrey Leech and Guy Cook. I have drawn on the work of literary critics, sociologists, social historians, social psychologists, philosophers, journalists, novelists, and even the occasional advertising copywriter. I have also benefited from being internal examiner on Ph.D. dissertations by Mary Talbot, Olumide Osinubi, and Kan Qian, and from having supervised undergraduate dissertations by Eloise Mackirdy, Vera Tang, Nicola Mullarkey, and Anne Marie Greisen, though I have been careful not to poach their examples. My thanks to Dan Calef of Oakland, California, for taping ads during late night movies, and to Carol Rhoades of Austin, Texas, for back issues of *The New Yorker*; thanks also to Kan Qian for her tape of 24 hours of Granada ads, and to Nicola Mullarkey for her tape of independent radio ads.

This book was written because Lesley Riddle, of Edward Arnold, suggested it. It is based on lectures on the Culture and Communication first year course at Lancaster University; my thanks to the many students in my seminars who brought in examples and made suggestions, and to my colleagues on the course: John Soyland, Dede Boden, Suzette Heald, Norman Fairclough, Mark Sebba, David Lee, and Kan Qian. Special thanks to Bron Szerszinski for help with Chapter 11, and to students and staff at Georgia Tech (Department of Language, Literature, and Culture) and the University of Texas at Austin (Division of Rhetoric) who discussed versions of that chapter. I received helpful comments on parts of this book from Mary Talbot, Elena Semino, Jonathan Culpeper, David Lee, Kan Qian, John Soyland, and Lester Faigley; thanks especially to Elena and Jonathan for their help with the Glossary.

Personal thanks to Tess Cosslett, for putting up with endless dinner table talk about ads, and to Alice Myers, for calling me to look at the telly whenever she saw an ad she liked. This book is dedicated to my father, who found it interesting to read Judith Williamson at bedtime, and to my mother, who helped by taping ads during NBA games.

Greg Myers

Epigraph

On the whole, there is no denying that Advertisements constitute a class of composition intimately connected with the arts and sciences, and peculiarly calculated to illustrate the domestic habits of a people. Porson used to say, that a single Athenian newspaper would be worth all the commentaries on Aristophanes put together. Surely, then, a brief analysis of modern puffery will be no unacceptable bequest to posterity.

A. Hayward, 'The Advertising System',
 Edinburgh Review 77 (February 1843).

1

The Air in Your Aero
Introduction

Dorothy L. Sayers worked for 11 years as an advertising copywriter at S. H. Benson in London, before going on to fame as a detective writer. In 1933, after she'd left advertising, she wrote a novel, *Murder Must Advertise*, in which her detective hero had to take on a job in an ad agency to investigate a crime. What he learned in a week as a junior copywriter is summed up in one sentence:

> He learned the average number of words that can be crammed into four inches of copy; that Mr. Armstrong's fancy could be caught by an elaborately-drawn layout, whereas Mr. Hankin looked on art-work as a waste of the copy-writer's time; that the word 'pure' was dangerous, because, if lightly used, it laid the client open to prosecution by the Government inspectors, whereas the words 'highest quality', 'finest ingredients', 'packed under the best conditions' had no legal meaning, and were therefore safe; that the expression 'giving work to umpteen thousand British employees in our model works at so-and-so' was not by any means the same thing as 'British made throughout'; that the north of England liked its butter and margarine salted, whereas the south preferred it fresh; that the *Morning Star* would not accept any advertisements containing the word 'cure', though there was no objection to such expressions as 'relieve' or 'ameliorate', and that, further, any commodity that professed to 'cure' anything might find itself compelled to register as a patent medicine and use an expensive stamp; that the most convincing copy was always written tongue

in cheek, a genuine conviction of the commodity's worth producing – for some reason – poverty and flatness of style; that if, by the most far-fetched stretch of ingenuity, an indecent meaning could be read into a headline, that is the meaning that the great British Public would infallibly read into it; that the great aim and object of the studio artist was to crowd the copy out of the advertisement and that, conversely, the copy-writer was a designing villain whose ambition was to cram the space with verbiage and leave no room for the sketch; that the layout man, a meek ass between two burdens, spent a miserable life trying to reconcile these opposing parties; and further, that all departments alike united in hatred of the client, who persisted in spoiling good layouts by cluttering them with coupons, free gifts offers, lists of local agents, and realistic portraits of hideous and uninteresting cartons, to the detriment of his own interests and the annoyance of everybody concerned.

What interests me is just how much of what the detective learned about advertising has to do with language: the demands of brevity, the relations of text and pictures, the semantics and associations and legal status of words, the implications of phrases, the effects of style, the side-stepping of taboos, and most of all, the unpredictability of the effects. But these questions are inseparable from other practices of copy writing – dealing with other parts of the agency, and with the media, and (worst of all) with the client. Lord Peter Wimsey being who he is, he not only solves the murder case, he also comes up with some great copy and a successful promotion scheme (and bowls brilliantly at the inter-agency cricket match).

The aim of this book is to try to link the words in ads to social structure, not by going into an agency, as Lord Peter Wimsey did, but by stepping back from the ads and seeing them as texts. Advertising makes us aware of language, the way poetry does. But it also makes us aware of social structures, in a way that poetry, as it is conventionally taught, does not. One way of tracing these connections of language to social structure is to look at the ads in a way different from our usual reading as consumers, to make them strange.

In this chapter I will use two television commercials to introduce some of the approaches that run through this book. Here is a description of an advertisement for a chocolate bar that appeared in the middle of a broadcast of Disney's *The Reluctant Dragon*.

> The ad begins with the pop song 'Oh oh oh it's magic', and the O on the screen becomes lips. Then it runs through a series of snatches of songs and phrases, each with an 'Oh' in it, each for just a few seconds (a doctor saying 'Say oh,' a reggae song, Mendelsohn's 'Oh for the wings of a dove', Al Jolson, from *The Jazz Singer*) and for each the

cartoon O is transformed to illustrate the soundtrack. The slogan 'It's the air in your Aero that makes you go O' comes with a picture of the chocolate bar at the end.

Now you could argue that with so much else going on, language was not very important to this ad. It would certainly fall flat if you just read the script for it, or just had the slogan. But it makes extraordinarily deft play with language at a number of levels.

My first point is that

1. Ads are made up of patterns of textual choices

We could start with the slogan

It's the air in your Aero that makes you go O.

This plays on the relationship between *Oh*, the exclamation, the shape of the letter *O*, and the sound /o/ as part of the product name. (Linguists write symbols between slash marks – /o/ – when they are talking about a sound, not a written letter). The pattern of these *Oh-O-/o/s* relies on linked choices. The sounds that go with the letters *air* and the *o* are both repeated.

It's the air in your Aero that makes you go O.

Not only that, the pattern of stresses makes a regular metre – two unstressed syllables followed by a stressed syllable. (You will have to read it aloud to check this.)

It's the AIR in your AERo that MAKES you go O.

This sort of regular patterning is part of what attracts linguists to ads – the copywriters are very self-conscious in their use of language. You can test the effect by trying to rephrase the ad without the poetic effects

An Aero is full of holes that make you say Ah.

The point is the same but it's not very catchy. And as we will see in the next chapter, when there are many ads competing for the audience's attention, there is an enormous premium on finding patterns of language that are unusual or memorable. The rest of the ad is an elaborate series of plays on the slogan. It starts with a metaphorical relation between the *O* at then end of the product name and the mouth that eats the product. This provides the basis for a series of phrases, all linked by an *Oh*. This is the sort of play with sounds and letters I will discuss in Chapter 3. We would expect to find such play in some periods and markets, and not in others.

The structure of this slogan is also crucial to its effect. It is constructed to put the product name near the end, where it will have maximum weight. But the Aero slogan is a statement. It doesn't tell us or ask us to eat Aero chocolate but states something about the Aero bars we already eat. This choice of sentence type, and the structure of sentences, will be dealt with in Chapter 4. One important result of stepping back from the ad this way and analysing the language is that we learn to see choices; we realise even with a slogan that has been thoroughly drummed into us, it could have been otherwise.

We can get that far just looking at the linguistic features of the ads in isolation – in some ads there will be very complex formal play with these patterns, and in others not much. But of course the effect does not just arise from a repeated *O*, from the regularity in the occurrence of a letter. Each variation of the *O* has different associations – medical language, a concert recital, rock and roll, reggae, soul. They are not only different kinds of music, they are done with identifiably different social varieties of English. It's an effect like flipping the channels on a TV, or like the snatches juxtaposed in house music, or like leafing through some pop music magazines. And the different voices alternate male and female, high and low, ending with a very deep voice with exaggerated intonation, and a very feminine voice, also with exaggerated intonation.

These associations and meaning are confirmed by the little sketches that flash around the *O* – palm trees or hands or a mirror or wings. Analysing these associations with words and phrases and visuals will be the topics of Chapters 5 and 10. The associations are crucial to the effect of the ad – for instance the suggestive mock sexiness of the last two voices. It's not sex it promises; it's a kind of excitement – as if adding holes was adding something. There are also double meanings, so that the Os are at the same time holes, letters, and exclamations. Puns like this are particularly common in contemporary British advertising, but I will show they turn up in all sorts of places. This leads to a second point that runs through this book.

> 2. *Linguistic features in one text are interpreted in relation to those in other texts.*

Part of the effect of these ads is their relation to other cultural artefacts – what is called *intertextuality*. You may not be able to trace all the linguistic and musical allusions in the Aero ad (I had to ask for help from several people), but you do recognise them as allusions to different periods and subcultures. All ads, even those making no explicit allusions, carry associations from other texts: ads, movies, novels, everyday talk. Language in ads comes to us used.

We can see this intertextuality more clearly if we look at the next ad in the same commercial break, which is for a breakfast cereal. It includes a song that is recognised by British audiences as the theme song of a television programme – any group of schoolchildren can sing it, though it was broadcast long before they were born (perhaps because it was also parodied by Monty

Python). The music opens with a fanfare. The visuals start with a spinning picture, such as used to indicate a change of scene in the conventions of 1950s television editing, and an arrow sailing through the air and hitting a tree. With the first stanza, Robin Hood rides through the wood, crowds cheer, Maid Marian waves a handkerchief from the tower of a castle. The second stanza, of course, was not part of the television theme song. While it is playing, Robin Hood sees the Sheriff of Nottingham eating the cereal that will presumably make him invincible. He pauses. Then he rides away, Maid Marian sighs, and the crowds jeer. The commercial ends with the product slogan. Without knowledge of Robin Hood, and more specifically, the television programme and its song, this ad does not make much sense. The intertextuality includes not only the parody of the song, but a parody of now somewhat dated visual conventions, and the exaggerated hamming of the players. But intertextuality is not just a matter of such specific references to other texts; it can involve references to whole subject matters of language.

We can see that it makes no sense to isolate the language of advertising, expecting it to contain certain words used in certain ways that would distinguish it from the language of medicine, education, fairy tales, sports, child-raising, or seduction. I will use the term *discourses* for these languages linked to a specific subject matter, social group, and setting. We could not make sense of ads unless we came to them with experiences of various discourses. That is why the ads of a different culture or subculture or a different period can be so strange to us. When I moved from Texas to Britain, I found it impossible to understand most billboards (or posters on hoardings as they are called here). That is not because the words in American and British English are so different, taken in their isolated, dictionary meanings, but because the ads typically drew on daily uses of language I had not yet encountered (see Chapters 5 and 7).

If advertising is not a particular, predictable kind of language, if there is no discourse it cannot incorporate, what makes it distinctive? To answer this, we need to step back and ask what the ads are doing. That's easy, you say, they're selling something. Of course they may be doing this very indirectly, selling us a service or an attitude towards a corporation, or trying to get us to change our behaviour. And their effect may be quite different from that intended. They may entertain or annoy use, without causing us to buy anything. With the act of selling goes a stereotypical form. This form, for instance, is what leads us to expect that these television ads will end with the name of the product and the logo or slogan. Some ads do not do this, but they gain their effectiveness by playing off our expectations. This leads us to another assumption underlying the analyses in this book:

3. Advertisements are stereotypical acts of communication – a genre.

The study of a genre leads us to some of the typical practices that constrain the way an advertisement is produced. My analysis so far has treated the ad as if it was a poem in a literature anthology, as if we might attribute all the linguistic choices to an individual poet. But we know that these choices are shaped by the way the business works. For instance, in the passage from *Murder Must Advertise*, Dorothy Sayers mentions the rival interests within the agency, the problems of media, and the intervention of the client. (Similar social constraints shape poetry, but that is not usually stressed in teaching literature.) The result is that ads are in some ways very much alike, but that each tries to play off in some way against our expectations of the genre. For example, the form of the cereal ad is funny because we are familiar with ads in which the product helps the hero defeat a villain. Here the villain has the product, and mocks the hero. We are familiar enough with the genre to enjoy the violation of our expectations.

If genres are social actions, it might seem that the only way to investigate genres would be to look in detail at how advertisements are produced, and there have been a few books of this sort. But one must also be cautious with such accounts. For one thing, the successful advertisers who write about their work often write in a rather oracular style. Like Nobel Prize winning novelists or scientists, they offer a retrospective account that is fuzzy on the details and that reads backwards from their demonstrable success. The meaning of an ad (or a poem or a movie) is not just what the creator intended. This is as true for an articulate advertising writer like David Ogilvy or Peter Mayle as it is for a novelist like William Faulkner or a director like John Ford. If the creative team was given the brief to promote Aero on the basis of it having more holes than chocolate in it, I don't imagine that someone said, 'Let's try a line in anapaestic tetrameter with two kinds of assonance and some graphological deviation, and then add some intertextuality.' But they would say, after they came up with this way of putting the slogan, that it was catchy. That is where I come in. Authors are not necessarily the best people to understand the complex web of texts around them, the constraints of production, or the interpretations of readers. If they were, advertising would be a much simpler business – we could just find the gurus and listen to them.

We cannot understand the genre of advertisements just by looking at how they are produced. The stereotypical act of communication that they embody also requires readers and viewers. This requirement leads to another key assumption of this book

4. Ads construct positions for the audience.

We can start with the simplest indication of audience, the pronouns (which I discuss in chapter 6). Who is *you* in the Aero ad? Well it is possessive – it refers to people who already own the product. This may not seem odd. But ask yourself, do you at the moment have an Aero chocolate bar in your pocket? The ad constructs a position in your interpretation whether you actually step into it or not. But the ad goes beyond the use of the pronoun – for instance it is the female voice that addresses us in the Aero ad in the sexy voice as *you*. It is important to note that this position constructed in a text does not necessarily correspond to a real audience, or on the other hand to some idealised market sector. In the rest of this three minute commercial break, you are put through a whole series of roles that are unlikely to be embodied in one viewer at one time: chocolate eater (Aero), breakfast eater, cat owner (Wiskas), parent (Fairy liquid), adolescent (acne medication), YUPPIE (Ferrero Rocher chocolates). Being able to watch television means taking up or rejecting a whole series of positions in rapid succession.

As I will explain in the next chapter, it was a crucial change in the history of advertising when the advertisers realised that selling might not focus on virtues of the product, it might focus on offering possible new positions to the consumer. And ads since the beginning have been criticised for having this effect on a helpless audience. It's not just critics who say this – the ad industry itself is sometimes happy enough to emphasise its powers (as McCann Erickson argue that its Nescafe ads, discussed in Chapter 8, led to an increase in sales), while at other times presenting themselves as helpless servants of larger social forces (as Lowe Howard-Spink present themselves in defending a cigarette ad, in Chapter 13).

The important point for us is that viewers of these ads are not constrained to take from them what the advertiser intended. That brings me to my fifth key assumption:

5. Audiences reconstruct ads in diverse ways.

Let me give an example. The cereal ad that I have described is a favourite of my daughter's. Though she is too young to have seen the original programmes, she knows who Robin Hood is and enjoys singing the song, and she realises there is something funny about Robin Hood turning and running away. So I asked her why he runs away. 'Maybe he doesn't like [this cereal] for breakfast,' she said. I doubt very much that that is what the company wanted the audience to think. But it is a possible interpretation of the text. The ad requires viewers to be active, to think of some relationship between the story constructed by them and the slogan with the box of cereal at the end. Viewers do not simply sit in front of the TV and think – 'I'll buy that, I'll buy that' (not adult viewers anyway). They notice some things, don't notice others, and link what they do notice to their own sense of the world.

Ads are not consumed alone: they depend on interactions with others, as my daughter would sing the song to friends. They may enjoy parodies of the ads, jokes with their friends; they may alter posters or slogans. In Britain one can ask someone about the Nescafe ads, or British Telecom ads, or others people talk about ; in America phrases from ads even enter presidential debates ('Where's the beef?'). Ads are common culture in a way that even the most popular movies or books are not. I can refer to 'the Heineken ad' and expect everyone in the room to know what I am talking about, and I would not do the same with even the most popular book on the best-seller list. I take up these effects in Chapter 13.

Just as I don't imagine copywriters talking about ads using the terms I do, I don't imagine that viewers of the ad write the slogan down and pore over it, underlining some letters, and then listing the variations, the way I have. They may ignore it, or misremember it, or leave the room, or hum bits of it. I am saying that this kind of close linguistic reading provides a vocabulary for talking about what happens in everyday experiences of ads. And perhaps the distance between my close reading and the everyday experience is not always so great. After all, someone who watches much television will watch some ads, or at least see them, many many times. Still, we need to remember that the exercise of analysing an ad does not lead us to a definitive interpretation. But it is a worthwhile exercise, if only because it leads us to the unpredictable diversity of effects of language.

I have talked about the practices of advertisers, and the practices of readers. What larger social system holds these together? Here is one way of defining it:

6. *Advertisements offer a relationship between the advertiser and audience members based on the associations of meanings with commodities.*

This may seem obvious enough, but it is crucial to the way we interpret ads. For instance, the British ads for Silk Cut cigarettes that show enigmatic pictures of mutilated purple silk would be incomprehensible unless we assumed that they must be trying to sell us *something*, and that, because of that health warning that is the only text, the something must be cigarettes. To do this the ad must define a commodity, something distinctive to buy and sell. But, as with chocolate bars or breakfast cereals, the brands may be virtually identical. The ads make them different by giving them meanings, for instance, the sexiness and sophistication of the Aero advertisement. Ads make sense in a system in which we work to get money and define ourselves by the things we buy. As I will show in chapter 2, this system is not natural or inevitable; it came into being over time, in response to changing systems of production and communication.

Sometimes I may seem to be uncritical, or at least not as hard on companies and advertising agencies as I could be. This is not because I think that the advertising system gives us the best of all possible worlds. But I do not accept all the assumptions that underlie some common criticisms of advertising. The main line of critique has been that ads make us buy things because we are deluded into giving the things meanings they don't have. Real meanings, in this view, are based on relationships of work and production. Advertising plays on and conceals the real alienation of life in capitalism and in a commodity culture. It replaces real human relationships with relationships based on things. It uses the sense of incompleteness that goes with our work in this system to offer commodities as a way of fulfilment. More recently, though, there has been interest in just how we give ads meanings. Cultural analysts have been more interested in consumption, and are less certain that the basics of production and necessities of life are the realities determining cultural change.

When we say that the purpose of ads is to sell things and increase profits, we have said something essential, but we have not said everything there is to say about their social effects. Similarly, we could say that the purpose of universities is to produce and transmit knowledge and certify learning, and one cannot understand the work of lecturers without seeing this purpose. But universities are also places where people find lovers, play football, drink to excess, come out, learn to cook, none of which activities come under the functional definition of producing and transmitting knowledge. Whatever ads were intended to do, they may also entertain, subvert, annoy; they may provide the occasion for other texts and all sorts of uses. In this book, I start with the pleasure I take in ads, with the sense I have that they can be fun, and I follow this to some of the diverse interpretations that might be possible.

Let us take one striking example of the multiplicity of interpretations. This is a full page newspaper ad with a picture of a duck covered in oil. The text is as follows:

Shetland Islands
January 1993
United Colours of Benetton.

At the time it appeared, its interpretation was fairly straightforward for most newspaper readers. Now much of the context that made it interpretable has faded. The slogan 'United Colours of Benetton' tells us that it is advertising a clothing chain. But it is not telling you anything about jumpers. Indeed, the juxtaposition of the slogan with the blackened oily duck seems ironic – all colour has been erased. You need to know that it appeared in British newspapers days after the Braer oil spill in the Shetland Islands. You have to be aware of some of the images in other Benetton ads; this duck can be paralleled to the AIDS patient, the flood, and the other symbols of human suffering used in other ads. It is part of a controversial campaign that tries to associate the name of a retailer with concern for social problems.

Some of the comments on this ad suggested it was opportunistic, since Benetton was not an organisation that did anything about the oil spill. Other comments suggested that it was no more opportunistic than other organisations that used pictures of oily birds to make appeals for money, such as the Royal Society for the Protection of Birds, or the Friends of the Earth. Seasoned Benetton watchers pointed out that the same duck had appeared before, after the oil spill in the Persian Gulf during the Gulf War. A Benetton spokesperson admitted this, and said that the reuse of the image only suggested the universality of the problem.

Discussion of the Benetton campaign has focused on whether it is exploiting social problems, or increasing awareness of them. All journalistic comments, and most people surveyed, say they are exploitative. But the firm's sales have still increased spectacularly since the ad campaign began. The point is that the stated revulsion of a large part of the potential audience probably doesn't matter to Benetton; certainly the attitude of a middle-aged university lecturer does not. The ad is not supposed to make me run out and buy a jumper. It is part of creating an image for the company, as different from other retailers, or more important, creating an image for its consumers. Benetton's ads differ from earlier image ads because they do this by being talked about, not by any direct association with, say, pictures of elegant people. But it is still drawing on our expectations about how this genre of newspaper advertising works.

The main point of this chapter is to suggest that the subject of words in ads includes such topics as assonance and rhyme (Chapter 3), and sentence structure (Chapter 4), but it also leads to basic social issues in how we define our identities, our relation to each other, and our ability to act. I listed the following assumptions that I will make through the book.

1. Texts are made up of patterns of textual choices.

2. Linguistic features in one text are interpreted in relation to those in other texts.

3. Advertisements are stereotypical acts of communication – a genre.

4. Ads construct positions for the audience.

5. Audiences reconstruct ads in diverse ways.

6. Advertisements offer a relationship between the advertiser and audience based on the associations of meanings with commodities.

But before exploring contemporary texts in detail, it will help to sketch out briefly how ads came to be the way they are.

Further reading
Approaches to analysing ads

There are two major books in the linguistic analysis of advertising, Geoffrey Leech's *English in Advertising*, and Guy Cook's *The Discourse of Advertising*; both are excellent, and offer much more detailed treatments than I can give here. Cook gives a thorough bibliography. Torben Vestergaard and Kim Schrøder, in *The Language of Advertising*, take a somewhat different view from mine: their book is more about critical commentary than about detailed linguistic analysis. Shorter introductions to different approaches can be found in Gunther Kress, 'Educating Readers: Language in Advertising'; Walter Nash and Ronald Carter, *Seeing Through Language*, and Michael Toolan, 'The Language of Press Advertising.' To see what a great philologist could do with an ad, see Leo Spitzer, 'American Advertising Explained as Popular Art.'

Approaches through cultural studies give less detailed analysis of the language, but explore more thoroughly the issues of social theory that I have touched on here. The classic study is Judith Williamson, *Decoding Advertisements*, and all later studies are indebted to it, even when they criticise it. Gillian Dyer, *Advertising as Communication*, is perhaps the most readable introduction to this kind of analysis, and Kathy Myers, *Understains . . . The Sense and Seduction of Advertising*, has witty and thought provoking case studies; I have drawn on both of them. Robert Goldman, *Reading Ads Socially*, is in part an extension of Williamson, showing how analysis of advertisements can help us understand the commodity system. The theory may be difficult, but the examples are clear and well presented. Michael Schudson, *Advertising: The Uneasy Persuasion*, is an excellent and complex study of the social background of advertising, but it is not particularly concerned with language.

My underlying assumptions about genre and social practices in this chapter owe a great deal to Gunther Kress, *Linguistic Processes in Socio-cultural Practice*, and to Norman Fairclough, *Language and Power,* and *Discourse and Social Change*; all three books analyse some ads as examples. Attitudes in recent cultural studies can be seen in Paul Willis, *Common Culture*, in John Fiske, *Understanding Popular Culture* and *Reading the Popular*; and in Lawrence Grossberg, Cary Nelson, and Paula Treichler, eds., *Cultural Studies*.

2

7 Shades Whiter
Some Advertising History

Here are four sections of advertising copy. In which decade do you think each of them appeared?

A. *The afternoon concert – and the washing done*

[picture of two women, one sitting by a radio and the other standing, looking on in astonishment]

With Persil, washing is done almost as soon as breakfast.

You want five minutes to get ready; then Persil takes thirty to make the clothes spotlessly clean. No work, no worry; Persil does it all, and without harm to anything. As soon as the concert starts you can start to listen in without the faintest feeling of duty neglected, thanks to Persil.

Write for a free booklet which tells how to use Persil.

[in small print at the bottom]

Persil is full of oxygen which is set free in the washing. The Persil oxygen eats up the dirt, leaving clothes clean and unharmed.

[picture of the package]

B. [picture of a woman hanging out wash, with a large cake of Sunlight Soap on the ground, against a snowy background, while a boy tries to trap a bird under a basket]

The afternoon concert—
and the washing done

With Persil, washing is done almost
as soon as breakfast.

You want five minutes to get ready; then
Persil takes thirty to make the clothes
spotlessly clean. No work, no worry;
Persil does it all, and without harm to
anything. As soon as the concert starts
you can start to listen-in without the
faintest feeling of duty neglected, thanks
to Persil.

In 3½d and 5½d Packets

Persil is full of oxygen
which is set free in the
washing. The Persil
oxygen eats up the dirt,
leaving the clothes clean
and unharmed.

Persil

Write for free
booklet which
tells how to use
Persil.

Sunlight gets the washing done
Leaving time for sport and fun.

C. Whose mother hasn't jumped to this year's news about Persil?

[picture of two girls skipping rope, one in a grey dress and the other in white]

Always tops for whiteness, Persil now has a new quality – a special quality which gives a *radiant, respondent finish* to white clothes.

Persil perks up tired whites marvellously. It even renews the appearance of those that have become dingy after chancy washings when you couldn't get Persil. Scientific tests prove that Persil now makes whites up to 7 shades whiter. Persil is best and safest for the whole wash.

　　PERSIL WASHES 7 SHADES WHITER

D. [gilt-framed painting of two women sitting outdoors, with a bright spot over one woman as if the painting had been cleaned there]

Restore your clothes to their former glory

No matter how much care you take each time you wash your clothes, sooner or later colours dull and whites lose their 'just off the rail' brightness.

Now Improved Biological Action Concentrated Persil changes all that. Its special action helps rejuvenate your clothes with every wash. This new Persil formula will actually remove accumulated dirt and greasy stains, which over time can noticeably dull colours and whites.

Now, with Biological Action Concentrated Persil, your clothes will stay not just cleaner but visibly whiter, instead of becoming faded memories.

[picture of the box, held up by a woman's hand]

You could probably date these ads right away from the accompanying pictures – visual styles are clearly tied to a medium and a period. The changing product names may give the dates away. But the texts are harder, because some of the same appeals ('washes whiter') continue through the periods. In addition, there are some linguistic turns that you might consider antiquated now, maybe without being sure exactly why. The rhyme in B, for instance, may sound dated, and the pun in C may seem fairly current. But some of the same appeals persist surprisingly. I am going to try to provide an admittedly oversimplified framework for interpreting these historical ads, as a way of relating the ads to the present. (By the way, A is from 1927, B is from 1891, C is from 1947, and D is from 1992).

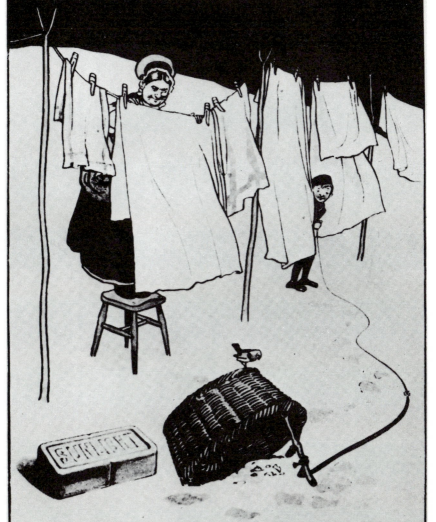

SUNLIGHT SOAP

Sunlight gets the Washing done
Leaving Time for Sport and Fun.

Whose mother hasn't jumped to this year's news about Persil?

ALWAYS tops for whiteness, Persil now has a new quality —a special quality which gives a *radiant, resplendent finish* to white clothes.

Persil perks up tired whites marvellously. It even renews the appearance of those that have become dingy after chancy washings when you couldn't get Persil.

Scientific tests prove that Persil now makes whites up to 7 shades whiter. Persil is best and safest for the whole wash.

PERSIL WASHES 7 shades **WHITER**

Conventional histories of advertising, especially if they are written by advertising people, usually stress the constant improvement of the marketing strategies and copywriting. Each new decade becomes a new age that sees discovery of new and improved methods. We may tend to treat earlier ads as just quaint because of their superficial differences, failing to see the basic ways they are like current ads. In this limited view, if ads are seen as having a relation to a changing society, it is because of their *content* – the way these ads refer to listening to the afternoon concert, or to hand washing, or to whites rather than colours, and others may refer to unemployment in the 1930s, rationing in the 1940s, or the Cold War in the 1950s. Rather than focus on that kind of change in *content*, I will look at what their *form* tells us about society.

To do this I am going to divide the history of advertising into three periods, focusing on

- the 1890s and the period before World War I

- the 1920s and the period between the wars

- the period from the 1960s to the present.

I am going to compare those periods, starting with the problems of producing and selling things, and seeing how these relate to the linguistic features on which we might focus later in the course. In each of these periods I will look at

- changes in what is advertised and where

- changes in how we read

- changes in the ways ads relate to other ads and other texts

There were changes on all these levels in all three periods, but I will stress the first in looking at the 1890s, the signs and meanings in looking at the 1920s, and the uses of discourse in looking at the 1960s. I will take most of my examples from advertisements for soap, which has been one of the most heavily advertised products in all three periods, focusing on those by Unilever, the largest advertiser in the United Kingdom, and Proctor & Gamble, the largest advertiser in the United States.

This short history focuses on the making of *commodities*, of things to sell and buy. It was Karl Marx who said, in the first chapter of *Capital* :

> A commodity appears at first sight an extremely obvious, trivial thing. But its analysis brings out that it is a very strange thing, abounding in metaphysical subtleties and theological niceties (p. 163).

Marx's central insight, for our purposes, is that commodities aren't just useful; they are part of a system of exchange in which they take on different

Restore your clothes to their former glory.

No matter how much care you take each time you wash your clothes, sooner or later colours dull and whites lose their 'just off the rail' brightness.

Now Improved Biological Action Concentrated Persil changes all that. Its special action helps rejuvenate your clothes with every wash.

This new Persil formula will actually remove accumulated dirt and greasy stains, which over time can noticeably dull colours and whites.

Now, with Biological Action Concentrated Persil, your clothes will stay not just cleaner but visibly whiter, instead of becoming faded memories.

kinds of values. Soap isn't just a thing for cleaning clothes; it can be freshness, modernity, leisure, tradition, ecology. I use the word *commodities* rather than a common word like *things*, because this term can remind us of how advertising is linked to other systems, of production and distribution. Many quite capitalist advertisers would agree with Marx that commodities can change their meanings in the course of exchange, and that changes in production can have effects all through the market.

The 1890s: making brands and getting attention

The first ad for Ivory Soap (dating from 1882) can illustrate the sort of language found in ads a hundred years ago. Procter and Gamble had been selling soap for 20 years, but this was their first exercise in large-scale branding and marketing. The ad has at the top an engraving of two hands (a woman's) tying a thread around a block on which the name IVORY is visible. The text reads:

> THE 'IVORY' is a Laundry Soap, with all the fine qualities of a choice toilet soap, and is 99 44/100 per cent. pure.
>
> Ladies will find this Soap especially adapted for washing laces, infants' clothing, silk hose, cleaning gloves and all articles of fine texture and delicate colour, and for the varied uses about the house that daily arise, requiring the use of soap that is above the ordinary in quality.
>
> For the Bath, Toilet, or Nursery it is preferred to most of the Soaps sold for toilet use, being purer and much more pleasant and effective and possessing all the desirable properties of the finest unadulterated White Castile Soap. The Ivory Soap will 'float'.
>
> The cakes are so shaped that they may be used entire for general purposes or divided with a stout thread (as illustrated) into two perfectly formed cakes, of convenient size for toilet use.
>
> The price, compared to the quality and the size of the cakes, makes it the cheapest Soap for everybody for every want.
>
> TRY IT.
>
> *SOLD EVERYWHERE*

The main claim for the product is that it can perform two functions, washing clothes and washing skin, that previously required two separate products; it is a familiar form of claim used for other products today (shampoo/conditioner, detergent/fabric softener, sports car/family car). A further appeal is that it can replace an expensive imported soap. The copy uses vague comparatives such as 'more pleasant and effective'. The two most famous slogans of the Ivory brand are both here in the beginning. First, it was claimed that it was '99 44/100 percent. pure'. And, linked to this, is the odd and apparently irrelevant claim that 'it floats'. This quality – due to air spun in – was associated with the claimed purity. It is what Rosser Reeves would call in the 1950s a 'Unique Selling Proposition' – the single attribute that would differentiate this brand from others in the mind of the consumer. All the claims, then, are linked to properties of the product, and its price and availability.

But ads were already trying to sell through favourable associations, rather than just through claims about the product. For Ivory, Procter & Gamble did not just use the name of a traditional type of soap, such as 'Mottled German,' the way they had in the past, or give it the names of the founders. Instead they chose a new brand name with favourable associations. The story has it that the name 'Ivory' came from Psalm 45, verse 8, but quite apart from any specific allusion it suggests whiteness and luxury. The Sunlight poster already quoted, early as it is, tries to build up similar associations. A woman is hanging out the wash, while a boy peeking from behind the sheets tries to trap a bird – apparently this is the 'fun' referred to in the rhyme. The only product claim is visual: implied by the laundry being as white as the snow. The main claim here is still a common one: that the product allows one to have more leisure time (free to harass animals, presumably).

We could start our history of advertising much further back than the ads for Ivory and Sunlight soaps. But the late nineteenth century marks a crucial stage in the development of some commodities and markets, a period when many current brand names began. That's because of a simple fact: the nineteenth century was the first period in history when it became possible to make far more of common things than anyone needed. Before that, for instance, households or local makers would have made just enough soap or cloth or pins or matches for the local needs. There would have been no need for branding – soap was soap, and its quality was assured, if at all, by the shopkeeper. As the factory system developed, it became possible to make billions of pins or matches in one place. These economies of scale could be applied only if one could sell vast quantities. It wasn't enough to make the stuff cheaply, because competition over price led to decreased profit margins. One had to increase sales enormously by creating new needs (for instance patent medicines), replacing home-made and locally made products (like bread), increasing market share (soap), or increasing use of the product (such as getting women, as well as men, to ride bicycles).

But to make these changes in the market, producers had to make their products into branded commodities – things that people would recognise as distinctive from other, similar products, and would choose for reasons other than price alone. That is why there is huge attention in ads of this period to uncounterfeitable trademarks and packaging. The depression of the 1870s and '80s had destroyed smaller producers, and huge centralised corporations were emerging, like Procter & Gamble and the predecessors of Unilever. Just as earlier in the nineteenth century, the first producers to use the factory system on calico or matches or guns had made huge profits, later the first company to put large amounts of its budget into advertising rather than production reaped huge rewards. The first innovation, mechanisation, depended on large spending on machines, but then making a lot of extra money on the work of each worker. The second innovation, marketing, depended on large spending on ads, but then making extra money from an enlarged market.

The 1890s were also a turning point in advertising media and the advertising business. Posters and handbills were reaching saturation point, as you can see in many Victorian paintings and drawings of street scenes. The advertisers were just getting a major foothold in newspapers and magazines. For instance, earlier ads had been restricted to the width of a newspaper column, and this was the first period in which it became possible to buy a full page ad. The new magazines were the first medium really created for advertising, to fit its needs. With higher quality of reproduction, it was possible to experiment with the complex interactions of language and image that are common today. With more differentiated publications, it also became possible to tailor ads to specific audiences. The advertising business underwent a crucial reorganisation. Previously, advertising agents had worked for the publications, selling space. Now they began to work for the producers, so they were able to make advertising outlets compete against each other, to plan coherent campaigns, and to begin to specialise such functions as writing copy.

How does this view of branded commodities help us understand the language used? These ads focused on *making a brand* and *getting attention*. They were essentially built on repeating the name and claims and picture of the product. They said:

BUY OUR SOAP

If such ads were successful, it was largely because they were seen more often – posted on more walls, or in bigger letters, or repeated more times in a newspaper column. It was above all competition for the consumer's notice, and thus for space. Some of the responses to the problem were non-linguistic. The artist could simplify, as in the Sunlight ad, to offer a relief from the clutter. Other responses were to associate the product with images currently popular in the press: a general, an elephant, even the Pope. Pear's Soap bought a painting by the most notable of the pre-Raphaelite artists, John Everett Millais, and used it to lend high-culture status to their name. (The picture, with a boy blowing bubbles and the name Pear's across the top, can still be seen framed in many British living rooms.) Ads could even draw on literature: an early Ivory promotion was a booklet of 'Poetical Selections' with ads.

Linguistic strategies for cutting through the clutter that we have seen in the Sunlight and Ivory ads include:

- having a catchy rhyme or slogan, as in the Sunlight ad
- choosing a product name with favourable associations
- using repeated claims leading to elaborate parallelism
- using vague comparatives
- drawing on scientific and technical discourse.

All this means a sort of linguistic diversity that is reflected in the typography of the period. But we won't find the full range of play with language that we would find in later ads; for instance, puns are rare. There had to be further economic transformations to push the experimentation in new directions. When advertising is not under the same sorts of pressures, in local publications or non-capitalist countries, the same format of listed claims persists.

The 1920s: creating an image for consumption

Let's look again at the 1927 Persil ad. The heading gives you the main selling point.

> The afternoon concert –
> and the washing done

The claims for the washing qualities of the product, which filled soap ads in an earlier period, are in tiny print at the bottom, or you can send for a booklet. There is no need for elaborate claims, because this ad is not selling you washing powder, it's selling relaxation. It sets up the opposition of washing and improving leisure that runs through the copy. It also sets up the opposition of one woman, wearing leisure clothes, and another still wearing an apron, astonished – a simple social contrast.

A key shift has taken place, from emphasising production and use of the commodity, to emphasising meanings associated with consumption. Gone were the pictures of vast factories that assured respectability in earlier ads; gone were the pictures of women washing: now we would see the kind of life associated with using (or failing to use) the product. And once advertising starts to do that, it starts to touch every part of our conception of reality, not just our conception of soap. In this case, it gives definition of what women do when they get free time in the afternoon. No, they don't have an extra-marital affair, or go to the movies, or take a walk, or read Proust, or even go shopping. They sit down to the dreadfully-good-for-you BBC, and do some needlework.

The 1948 Persil ad used a simple poster style of illustration that is still associated with the Persil brand today, with the headline:

Guess whose mother hasn't jumped to this year's news about Persil?

And at the bottom, the slogan

Persil washes 7 shades whiter.

There are several devices at work here. The question assumes we already know the product and its superiority. The pun on *jumped* suggests a playfulness not found in the earlier ads. The slogan repeats /w/ sounds. But the main effect is the visual comparison, and the implied criticism that the grey frock is seen as an accusation of the mother. Each Persil ad focuses on something other than the soap powder: pleasures of leisure time and fear of social comparisons.

This new strategy in ads, like the earlier one, can be traced back to changes in production. Business leaders after World War I were terrified that there would be a larger-scale depression as war consumption ended and soldiers went back to work. And in America, at least, there were new things to consume because of assembly line production: cheap automobiles, radios, refrigerators, bathroom fixtures. Products that were already mass-produced and advertised, such as soap, found that their markets were no longer expanding. One answer to this problem might have been to distribute wealth more evenly. But the answer industrialists proposed was that the consumers should consume more. At the same time, there were changes in the media. In the US, the new medium of radio was shaped entirely by and for advertisers. And advertising agencies became big businesses, with the sort of organisation they have today: market researchers and account executives separated from copywriters and artists, and many firms competing for hugely lucrative accounts.

We have already seen two ways of increasing sales: by substituting a sign of something desired (such as leisure) for a branded product, and by substituting a sign of something feared (comment on one's child's frock) for lack of the branded product. My favourite scare ad from the 1920s is that for Scott toilet tissue, which showed surgeons peering down over a patient on the operating table, with the headline:

. . . and the trouble began with harsh toilet tissue.

Here is another headline, above a portrait of a patrician doctor:

'Civilization's curse can be conquered' says England's Great Surgeon Sir W. Arbuthnot Lane Bart. C.B.

What do you suppose 'Civilization's Curse' was? (The answer is at the end of the chapter).

Another way of increasing consumption was to create a new problem: 'halitosis' (for Listerine), 'BO' (for Lifebuoy soap), 'Iron-Poor Blood' (for Geritol), or 'Night Starvation' (for Horlicks), all of which were fantastically successful at moving rather dull products. Other advertisers increased consumption by broadening the range of choices and trying to associate different meanings with the different styles. For instance, almost all bath towels up to the 1920s were white. Cannon did ads treating towels and bathrooms as fashion accessories, in need of constant change and harmonisation, thus opening up the possibility of people buying more towels than one per family member. Western Electric did the same for telephones. General Motors overtook Ford in the 1920s by bringing out cars in colours, and in yearly models, so that those who wanted to keep up would need to buy one frequently, what critics have called 'planned obsolescence'. This has provided the pattern for the automobile industry ever since.

All these innovations draw on the simple idea that if one is selling soap, one's markets are limited, because the world can only use so much soap. But if one is selling a better life, there will be endless markets, because people can always be dissatisfied. The appeal was not

BUY OUR SOAP

but rather

BUY a better life by buying OUR SOAP

So what do we look for in the texts of ads from this period?

- They often contained embedded narratives and mock conversations.
- Images depended on substitution of one referent for another (radio for soap).
- Ads used the new media – for instance radio and comics – but also drew in print ads on the language used in them. They even anticipated in their form the medium that was coming – TV.

A surprising number of ads today have predecessors in this earlier period. But their style is still recognisable today as that of an earlier period of production.

The 1960s to the present: addressing the jaded consumer

I'll talk only briefly about this period, since it extends to our own time. The Persil ad quoted at the beginning of the chapter, now running in magazines, does a more elaborate variation on the grey and white posters of the 1940s. It shows a framed painting of two women sitting in a field. The colours are yellowed, except for one patch in which the painting has been restored to show the brilliant white of one woman's dress. The headline is

Restore your clothes to their former glory.

This seems to recall posters like that of the two skipping girls. But here the illustration is not showing Persil at work: it is showing the effect of picture restoration as being metaphorically like the effect of the product. Other ads may still hold up shirts washed in Brand X, but here the demonstration is put in a frame, treated as something too old-fashioned to show literally. Another current Persil ad that assumes knowledge of earlier ads shows two rows of kids in the blue cardigans used in school uniforms. One cardigan, though, is light blue, while the others are all a darker shade. The text says:

Guess whose mum isn't using Persil Colour?

It is the same pitch as in the ad with the two skipping girls, but with the claim now for colours rather than whiteness. Mum is still supposed to feel guilty.

Like many ads today, these are ads about ads. So are a lot of the famous ads of the 1960s. One of my favourites is the famous Doyle Dane Bernbach slogan for Avis:

We're only Number 2. We Try Harder.

The ad depends on our knowing that corporations like to advertise they are the largest of something. Thus we take it as a surprise that they say they are only Number 2 – though of course that still means they are huge. Similarly, in one of the early Doyle Dane Bernbach ads for Volkswagen, Americans were startled to see a car company using the word colloquially used for defective cars. The heading said simply:

Lemon.

People were startled because they had come to expect only words of praise in ads. The copy below explained that this beetle had been rejected by Volkswagen's quality control because a metal strip on the glove box was loose, thus reaffirming the product's reputation for quality. The long and very successful line of ads stressing understatement combined with product claims enabled Volkswagen to give favourable meanings in the US to an odd-looking German car.

These ads emerged from new, smaller, 'creative' firms in the 1960s. The tendency to humour and play was much derided by the next generation of copywriters, in the 1970s. But the reason for this play is again related to the changing nature of commodities, not just to the personalities of ad agents. As ads of the 1920s tried to deal with saturation of the market, ads of the 1960s tried to deal with saturation of the consumer. Ads now compete for attention in a world where they are ubiquitous, and where it is taken for granted that they are not to be trusted. One solution for the advertiser is to treat the consumer as an active and disenchanted interpreter. We will see this again and again in the examples of current ads in this book.

These ads start with the assumption the interpreter doesn't believe ads. Having acknowledged that, they then go on to make their pitch. So if ads of the 1890s said

BUY OUR SOAP

and those of the 1920s said

BUY a better life when you buy OUR SOAP

the ads of the 1960s said something like:

> There are so many ads telling you to BUY OUR SOAP, and we know you are too smart to fall for ads, so we won't tell you to BUY OUR SOAP, but will let you consider for yourself, and anyway we will assume you have already BOUGHT OUR SOAP

At the same time as this change in strategy by some advertisers, there has been an extension of advertising to new kinds of commodities. The ads of the 1920s sold things. As we are constantly being told, the commodities of today are services. So there are ads for things that even the most aggressive advertiser of the 1920s would have thought unlikely commodities: university courses, hospitals, long-distance telephoning, political figures, radical movements like Greenpeace, medical charities. And there has been an extension to new media – not only television, which works like radio in many ways, but sponsorship of sports, the arts, and university chairs. The line between advertising and the rest of culture is now very hard to define. Feature films like *Jurassic Park* promote products, and we saw in Chapter 1 that Benetton runs ads that have no discernible sign of their business as a clothing retailer.

So what do we look for in the texts of ads for the jaded consumer?

- Puns and play with sounds (see Chapter 3)
- Parodies and ironies (examples in Chapters 5 and 9)
- Relation of ad to ad (examples in Chapters 8 and 13)

- Dominance of the image over the text (see chapter 10)
- All other discourses are incorporated into advertising (examples in Chapters 8, 11 and 12).

I have been treating these periods as discontinuous stages, separated by sharp economic changes. But we should also remember that there is a great deal of continuity in advertising history. Instead of moving on along a road to some goal, as in the popular idea of progress, advertising history piles layer on layer, with the earlier periods still there. Many of the most common appeals of advertisers persist through all the stages I have discussed. For instance, rhymes persist in slogans today. In illustrations, the commodity is often shown as grotesquely enlarged. We still see celebrity endorsements, which were used a hundred years ago. The association with high culture can be seen in the Pears 'Bubbles' ad that uses a real Millais painting, or in the recent Persil campaign parodying impressionist paintings. The boundaries between advertisement and editorial content, blurred in the 1920s, are still regularly breached by 'advertorial' in some magazines today, when, for instance, a feature describes a cosmetic problem addressed by products that are also advertised.

As a general rule, it might be good to resist our sense that old ads look funny, and start any interpretation of an ad from a earlier period with the question of what is similar to ads of today, as a prelude to seeing what is really different.

Conclusion

So what do we learn from ads from earlier periods? They make us aware of the ongoing process of the making of commodities and the making of meanings with them. It is hard with contemporary ads alone to see just how odd it is that soaps should be marketed with sex, or that coffee should be marketed with jokes, or that cigarettes could be marketed with no copy at all. We have to go back to a different era of production and marketing to understand the changes the language and styles of advertising.

Let's review here the main points I have made about each period:

- In the period beginning in the 1890s, ads made brands, and had to get attention in crowded media. They did this with rhymes, repetition, parallelism, scientific and literary language.
- In the period beginning in the 1920s, in a saturated market, ads associated social meanings with brands. They did this with conversational and narrative formats, associative language, and metaphorical substitution of one thing for another.

- In the most recent period, beginning in the 1960s, ads addressed a jaded consumer saturated with ads. They did this with ironies, parodies, ads on ads, puns, and juxtaposition of competing discourses, in the text and the images.

By the way, 'Civilization's Curse,' referred to in the Fleischman's Yeast ad, is constipation. Fleischman's in 1920 faced a declining market for its product. People weren't baking at home as much, and Prohibition had cut off any legal demand by breweries. The marketing solution was ingenious – it was suggested that people should just eat the stuff three times a day. The company spent one of the largest of all advertising budgets, with the most prestigious of all firms, telling people that yeast eased constipation, improved muscle tone, ended depression. At first they got doctors to endorse it, but the American Medical Association objected that it was nonsense that yeast ended constipation. So they paid British doctors to endorse it.

Further reading
Advertising history

The main ideas of this chapter are derived from Raymond Williams, 'Advertising: The Magic System'. The section on the 1920s draws heavily, for ideas and examples, on Roland Marchand, *Advertising the American Dream: Making Way for Modernity 1920–1940*. The best short account of the history of advertising, in relation to texts, is in Gillian Dyer, *Advertising as Communication*.

Other social histories of advertising include Stuart Ewen, *Captains of Consciousness: Advertising and the Social Roots of Consumer Culture*; and for a more favourable view of advertising, Stephen Fox, *The Mirror Makers*. Armand Matellart, *Advertising International*, is a useful and highly readable introduction to the global advertising networks since 1980. Russell Keat, Nigel Whiteley, and Nicholas Abercrombie, eds., *The Authority of the Consumer*, surveys recent cultural changes in relation to the marketplace. Jennifer Wicke's *Advertising Fictions* links the development of advertising to the fictions of Dickens, James, and Joyce; it also includes many insights into advertising itself, and especially into the use of intertextuality and allusions to high culture.

Fictional accounts, journalism, and memoirs, give a better idea of what advertising agencies were like than do these histories. Martin Mayer, *Madison Avenue USA*, though it is about the 1950s, gives a vivid portrait that seems to remain true in some respects. A readable British account from the same period is John Pearson and Geoff Turner, *The Persuasion Industry*. Michael J. Arlen, *Thirty Seconds*, is a zippy series of vignettes tracing the history of one

AT&T commercial. Advertising agencies seem (like universities) to be prime settings for murder mysteries; as well as Dorothy Sayers, *Murder Must Advertise*, which I mentioned in the introduction, there are two by Julian Symons describing the ad world of the late 1940s, *The Thirty-first of February* and *A Man Called Jones*. There are many many memoirs by famous advertising writers, such as David Ogilvy, *Confessions of an Advertising Man* and Peter Mayle, *Up the Agency*. Both are witty, bitty, informative, and rather smug.

If you are looking for old advertisements, and can't find old magazines, corporate histories are often a good source, though of course they can highly biased and absurdly eulogistic in their coverage. Most of the ads in this chapter came from W. J. Reader, *Fifty Years of Unilever*, and a book by The Editors of *Advertising Age*, *Proctor and Gamble: The House that Ivory Built*.

3

Beanz Meanz Heinz
What Makes Slogans Stick?

Let's compare two slogans, both of which try to get us to think of chocolate products as healthy foods rather than as indulgences. The first is for Van Houten's Cocoa, and appeared in an ad in 1904.

A COCOA YOU CAN ENJOY. SUPPLIES THE ENERGY FOR WORK AND STUDY

Even with some very nice allegorical figures of work and study accompanying it, this is an unmemorable slogan. The second example is a slogan recognisable to most British people:

A MARS® A DAY HELPS YOU WORK REST AND PLAY

Why is this more memorable? To begin with, it rhymes, and runs in a fairly regular rhythm (though the regularity follows some rather complex metrical rules). The sentence structure places work, rest, and play as parallel activities (see Chapter 4) and the rhyme comes on *play*. And of course it echoes an even older saying, 'An apple a day keeps the doctor away', which gives it a sound of familiarity and perhaps inevitability.

The Mars® slogan sticks with us because it draws attention to its form. Most of our daily uses of language do not draw attention to the form of the language itself this way. If I tell my daughter, 'Have a Mars® bar', she is interested in what is said (and eaten) and not how it is said. We usually assume that language is transparent, that we can express ourselves through it without the exact words and sounds mattering. Poetry often tries to break down this transparency, with rhythm and rhyme and other patterns that make us respond to the form, even if we do not analyse it. Jokes, too, often play on the forms of language; most jokes fall flat when the punch line is changed even slightly. It is part of the fascination of ads that they play with language in similar ways. And in ads, as in poems and jokes, the patterning of the form of the ad – the product name or the jingle or the headline – may lead us to important meaning relations – as in the way *play* is stressed in the Mars® slogan by being last.

Theorists of literature writing in Russia in the 1920s, who have been very influential on later writers, suggested that literature is distinguished, not by its subject matter (heroes, heroines, romantic or tragic events) but by a use of language in a way that would stand out against ordinary uses. Literature would make the language strange to us and thus renew our perception of it. Their term for this standing out is translated as *foregrounding*, drawing on a metaphor from painting, the way some things in the composition draw our attention while others fade into the background. Foregrounding in language can be achieved either by unexpected regularity or unexpected irregularity. An unexpected regularity is called *parallelism*, and an unexpected irregularity is called *deviation*. (The terms here are not important in themselves, but the patterns they describe are important in most theories of poetry.) The rhyme in the Mars® slogan is a example of parallelism, because we don't expect the first part of a sentence to rhyme with the second part. An example of deviation would be the name for what was once the Standard Oil Company of New Jersey, or Esso; *Exxon* is deviant in that we do not expect double *X*s in English words or names.

Most critics would now question the idea that literature can be defined as a special type of language; they would see it as a special way of using language. After all, we have just seen two of the best known literary devices, rhyme and rhythm, in a decidedly non-literary text, the Mars® slogan. Instead of trying to fence off kinds of language, we can look at how any text builds up and defies expectations. In this chapter, I will point out some of the most common kinds of patterning in ads at the most basic level of sounds and letters. Most readers can agree that these patterns are there, so they are a good place to start any analysis. But the meanings with which they are associated can be highly complex and variable, as you will see if you groan at some of my examples.

Catchy sounds

Alliteration

The basic move in many advertising slogans is to build up a pattern of similarity, so that they can break it for effect. The simplest and by far most common technique is to repeat a sound. When the repeated sound is a consonant, the effect is *alliteration*. One example some people still remember, though it was only used for a period in the 1950s and early 1960s

Top People Take *The Times*

The Times had just begun to advertise; this slogan replaced an earlier one that seemed to say the same thing, but that no one remembers:

Men who make opinion read *The Times*

Saxon Mills, the copywriter who made the change, had to sell it to those in the management who thought the new slogan was vulgar. But it worked, partly because the catchy alliteration (and the colloquial phrase 'top people', and the boast) suggested the liveliness of the newspaper, while the explicit message said it was read by people who are a bit dull.

In many cases the pattern of similarity in sound in a slogan will play against a dissimilarity in meaning, making us more aware of the contrast. For instance, this is the headline on an ad for olive oil, above a picture of a pot of paella:

For a *moment*, Morecambe be*came* Madrid

This is not just playing on the opening letters – if it was, they could have used 'Manchester became Madrid'. Morecambe shares the /m/ with *moment*, and /m/ and /k/ with *became*, as well as the /m/ with *Madrid*. The joke for the British audience is that *Madrid* is the capital of the exciting country in which the British like to take their holidays, and *Morecambe* (pronounced morkum) is seen (unfairly I am sure) as a gloomy, rundown, and terribly ordinary working-class seaside resort, popular in the 1950s. The parallelism links two places with completely different associations, two places that can only be linked by using olive oil; there is a kind of wit in being reminded that they share some accidental similarities in sound.

But just repeating sounds may not be enough. For one thing, there are only about 20 consonant sounds in English, and most of them get repeated fairly often anyway. If you find a repetition of /s/ in a text, it may go unnoticed in normal reading, because /s/ is very common in English. So when writers want to draw attention to sounds, they are more likely to use certain sounds, and place them in certain prominent positions. Some sounds stand out more than others – for instance those that are made by stopping the air-stream completely with your tongue or lips and then releasing the air. The sounds in this class are those made for the letters *p, b, m, n, t, d, k,* and *g,* and you can see from my examples so far that they tend to be repeated where the parallelism is supposed to be noticed. Also, repeated sounds are more likely to stand out at the beginnings of stressed syllables than at the end.

But many slogans don't want the repetition to stand out so strongly. For instance, this slogan for the largest British supermarket chain –

Good food costs less at Sainsbury's

– repeats the /s/ sound rather subtlely, so that I doubt if even those reading it many times while standing in the queue at the checkouts notice any repetition.

This Sainsbury's slogan also shows how alliteration can work with similar, as well as identical, sounds. Though the letter *s* is repeated, not all the letter *s*'s have the same sound, and the way I say it, the last two *s*'s in *Sainsbury's* sound like *z*. Does that mean there is no alliteration there? No, because the two sounds are very closely related. For instance, the sounds that go with *s* and *z* are formed the same way, but one involves a vibration of the vocal chords and the other doesn't. The same is true of some other pairs: *p/b, t/d, k/g,* the *sh* in *shoe* and the *s* in *leisure*. The sounds that go with the letters *m* and *n* are related in a different way – they both involve air going through the nose, which is why you can't say them when you have a cold. So there is a pattern of repetition in this Heinz poster:

Before it can become a Heinz bean, every raw bean is tested by a light beam

I'm told that the *n* in *can* will actually sound like /m/ before a /b/ (you might check this suggestion out by reading this out loud, if you are reading this somewhere where no one will overhear you and think you strange). There will still be a repetition of the two sounds. Still, I don't think passers-by seeing the slogan would think of this as an obviously repeated sound like 'Top People Take the Times'. But my wife thought it was a tongue twister, and that is likely to be the effect of alternation of such closely linked sounds. (Think of 'She sells seashells … ', in which the sounds that go with *s* and *sh* get tangled up.)

Assonance

So far I have been talking about the repetition of consonant sounds, *alliteration* . Linguists and literary critics usually distinguish this from the repetition of vowel sounds, *assonance*, and it is worth maintaining this distinction when talking about advertising because the effect of assonance is usually more sub-tle. There are many vowel sounds (how many depends on which variety of English you speak), all made by changing the shape of the lips or the mouth cavity; they are represented by the letters *a, e, i, o, u,* and various combina-tions. Because the effect is subtle, I had a hard time finding examples at first. Here is the current Gillette slogan:

Gillette – the best a man can get.

I haven't underlined the *e* in *the* or the *a* in *can*, even though they are spelled with the same letters, because assonance only works with the vowels in stressed syllables (the syllables we pronounce more loudly and at a higher pitch). That's because in English all the vowels that aren't stressed tend to sound much the same, the sound of the *e* in *the*. In the Gillette slogan, sung at the end of the ad, the music puts stress on GiLLETTE, the BEST a MAN can GET. The stressed syllables alternate with the unstressed, as they do in the most common meters of English poetry.

Once I started looking for assonance, it was not so hard to find. The Heinz ad I just quoted has (at least in my accent) assonance of the vowel sounds in *Heinz* and *light*, and *bean* and *beam*:

Before it can become a Heinz bean, every raw bean is tested by a light beam

One of the most famous American political slogans has the same vowel sounds in all three words. Dwight Eisenhower was known as Ike, so his sup-porters wore buttons saying

I like Ike

Despite this, he won two elections. (But then this slogan was running against 'We're Madly for Adlai'.) Assonance is also very common in product names:

PrittStick (a roll-on adhesive)

Super Noodles

Coca-Cola.

Rhyme

I started this chapter with an example of rhyme. Even three-year-olds recog-nise rhyme when they hear it, but it is a bit more complicated to define it. Rhyme is the repetition of ending sounds; technically it is the similarity of all the last sounds of two words, from the ending of the last stressed syllable on. (This is a complicated way of saying that *motion* is a full rhyme with *lotion* but only a half rhyme with *caution*.) Rhyme was used in ads from the beginning, so that it was taken as part of the genre. At the turn of the century, Elmo Calkins wrote a series of ads for the Lackawanna Railroad starring a character names Phoebe Snow, and stressing how the use of hard coal in the steam engines meant less soot on the passengers. Here is a sample showing how much rhyme he could pack in:

Says Phoebe Snow
About to go
Upon a trip to Buffalo:
My gown stays white
From morn to night
Upon the Road of Anthracite.

Later, when radio advertising began in the 1920s, rhyme became the main component of the jingle, which has been popular in advertising since the mid-nineteenth century. So parodies of ads often play on the excessive use of rhyme.

Rhymes are used today more cautiously, perhaps because they carry associations with the mindless hard sell. In some cases, they are presumably meant to sound over insistent, as in this ad that appeared around Christmas.

IF MEN ARE WISE THEY SOCIALIZE WITH APPLETISE

Part of this oddity comes from the fact that the last two rhymes (*ize* and *ise*) are on less stressed syllables, so to make the rhyme come out you have to stress them more in your reading. A more subtle example –

Timotei: A breath of fresh air in skin care

–involves alliteration (*skin* and *care*) and assonance (*breath* and *fresh*) as well as rhyme (*air* and *care*).

One important point to remember with rhyme, as with the other patterns of repeated sounds, is that it refers to *sounds*, not spellings. By the time we get through school, we sometimes get so used to spelling that we forget that most letters have several sounds, and most sounds can be spelt with several letters. For instance, in –

Pilkington Glass. Amazingly Pays in Your Glazing.

– a company that makes double glazing gets in three rhyming words, with two different spellings.

Rhyme, like assonance, often works in some accents but not in others. In many British accents, the *g* at the end of *glazing* would not be sounded, so the rhyme with *pays in* would be exact. This British ad for Nokia portable telephones lost me because while British people do not pronounce *r* after a vowel, I still do.

> Smaller – Easier – Closer – Nokia

There is parallelism here at the ends of all four words, but not in American English.

Tunes and Intonation

Of course words don't always stand by themselves on the page; the most insistent slogans are in broadcast ads, where words often work with and against music. Advertising music has been criticised for its limited range of melodies, harmonies, rhythms, and timbres; its sole remarkable quality is that one can't get the tune out of one's head. An admiring review of a Heinz Baked Beans ad in *Campaign* (the advertising industry's weekly newspaper) says, 'For those who thought the jingle was on its last legs, a ditty from hell which I guarantee you'll be singing on your third hearing'. It's a good bet that all of us know more lines of advertising jingles than we do of poetry. Where the music is written for the ad (instead of borrowed from an already popular song, a currently popular form of intertextuality), it often sets up patterns of similarity and difference in the same way as the words. Let us take one jingle playing on local radio.

> Winstons for delicious pizza
> Winston's can't be beata

This falls rather flat, partly because I would accept *pizza* and *beat* as rhymed only on a bad day. (It's not so far-fetched: if you listen closely, you will hear that there is a /t/ sound in *pizza*.) The tune is not particularly catchy in itself. But it brings out both the parallel and the difference in the rhyme. The tune shifts the way we would emphasise syllables: for instance, the *de* in *delicious* gets stressed. It also makes patterns of its own. Without using musical notation (and without you being able to hear my singing), I can show it like this:

```
                                                      beat

                                    stons can't              a

     Win         de         piz         Win           be
        stons       lic         za
           for          ous
```

The first line sets up a pattern of syllables falling in tone from one note. The second line starts with the same syllable and same note, but rises. The falling tones of *beata*, ending on a note higher than the beginning, repeat the interval of *pizza* as the rhyming sounds are repeated. So the pattern of variation and parallel in the music pulls together a rather forced rhyme.

The loudness, pitch, and grouping of the spoken voice can also interact with what might be the expected patterning of a slogan; these aspects of pronunciation are called *intonation*. In the intonation of radio advertising, some words that would not be stressed in normal reading (such as *so* and *the* and *and*) are stressed to shift emphasis:

I exercise, *AND* I eat the right sort of breakfast.

SO, if ordinary shampoos don't fix your problem, try this.

You have the Bible, but do you have the *OTHer* Testament of Jesus Christ *[it's the Book of Mormon]*

Intermountain Design Inc., 521 South 8th Street, *IN* Boise

In each of these cases, the emphasis on a usually unstressed word shifts attention to some relevant relation: the need to link exercise to diet, the link between dandruff and trying a new shampoo, the existence of another religious book, the nearness of the location.

The effect of grouping, with one stressed syllable for each group, can be heard most clearly with the presentation of telephone numbers, which play an important role in some ads. In the US numbers are usually grouped already by the parentheses around the area code and the hyphen after the first three digits, but in the UK, numbers are of different lengths, and may be remembered in different groupings. The London *Evenings News* once advertised its number, 3535000, as –

Three five three, five thousand

–which is simple enough. Their advertising agency suggested reading it as

Three five three five oh oh oh.

This seems to have been demonstrably more catchy (more people phoned), even though it gave more separate elements to remember. Many other phone-in numbers have since been designed with similar patterning. Intonation of slogans and names is not so easily shifted, but they too are affected by the way they are spoken, as well as the way they are written.

Catchy print

Some advertisers try to get attention for print ads by making the ad as much as possible like face to face interaction; I will deal with that strategy in Chapter 8. But another approach is to call attention to the printedness of it, to the artificiality of the symbols. This section is about how the letters (not the sounds) are presented, what is called in linguistics *graphology*. Just as repeated sounds attract attention, so do repeated letters. In print, they can be emphasised by enlarging them, or using one letter to fill several slots. So if a firm has a name like Kopy Kwik, it may appear on the logo with a huge K in front of *opy* and *wik*. Where alliteration arises by chance, as with Minnesota Mining and Manufacturing, it can be brought out in the print version, so the company name becomes 3M.

But the simplest way to call attention to the printed form is to use unexpected letters. They can be unexpected in two ways – because they are infrequent in the language as a whole, or because they are unpredictable in a particular sequence (for instance, breaking with conventional spelling). One of the most predictable features of English texts is that some letters will be much more common than others. If you play Scrabble®*, you will know that you get only one point for using one of the letters that occur in many words, such as E, A, S, or T, and 4, 8, or 10 points for using letters like Q, Z, X, or J. I never have figured out why one gets 4 points for using H. . Remember that it is the *letters*, not the sounds, that are unusual. The uncommon letter *z* is a very common sound in words like *cause*, but it is usually spelled *s*, while the uncommon letter *x* is also fairly common as a sound, spelled *cks* as in *stacks*. That means that an advertiser can attract attention by using surprising spelling without producing something unpronounceable (the way the name of the villain Mr. Mxtplx, in *Superman*, is unpronounceable).

Frequency of letters

If you played Scrabble® with established brand names instead of words, it would be much easier to get rid of your high-scoring letters. When advertisers make up names (instead of keeping the name of, say, the founder) they very often use these less common letters to make the name stand out. X is particularly popular. I tried the experiment of going down the aisles at our local supermarket, and found *Radox*, *Dettox*, and *Biotex*. And of course there's the beef stock cube OXO, which has the advantage of reading the same, not only backwards and forwards, but upside down and right way up. Other names used in marketing include *Dulux*, *Halifax*, *Kleenex*, and *Exxon*. Now you might object that the Halifax Building Society was not named by a clever advertiser (it is the town in West Yorkshire where the society originated). But note that when they recently came to choose a logo, they chose the uncommon *X* and not the more common *H*. *Z* seems to work almost as well as *x*: I found in the household cleaners aisle *Daz* and *Oz*, and in other products there's *Jazz* (software) and *Lucozade*. *J* works for *Jif* in English, but the same

---

* Scrabble® is a registered trademark of J. W. Spear & Sons plc

product is *Cif* in Austria, perhaps because the letter *j* is more common in German, and the letter *c* much less. *Jif* would be pronounceable but less striking.

Unpredictable spelling

Even when the advertiser is stuck with an existing product name, it may attract attention by deviating from expected spelling. I think the most famous British example is:

Beanz Meanz Heinz

This is a good example of deviation in graphology, that is, attracting attention by spelling, because read aloud it doesn't sound odd. This spelling emphasises the fact that the three final consonant clusters sound the same, even if they are spelt differently. (To get this parallelism, one has to read it as referring to the word *beans*, as singular.) The deviation brings out what is unusual, and therefore memorable, about the brand name. (The current example, *Heinz Buildz Britz*, is rather less catchy– I'll leave it to you to decide why.)

Simplified spellings remind us that the usual sound/letter correspondence in English is by no means simple. Other simplified spelling include *IRN BRU* (a soft drink), *Kitekat* (a cat food), and *Sunkist* citrus products. Some of these spellings have become so common through advertisements and highway signs that they have almost become second spellings of the words: *Kwik, Nite, Drive-Thru, Bar B Q*. (British linguistic purists seem to believe that this, like other signs of decay, is American in origin, but I doubt it. The brand name of our Made-in-England laundry basket is *Plysu*, which I guess is meant to be read *Please you*.)

Besides these phonetic spellings, there are many ads that alter spelling to make it represent sound. This ad from the association for research into stammering tries to convey the stammer:

IF YOU FIND
MY S-S-S-STAMMERING
F-F-F-FRUSTRATES YOU,
HOW DO YOU THINK
I F-F-F-F-FEEL?

This ad for Panasonic telephones tries to incorporate the hiss (as suggested in the accompanying picture, of a snake).

Introducing a cordless phone with something missssing.

It is interesting that most readers, without the clue of the snake, miss the fact that there is any misspelling here at all. We are so used to jumping to the whole shape of a word that we can miss play with individual letters.

All these examples alter the spelling to make it more like the sound. Another tactic is to treat the letters as just letters, moving them independently into new combinations. An ad for St Ivel low fat spread says simply

SUNF
    LOWER

to make the low fat content seem an inherent part of the name. A series of ads for Holsten's Pils beer depends on scrambled letters, as in anagrams.

HELTONS Lips

We can still recognise as advertising the product because of the typeface of the trademark; a picture (here a kiss mark) helps us decode the other meaning Once people got used to the anagrams, the advertiser could move on to more difficult plays, such as beer mats for the Christmas season:

TINSELL hops.

The ability to maintain this campaign over many different posters must be some sort of world record for copywriters' anagrammatic ingenuity. But some repetition of letters (not sounds) may not be consciously noticed. There is an anagram in –

Morecambe became Madrid

– but I didn't see it until I went over the headline very carefully for this chapter. So it first registered with me as catchy, not tricky.

Between languages

We may read English words without thinking of the spelling. Foreign words attract attention in ads when they provide unfamiliar spellings. The advertisers can either try to conceal the non-Englishness of the sequences, or emphasise them by juxtaposing them with English words. A current series of ads for videotape uses the line

YOU CAN FUDGI IT
OR YOU CAN FUJI IT

This uses the coincidental similarity between the transliteration of the Japanese brand name (which they want to have positive associations) and an English word *fudge* that has negative associations. The joke of the ad is that the first half of the text is shown with separated colours or wrinkled plastic or

OR YOU CAN FUJI IT.

The one tape with two magnetic layers.

otherwise distorted print, representing the fudging of the image with which we are threatened.

One would not think one could do this sort of play with a name like *Mitsubishi*. But a clever agency in Singapore brought out a juxtaposition with English words by rewriting it as

MI*T*
SUB
*I*SHI

With the name in white on black, the underlined letters in red, and very sharp art direction, it could be made to contain IT IS, as if this firm statement of something or other were a natural part of the Japanese name. The play works, of course, only in print.

Perhaps the best known example of this kind of spelling play between languages is the Perrier campaign that replaced the sound *o* with the French word, pronounced more or less the same in a bad French accent, *eau*. So the heading *H₂Eau* went with a bottle of water, *Picasseau* went with a cubist representation of the bottle, *Incogniteau* went with the bottle without a label (still recognisable by its shape), and *The Sole eau* with the bottle on stage in front of a curtain. They even managed to get the British version of *Cosmopolitan* to print its name on its spine as *Cosmeau*. As the series ran on and on, it became another test of the copywriters' ingenuity. Note that this deviation in spelling serves two functions, both of reminding us of the water and reminding us that it is French.

Names and shapes

One further kind of deviation with graphology occurs when the advertisers ask us to take an image on the page as both a letter in a word and a picture or name in itself. So in the UK public-information campaign to get parents to lay children on their backs rather than their fronts, to reduce the risk of cot deaths, the headings was

BACK TO SLEEP

with the B on its side, in the shape of a sleeping baby. In the Pork Marketing Board's

SWALLOW THAT JACK SPRAT

the O is an Edam Cheese, and the copy assures us that slices of pork have less fat. (Unfortunately for the advertisers, the picture makes the cheese more tempting than the meat.) A Prudential poster advertising personal equity plans (PEPs) substitutes a pound sign for an E in

I WANT A PEP THAT LETS ME INVEST MOR£.

Another way to draw attention to print is to the names of individual letters, as we call them when we recite the alphabet. Of course, this particular kind of play will be untranslatable. I was at first baffled by the name of a French pop radio station *NRJ* because I failed to give the letters their French names – it comes out sounding like the French word *energie*. A similar play in English, in an ad for Lucozade, says *NRG*.

Homophones

In English, there are many words that sound the same (or can be made to sound similar) but are spelled differently – what linguists call *homophones*. This kind of play works especially well in print because of the tension between the spelling and the apparent meaning; we have to work harder so the joke comes as more of a surprise. For instance when we read this –

Sainsbury's have discovered that the finest whisky is kept under loch and quay.

– the spelling and pictures make us think of the relevant Scottish meanings first, but we must also recall the idiomatic phrase that fits in this sentence, *lock and key*. (Such a set of words that goes together is called a *collocation* ; see Chapter 5.) In the same way, the picture of a huge male singer in evening dress in an Our Price Records/British Rail promotion makes us think of music.

Spend six pounds at Our Price and you can get a Young People's Rail Card for a tenor.

The jokes would not have the same wit if the words happened to be spelled the same, if there was just a double meaning. Part of the effect comes because of the outlandishness of the leaps we are asked to make – we come to the edge of a groan. Each of the two interpretations – as spelling or as sound – has some support, one from the picture of a singer in a dinner jacket, and the other from a familiar collocation, 'for a tenner'.

Conclusion

I have been pointing out some of the ways that slogans can be catchy relay on their sound and print forms, and some of the uses of this catchiness:

1. Ads may attract attention by unexpected parallelism in sounds (not just spellings), especially repetition of consonants (alliteration).

2. Repetition of some consonants and in some positions is more insistent.

3. Repetition may also work through similar, rather than identical, sounds.

4. The repetition of vowels is usually more subtle in effect.

5. Some rhymes work only in some varieties of English and not in others.

6. The effect of any foregrounding of sound can be brought out or played down by spoken intonation or by music in a jingle.

7. Advertisements can draw attention to the written form by using of letters that usually only occur infrequently, or by using unpredictable spellings.

8. Letters may be altered to draw attention to their shape or name as well as their place in a word.

9. Foreign names can be transformed into English words.

10. Homophones – words that sound alike but are spelled differently – work by forcing a switch between two interpretations. Often the interpretations are anchored by pictures or by set phrases.

One final point, to which I will return in later chapters: these patterns are not automatic in their effect. They require activity on the part of the hearer or reader, and the advertisers use this investment of effort to make their messages stick. Everyone can identify rhyme, but we may not notice it in any given jingle. We can show that an X is not common in written English, but we cannot say from that what the effect of a name like *Oxo* will be. We can say that this sort of play attracts attention to the physical form of the ad, spoken or written, while most daily language use leads us to ignore this physical form. Sometimes, as with the sillier jingles and altered spellings, that is all it does. But with most of these ads, the play led to some aspect of meaning to be associated with the product. Since we can't get them out of our heads, we might as well think about them.

Further reading
Foregrounding and deviation

Several linguists have produced very complex analyses of patterning of sounds and print. The most spectacular is Guy Cook's analysis of an ad for Tsar cologne in *The Discourse of Advertising*; there are also extended analyses in Geoffrey Leech, *English in Advertising*, Ronald Carter and Walter Nash, *Seeing Through Language*, and in Leo Spitzer's 'Advertising as an American Popular Art'. The 'I Like Ike' slogan was analysed with extraordinary thoroughness in Roman Jakobson's famous essay, 'Linguistics and Poetics'. For an introduction to the sound system of English (in general, not in ads), see J.

D. O'Connor, *Phonetics*, or Gerry Knowles, *Patterns of Spoken English*. For more on the literary theory underlying foregrounding, see Geoffrey Leech, *A Linguistic Guide to English Poetry*, and Geoffrey Leech and Mick Short, *Style in Fiction*.

There has been much less written on the relationship of these patterns to sound, music, or visual layout. I base my comments entirely on the only paper I know that studies the intonation of advertisements, Theo van Leeuwen, 'Persuasive Speech: The Intonation of the Live Radio Commercial'. Van Leeuwen also has an excellent paper on theme tunes that is not, unfortunately, easily accessible yet: 'Music and Ideology: Notes Toward a Sociosemiotics of Mass Media Music'. Helmut Rösing, 'Music in Advertising', may be easier to find. The comment on the Heinz jingle was from Michele Martin in *Campaign*, 18th June 1993, and the anecdote about the *Evening News* telephone number was given in a letter by Bob Walton in *Campaign*, 16th April 1993. For many examples of slogans illustrating the ideas in this chapter, see the collection edited by Nigel Rees, *Slogans*, one of the few books that requires an attention span of less than five seconds.

4

It is. Are You?
Sentence Type and Sentence Structure

One of the most insistent ads on television now is one for Ariel Ultra that says why other powders won't clean chip grease.

Because it's fat.

Part of the effect is that this is said in a deep male voice, in response to high-pitched women's voices. But the blunt insistent tone also arises from the structure of the utterance, the way it is just part of a sentence, responding to what the women have said. That's part of what makes it seem so annoyingly know-it-all. Even a print ad can suggest a voice, urgent or casual or dreamy, an attitude towards the subject matter, and towards you, the reader, in a number of linguistic choices. One of the important stylistic features in these effects is sentence construction, both the kinds of sentences used, and the ways they are put together.

Sentence types

One basic way of classifying sentences is to look at the way they function as statements, commands, questions, or exclamations. Statements assert facts about the world; commands seek to make the hearer act; questions seek information from the hearer; and exclamations express the speaker's surprise. If it were always that simple, this classification wouldn't tell us much about the style. But we can use it to show us what the advertiser is taking for granted, what is assumed in this type of sentence.

The most common sentence type in written English is the statement. For instance, statements make up nearly all of this chapter (this sentence is one of them; it asserts something about the sentences in the chapter). Philosophers treat statements as true or false assertions about conditions in the world, and they have devoted most of their study to this one type. But in everyday conversation we may make more use of sentence types such as commands, questions, and exclamations that are more directly concerned with interacting with other people (think back over your conversations so far today). The use of these types of sentences does suggest something about who is listening or reading. A question, for instance, is neither true nor false, but it does typically suggest that the hearer knows something that the speaker does not know. So instead of asking whether a question (or command or exclamation) is true, we ask what conditions would have to hold for it to make sense to this listener. The answer isn't always straightforward; a question can function as an indirect command:

Could you give me some cake?

And so can a statement:

I'm hungry.

So can an exclamation:

What a wonderful looking cake!

So we are always trying to figure out what the speaker is trying to do with this sentence type. In this respect, ads are more like everyday conversation, with a full range of sentence types, than like textbooks, which tend to stick to statements. (Don't they?)

Use commands

It could be said that the generic sentence type for the ad is the command, or imperative, because all ads are urging us to some action. For a guide to what has long been typical in ads, I will turn to an old copywriter's guidebook, Merrill De Voe's *Effective Advertising Copy*. De Voe urges his students to use imperatives (commands), in a passage that itself is made up of commands and questions:

Do you like to read sentences that are addressed directly to you as a reader, as this one is? Most people do. It gives the feeling that someone is talking to them from the printed page. Don't forget imperatives! They have a similar effect.

Note that advertisers use commands, not because telling you to do something really makes you do what they say, but because it will create a personal effect, a sense of one person talking to another.

The form of a command is recognisable even without a speaking voice because it typically leaves out the subject *you*. An ad for a skin bronzer urges you to

Brush up your tan.

One of the most famous of all headlines, from an ad for Plymouth written by J. Stirling Getchell in 1932, told us to

Look at all three

The problem was that Chrysler was running a poor third to GM and Ford, especially in its cheapest cars, the Plymouths, which had a reputation a little like that of Lada in the UK today: serviceable but cheap and style-less. The Chrysler executives were at first horrified at Getchell's suggestion; he seemed to be asking them to pay their advertising money to get people to look at Ford and GM cars. But that was just why it worked; it makes sense only if we assume it is good for Plymouth to have us try other cars; that is, if we assume their superiority. It has remained a favourite advertising strategy, in variations, ever since.

The underlying assumption of these commands is clear if we ask why they never say *please*. Normally in our culture we learn from about the age of three that almost all commands must be mitigated, with politeness words or qualifications or by changing them into questions:

Please hand your essays in on time

Could you lend me your 101 lecture notes?

Ads go on telling us to do things hundreds of times a day without any such politeness. One explanation may be that in our culture we cut out the politeness devices if we are asking somebody to do something that benefits the hearer, not the speaker.

Take a seat.

Have some more cheesecake.

This is how advertisers would like to present their commands, as benefits to us. If they said

Please brush up on your tan.

they would imply it was for their benefit, not ours. If they said

Would you mind looking at all three?

it would sound like whining. While most commands make sense as being for the benefit of the speaker or writer, these present themselves as benefits to the hearer or reader.

Why do ads use questions?

Questions, like commands, imply a direct address to the reader – they require someone to answer. That's why they are often used on magazine covers, like these from one issue of *Cosmopolitan*:

> *At long last love.* Are you sure it's the real thing?
> *THE CONDOM.* What's in it for you?
> *Hired or fired?* How to leave your job in style

We take them as requiring a response, like a ringing phone. There is another more subtle effect questions can have – they can contain presuppositions that are almost impossible to discard if one interprets the text. Again, you need to ask what conditions have to hold for this utterance to make sense. So, for instance, the question in my heading – *Why* do ads use questions – assumes that ads do indeed use questions. Here are some headlines from ads:

> Why does a woman look old sooner than a man?
> (Sunlight soap, 1900)
> Should a mother continue to model? (Ipana toothpaste, 1946)
> How do I stay fresh, clean and comfortable all day, every day?
> (Carefree pads)

Each of these questions contains presuppositions about a woman's role:

> A woman does look old sooner than a man.
> Being a mother is inconsistent with being a model.
> I do stay fresh, clean and comfortable every day.
> (And behind that, an assumption that women tend, without these
> pads, to become daily more stale, dirty, and uncomfortable)

You should watch for this sort of thing as a critical reader or hearer of any discourse; you may find yourself taking on all sorts of presuppositions that you would question if you made them explicit. When the interviewer asks

> How will Labour respond to its plunging popularity?

he or she takes the unpopularity as something given, and makes it hard to question.

Many of the questions used in advertising are rhetorical; that is, they assume only one possible answer. A woman in tight jeans just putting on her blouse looks over her shoulder; the headline says:

> Do I look like my period stops me wearing what I want?

In case you miss the fact that this is a rhetorical question, the first line of the body copy says

> Of course not. That's because I use Tampax tampons.

There is a more complex packet of assumptions in

> If your pay packet was £1 short each week who would really notice?
> (Christian Aid)

First, it implies that you are well off, that you can only answer no. It leaves open the question of 'who' would really notice, so that it can give an unexpected answer at the bottom of the page.

> You'll hardly notice the difference, but they will
> [photo of impoverished farmers hoeing]

It also implies, flatteringly, that you *wouldn't* notice because such charity is typical of you. I think you will see lots of questions in charity ads. That is because they are selling, not a service, but a version of yourself as a good person.

The assumptions invoked in these questions are not all benign. This is an ad for Macmillan nurses, who care for people with cancer. It shows a picture of a woman without hair, addressing us:

> Can you see me as a wife, mother, lover? Nor can I.

The first part, 'Can you see me as X?' is in a form that is usually a rhetorical question, assuming the hearer can't see them as X. Here it attributes to us the idea that a woman without hair, due to chemotherapy perhaps, is of course unlikely to be able to continue as a wife, a mother, or a lover. There are plenty of other ads in the same magazines suggesting that hair is essential to all these roles. Then why does 'Nor can I' come as a surprise? It must be that we expect her not to share this prejudice about herself. The body copy then tells how the Macmillan nurse could deal with this loss of confidence. But it all started with a prejudice attributed to us, and then a sympathy attributed to us. This example shows that the complex web of assumptions invoked by a question may be more important than any answer.

Exclamations!

There is one other sentence type that is proportionately over-represented in ads – the exclamation. Here is some examples from the cover of *Cosmopolitan* that I used earlier.

> *OUCH! IT HURTS!* When you're ditched for a bimbo
> Will you ever get over him? Oh yes you will!
> What men do wrong in bed (and we could use some sex tips too!)

In ads, as on magazine covers, exclamation points are sprinkled liberally. The only other writing that I can think of that has more of them is the personal letter. ('I'm here at the Uni. At last! I went to the first lecture on ads. What a bore!!') They are an attempt to recreate the intonation and facial expression that go with face to face interaction, so they make sense in letters that try to substitute for that interaction. But they are odd in other genres. For instance, I was rather surprised to come across a university admissions application full of exclamation points:

I love everything connected with Communication!

I can't remember whether we made an offer on this one. The reason exclamation points are common in letters and odd in application forms is that they suggest personal, face to face contact.

Unlike commands and questions, which typically have a different form from statements, exclamations depend on complex interpretation. If you think they are simple, try explaining why that mark is there to a child, or to an adult who is learning to read. Purists argue that the exclamation point should be reserved for written utterances that must convey spoken emotion to make sense, such as those beginning with *what* or *how*, or utterances in which something is left out. For instance, in a 1946 ad for Pepsodent:

Marrying My Jim!

The incomplete sentence only makes sense with the exclamation mark. It shows we are to take it in terms of the surprise expressed by the speaker, as a frustrated outburst from the jilted woman with the less white teeth. Most exclamations in ads violate the purists' rules; they could be read as simple statements. But the exclamation point tells us to read them emphatically.

IS YOUR CAR DAMAGED?

DOES THE INSURANCE EXCESS PREVENT YOU FROM HAVING THE REPAIR DONE?

WE CAN HELP!!

FOR A LIMITED PERIOD WE CAN OFFER YOU A 25% DISCOUNT OFF YOUR INSURANCE EXCESS ON YOUR NECESSARY WORK!!

(Accident Repair Centre)

The first exclamation is short, and is made up of short words, and I can imagine reading it with the exaggerated intonation of a radio voice-over. But try exclaiming that last sentence out loud. Even double exclamation marks won't make it emphatic.

In the typical cases, it is easy to tell when a sentence is not a statement: the subject *you* will be lacking (for a command), or the subject and predicate will be inverted (for a question), or it will end with an exclamation mark. In practice, as we've seen, it gets more complicated than that, when questions get used for commands, or statements for questions. But the choice of sentence type remains important. Try rewriting any of the examples I have quoted as statements and you will see the difference in effect.

Sentence structure

The chapter so far has been about the *type* of sentence – what its form says about what it is doing. The second part is about the *structure* within the sentence – how it does it. Here we are looking at the same patterns of foregrounding, parallelism, and deviation we saw at the level of sound in the last chapter, but we see them at the level of structure.

Parallelism

I have a blue sweatshirt that says on the front:

Rome [picture of the Coliseum]
Paris [picture of the Eiffel Tower]
London [picture of Big Ben]
Boise [picture of a potato]

Here the first three names set up a pattern of similarity: they are all great world capitals, shown with familiar symbols. The fourth term is parallel in being the name of a city with a familiar symbol, but deviates in that it is not a great world capital. (I should point out that even in Boise this sweatshirt is a joke.)

This ad for microwave ovens works on the same principle. There is a picture of children sitting at a table decorated for a birthday party.

The Samsung RE1200.
Grills
Browns
Bakes
Crisps
Microwaves
and Silences

Here the parallelism is established by a list of verbs for cooking processes. Then, as with the sweatshirt, the last item deviates from the parallel; one hopes that the children are silenced but not grilled, browned, etc. Note that the joke works partly because the thing grilled or silenced is left off the list. I will come to that sort of deletion later in the chapter.

In an ad for Jaeger clothes, whole sentences rather than just words are paralleled:

As a little girl, I hid behind my mother's skirt
In my teens I went red at the drop of a hat.
Quite frankly, these days I don't give a damn.

All readers can sense the repetition, but the only word repeated is *I*. It is the structure that is the same in each case. The sentences start with a phrase telling the period of life, then continues with what she did. It is a life story of maturation, like a lot of children's rhymes ('When Susie was a baby . . .'). The first two, because they are parallel, are taken as signs of timidity. (They both use idiomatic phrases referring to clothing, but not to the clothing advertised here.) Then the last sentence, in present tense, is by contrast a sign of her boldness, with an allusion to Clark Gable's line in *Gone With the Wind*.

Once a parallel structure is established, it allows us to interpret otherwise rather odd constructions. This text appears in block letters on one full right hand page of *Cosmopolitan*:

THE NEW YEAR'S RESOLUTION DIET
THE FIRST-REAL-DATE-IN-TWO-YEARS DIET
THE WEDDING DAY DIET
THE HONEYMOON DIET
THE IT-CAN'T-BE-SUMMER-I-HAVEN'T LOST-ANY WEIGHT-YET DIET
THE I-WISH-I-WAS-HER DIET
THE BEFORE-THE-BABY DIET
THE AFTER-THE-BABY DIET
THE IF-FERGIE-CAN-LOSE-IT-SO-CAN-I DIET
THE WHY-DOES-LYCRA-HAVE-TO-BE-SO-POPULAR DIET

If you stop here, what do you think this is an ad for? When one turns the page, one sees a picture of a woman running up stairs, and the headline

OR YOU CAN CROSS-TRAIN

It's an ad for Nike. The list treats various chunks of language as if they were names of diets, from nouns like *honeymoon* to rhetorical questions like *Why does Lycra have to be so popular?* The hyphens indicate that even these whole sentences are to be treated as if they were single words. The list has its own structure, starting with a relatively simple phrase (*The New Year's Resolution Diet*) and ending with a highly complex one (*The Why-Does-Lycra . . .*), and linking some items, wedding day and honeymoon, before and after baby. The list conveys the cyclical feeling of dieting, the hopelessness of it all, and the endlessness of the motivations. Then exercise is offered as an escape from this hopeless cycle, a way of taking control instead of just reacting to various pressures and anxieties.

Parallelism is also a structural principle of television ads. Since they involve visuals and music as well as language, a good rule of thumb is that where there are parallels on one level there will be on others as well. And as with linguistic parallelism, we usually find that a pattern is built up and then broken. Here is the spoken part of a Persil commercial. The backgrounds are of bright, uniform, poster-like colours, and each speaker addresses us directly. Each speaker gestures to a prominent spot on his or her shirt.

Boy: Oooo. Chocolate ice cream. Mum says she'll never get it out.
Middle-aged man sitting outdoors at a table: It's Bolognese. I don't know how I'll ever get it off.
Woman: Fondue. *[dreamily]* On our anniversary. It's ruined.
Twin women in field: *[one]* Take away spring roll. *[both]* But you can't take it away.
[An announcer and visuals demonstrate the virtues of Persil]
Yuppie male in night club: This is where Jerry Hall splashed me with gravy. *[holds up shirtfront]* I know you can't see it now.

Each utterance begins with a statement of the type of food stain, and expresses pleasure at the memory, and each except the last comments that the article of clothing is ruined. Each speaker provides a type, linked to the type of stain, so the first two contrast by age, the second and third by gender, the third and fourth by number. The last speaker deviates from the pattern by not having the stain visible, and in recalling a violent rather than a pleasurable event. But he deviates as well because he is the only one who wants the stain to remain, as a souvenir. Any part of this ad taken by itself is just odd, but taken together they can be read as parallel.

Ellipsis and substitution

Besides using the regularity of parallelism, an advertiser can throw in an unexpected irregularity. One of the most common ways of doing this is to leave something out which we the readers or viewers must supply. This is called *ellipsis* ; we have seen it already in the Samsung ad, which didn't tell us what was being grilled or silenced. The famous ad for Clairol

Does she or doesn't she?

was considered potentially suggestive, because we are not told what she does or does not do. Shirley Polykoff, who wrote it, thought that the client would not accept it. The suggestiveness would seem to demonstrate Dorothy Sayers' comment, that 'if, by the most far-fetched stretch of ingenuity, an indecent meaning could be read into a headline, that was the meaning the great British public would surely read into it'. But the suggestiveness is not just the result of the prurience of the British (or American) public; such interpretations arise with many ads in which a part of the sentence is left out, because it is just taboo subjects that we talk about in this way. In the case of hair colour, the elliptical question worked just because it could be taken as the sort of embarrassing topic that might be hinted at in this way.

The copy might also put in a word like <u>it</u> or <u>do</u> to substitute for what is left out, as in this Thomson campaign:

If Thomson don't do it, don't do it. But if they do, do.

This is substitution because there are words there, *do it,* to stand for the various possible verbs omitted: go to the desert, sail a boat, stay at a hotel. The compression is carried further by the omission of the *it* in the next part – that is ellipsis. The omission doesn't just let you fill in what you want. It makes you active in interpreting the sentence. Of course it also opens up all sorts of possible ambiguities, but the pictures of hapless hotels (for the 'don't do it') and lovely vacations spots (for the 'do') help guide our interpretations.

The risks of ellipsis are shown by another highly reduced example, for the *Independent*:

It is. Are you?

What is omitted here was supplied in posters by the picture of the newspaper's masthead. But of course other adjectives besides *independent* could go in that slot. As part of the promotion they made buttons saying 'I am. Are you?' and found they were worn proudly by the gay community in one town, but not to indicate which newspaper they read. Ellipsis and substitution aren't just ways of keeping the copy short and punchy. When the readers supply the interpretations, they write themselves into the ad. You might say that the ultimate ellipsis is where the words are left out entirely. I'll talk about that more in Chapter 10.

Incomplete sentences

Ads often punctuate phrases – that is, parts of sentences – as if they were whole sentences. One can read whole ads without coming across a main verb. One reason this is possible is that we turn to the pictures to interpret the relevance of these phrases. So we don't need the explicit signals of what's what that the sentence structure can give us. An Estée Lauder ad, for instance, shows a close-up of a woman's face, her eyes closed, a man's lips just visible to the right kissing her eyebrow. The text reads,

> More than lengthening.
> More than thickening.
> More than separating.
> Introducing *More Than Mascara*
> Moisture-Binding Formula Mascara

In the Estée Lauder ad we supply something like 'If you need' or 'This mascara does' or 'For those who want' before these phrases. The effect is to suggest that we already have these desires, that they are completing our own thoughts. I imagine the kind of voice that a radio announcer has, with huge range of intonation. An ad for Kleenex® facial tissue has a slightly different effect (®Registered Trademark Kimberly-Clark Corporation, USA). On the left, roses made out of tissues emerge from a tissue box. The text says

> Even softer facial tissues
> Just in bloom

The use of 'just in bloom' without a verb (such as *are*) to link it to the first phrase allows it to be ambiguous between the tissues and flowers.

Incomplete sentences may result, not from leaving anything out, but from punctuating with full stops what would otherwise be punctuated with commas. We can see this by looking in detail at one ad for Clinique soap, as it appeared in *Esquire*. I have italicised the phrases punctuated as sentences.

> In just one soaping, this man's skin will start living better.
> [picture here, a close-up of a man's hand gripping the top of a box containing a block of soap labelled 'Clinique Skin Supplies for Men']
> His face will be thoroughly clean. *Look fresh. Feel comfortable.*
> Because it's had an important meeting.
> With Clinique Soap that cleanses a face without overdoing it –
> *without leaving skin feeling taut, stiff, or dry.*
> Clinically formulated, this soap knows exactly what to do.
> *How hard to work. Where to stop.*
> Clinique Soap has a rich, robust lather that feels good on the face.
> *Works quickly. Has no perfume.* Its big brick-shaped bar lasts for months.

Find it – along with a fast, free skin analysis – at selected Clinique counters.

Clinique Soap is the first step in Clinique's 3-step system of skin care.

It's where better skin starts.

CLINIQUE SKIN SUPPLIES FOR MEN.

As I see it, the advertising problem is getting men to use beauty soap. The solution here is to show us an undoubtedly masculine hand, gripping an undoubtedly masculine brick-shaped block of soap. The ad talks about him, instead of addressing us. But if he can use it, it must be okay for less confidently masculine types like me. This punchiness is carried out in the punctuation of some phrases (shown in italic) as if they were independent sentences. With pauses distributed in that way, it gives a sense of toughness and brevity. This is a busy man, huh? Notice that after he has his important meeting with the soap, it takes over as the subject of all the sentences. *It* knows what to do. *It* knows how hard to work. The only thing the reader has to do is 'find it'.

One point of the Clinique example is that there is no direct connection between linguistic features, such as these incomplete sentences, and a single specific effect on a reader. The text works through our interpretation of the situation : who is talking, to whom, about what. It plays off our associations with other texts. So we can't say that these phrases alone make the ad sound tough and masculine, or dreamy and feminine. We can say they are a deviation from what is usual in written English, and that as readers we will look for some interpretation of the voice that makes sense of this deviation.

Conclusion

To review the analysis of sentence type and structure, let's go back to the ad with which I started, the television commercial with the repeated line

Because it's fat.

This hard sell is introduced indirectly, as an answer to questions from women.

Woman 1: Why won't my powder get this chip grease completely out at 40 degrees?

Announcer [and on-screen print]: BECAUSE IT'S FAT.

Woman 2: And butter? At 40 degrees my powder won't shift it. How come?

Announcer [and on-screen print]: BECAUSE IT'S FAT. And ordinary compacts don't stand a chance at 40 degrees.

Woman 2: And now?

[On screen] [the word FAT is broken up by a box of the product]

Announcer: Now there's new Ariel Ultra with fat digester, its re-markable new ingredient.

[On screen] [The words FAT DIGESTER dissolve into a powder that falls into the box]

Announcer: Look, on these fat stains at 40 degrees, ordinary compacts can have problems. But new Ariel digests fat, leaving clothes ultra clean. [picture of demonstration with the word FAT written on two squares of cloth]

[On screen] TWENTY MINUTES LATER

Woman 2: I hate to admit it, but Ariel's worked.

Woman 1: The fat had no chance, not even at 40 degrees.

[On screen] DIGEST THE FATTY FOOD STAINS ORDINARY COM-PACTS LEAVE BEHIND AT 40 DEGREES

[picture of the product]

The key line in the middle of the ad is a statement clogged with the words recommended by the oldest copy writing manuals. '*Now* there's *new* Ariel Ultra with fat digester, its *remarkable new* ingredient'. But the rest of the ad breaks the pitch up. It starts with the women's questions, rather than statements. Note that the only command here is *look*. We are not being asked to buy the product, just to compare Ariel with others, to pay attention to the demonstration being provided for our benefit. We might also ask why the second woman says 'I hate to admit it.' Why should she mind? The form of this statement sets her up as a sceptical audience for the detergent's claims, as a voice separate from the announcer. Then the first woman follows with an exclamation, 'The fat had no chance.'

What about sentence structure? First, there is a parallel between the questions of the two women, and the announcer's response. This sets up the parallels at the end. The elliptical 'And butter?' in line 3 suggests that the second woman is included in the conversation with the first, even though she is in a different laundry room. The 'because it's fat' is also incomplete. This sort of ellipsis leads to the sense of a tough, straight talking voice. Of course the announcer's deep pitch, and the white letters on black, also help.

Let me summarise the main points of this chapter. You can look to the construction of sentences for clues to how the speaker is supposed to be related to us, the readers. The most fruitful place to start is probably asking about sentence type, because sentence types are usually easy to recognise. Then you can go on to observe the parallelism, ellipsis, and incomplete sentences. But remember there is no easy and direct connection of a form to a style or purpose. For that you must read more closely, considering what the writer is trying to do. You can't, for instance, assume that the use of more commands means a harder sell. What you can talk about is surprising variations from expectations – for instance the fact that commands may be avoided, when they logically would be more common in ads.

I will end with one last example for you to try to reconstruct the voice of an ad, in a piece of superb, sneaky copy writing. On the left is a slightly yellowed photo of a chubby, smiling, naked one-year-old baby girl with a red bow in her hair, looking out at us. To the right of this is the line:

when was the last time you felt really comfortable with your body?

The copy includes commands, questions (including rhetorical questions), an exclamation, parallelism, substitution, ellipsis, and sentence fragments; you would think the copywriters had read this chapter. And of course the Nike slogan at the end is a powerful bit of substitution. But I am quoting it to show how all these stylistic devices are used to give the voice of a tough, close old friend, breaking out of the same magazine that it mocks (I've kept the layout, because the short lines are part of the effect):

What happened?
One day you're strolling
around in the buff and
looking the world straight
in the eye without
so much as a blush.
Then wallop!
Puberty. Boys.
Magazine images.
Suddenly the mirror is no
longer your friend.
So who defined your
template of beauty?
Who said you weren't OK?
Get real.
Make your body the best
it can be for one person.
Yourself.
Just do it.

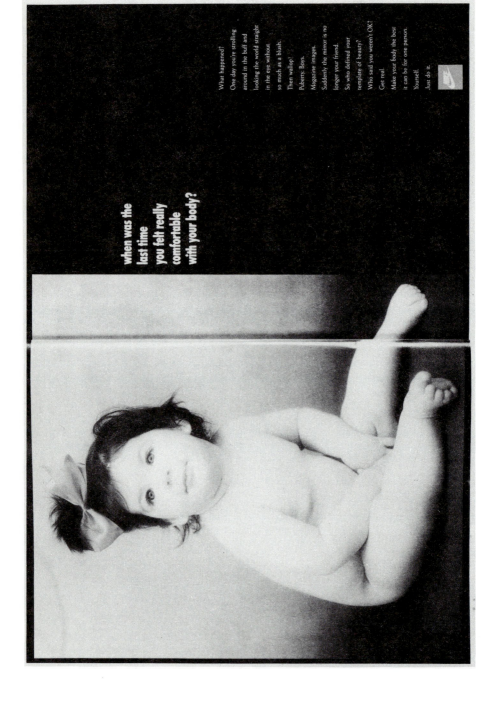

when was the
last time
you felt really
comfortable
with your body?

What happened?

One day you're strolling
around in the buff and
looking the world straight
in the eye without
so much as a blush.

Then wallop!

Puberty. Boys.

Magazine images.

Suddenly the mirror is no
longer your friend.

So who defined your
template of beauty?

Who said you weren't OK?

Get real.

Make your body the best
it can be for one person.

Yourself.

Just do it.

Further reading
Sentence types and functions

Guy Cook, *The Discourse of Advertising*, Chapter 6, has a particularly strong analysis of parallelism, with good examples, and more detailed theoretical argument. Some more complex issues of language in use, related to those here, are taken up in Paul Simpson, *Language, Ideology, and Point of View*, on pp. 147–156.

Linguists deal with the topics that I have covered in this chapter under two headings: grammar (for the structure of sentences) and pragmatics (for assumptions that enter in as language is used). There is more on grammatical description, applied to literary examples, in Geoff Leech and Mick Short, *Style in Fiction*; in Ron Carter and Walter Nash, *Seeing Through Language*; and in Roger Fowler, *Linguistic Criticism* (which focuses on social and ideological implications). The standard textbooks of pragmatics are Stephen Levinson, *Pragmatics*, which is rather difficult for non-linguists, and Geoffrey Leech, *The Principles of Pragmatics*, which explores politeness and irony in detail.

I have just touched on politeness in passing. The classic work on politeness in the construction of sentences (for example, the use of questions for commands) is Penelope Brown and Stephen Levinson, *Politeness*. For applications to literature, see Ronald Carter and Paul Simpson, eds., *Language, Discourse, and Literature*; that might be an easier place to start than with the rather heavy treatises and textbooks. For more on politeness in written texts, you could look at Greg Myers, 'The Pragmatics of Politeness in Scientific Articles', which has further references.

5

Players Please
Puns, Associations, and Meanings

Sometimes guidebooks to copy writing, as to other kinds of writing, suggest that the message should above all be clear and easy to read. Let's test an example. Can you guess what product this headline is advertising?

First shoot your dog then freeze it

This ad makes us work, guessing what the ad could be for (see the illustration for the answer). It is hard to guess without the illustration, because the headline contains two puns, in which a word can have two or more possible meanings. The ad is startling because the first meaning that might occur to the reader is offensive ('Shoot your dog'). Then the picture directs us to a second meaning, one that is less of a threat to the dog. Puns are very common in British ads now (much less so in US or French ads). Their usefulness arises from factors that I mentioned in the chapter on advertising history. First, they attract the attention of bored readers, saturated with ads. Since a pun is by its nature not considered serious, they disarm scepticism. And the pun can be used in image creation, with the second meaning, the one that the reader is meant to reject, lingering, or not, with the product.

Puns are one of several sorts of play with meaning used in advertising. Compare this famous cigarette slogan:

Players please.

First shoot your dog then freeze it.

You may have been led to believe that your best friend was furry with a wet nose.

In fact they have sag-sing and scream to the name of CVD3500.

In other words Sony's latest Colour Video Printer.

Hook it up to most camcorders or any video player and it will obediently produce a high-quality still print And so do near-high quality.

Being a Sony it's as faithful as a hound to the original This is achieved because it's digital frame memory holds twice as much information as most other printers.

passport-sized smiling portraits of the dog.

But less tender portraits of the dog-greet big birds, even portraits of the dog.

(You can see the quality for yourself at selected Sony dealers. Ring 0439 89000 for your nearest Sony Print Centre)

The exactly around 60p a print if not a fitting for it it can make multiple images.

Up to sixteen on one print. It can be up neatly enlarged and colour corrected. In fact there's not much it won't do, apart from chew your slippers.

All sorts of uses spring to mind.

SONY

Why compromise?

to the slogan used for an American cigarette that invites us to a land of cowboys and Western landscapes (I am not allowed to quote the slogan here).

The Players slogan is a pun, in which the same words can have different meanings in two different sentence structures, since the full utterance can be interpreted as:

Players please [you] [said by the advertiser]

or

Please [give me some] Players [said by the customer]

The other slogan depends on the vague associations we have, as suggested by the pictures of ruggedly masculine cowboys and Western landscapes. The two ads play in different ways with meanings.

Where do we go to untangle the meanings of words used in ads? We might look first in a dictionary. It will help us where the same word is used with two distinct meanings of the same word, as in *Players please*. I will look at different ways these meanings can be related. But a dictionary cannot carry all the information about ways in which we build up associations with words; it will not help with the cigarette slogan to look up *cowboy* or *country*. So in the second part of the chapter, I will look at different ways words can take on these associations.

The anatomy of puns

Linguists have several classifications for the ways multiple meanings of one word are related. For our purposes, the key point is that some pairs of meanings seem closely related, hardly noticeable as a pun, while others seem far apart and it may require considerable hinting for us to see the pun. The more distant the relationship of the two meanings, the more striking, but also more strained, is the pun. This is not to say that advertisers will avoid the more distant relationships of meanings; for some products they can use a groan just as well as a chuckle.

One kind of relationship is so common it might be considered the basic advertising pun. In it, the same string of letters refers both to the name of the product, and to a word with its own everyday meaning:

SUNLIGHT IS BEST (Sunlight soap, 1890s)

Don't rough it. [picture of cactus] Live life in Comfort
[picture of green sock matching the cactus] (fabric softener)

Here, both the light of the sun and Sunlight soap are best, and comfort is both a product (spelled with a *C*) and a feeling (with a *c*). This sort of pun is so common we hardly notice it, because of course the whole point of giving a product a name like this is that the producer wants us to carry over associations from the ordinary meaning of the word to the product name (as we saw with Ivory soap in Chapter 2). In a variation of this strategy, the ad may use the word as part of a phrase as if it already had an everyday meaning, even if it does not:

Get that Pepsi® feeling

TDK it

Pepsi is used as if it were an adjective, like *happy* or *excited*; *TDK* is used as if it were a verb, like *record*. This sort of play on the product name must be effective, since it is still used after a hundred years. But it is very boring.

Many of the puns in ads use two unrelated existing meanings of a word. Linguists call this *homonymy* (using the same name for two things) and argue about which meanings can be said to be unrelated. Dictionary makers try to put unrelated meanings in separate entries. But how do you tell? In some cases the distinction is clear, as in this old ad for B. F. Goodrich:

Is this the little flat you promised me?

The meanings of *flat* as 'an airless tyre' and 'an apartment' are, as far as I know, unrelated. Let's look at a common advertising pun, on senses of *light*.

You can tell when the cook's seen the light. (olive oil)

Essilor Transitions lenses. As dark as it's light and as light as a feather. (Boots Opticians)

The meanings of *light* as as 'not fattening', and as 'not heavy' may be metaphorically related, but neither is related to the meaning as 'that which shines', which gets a separate entry in a dictionary.

The pun will seem particularly strained, but particularly striking, if the word can fill two different grammatical categories. For instance, in the Penguin books poster on railway platforms,

Book at any station.

Book is both the verb ('reserve a ticket') and the noun ('a bound volume of reading matter'). The picture of the trademark Penguin at a station links the two. In an ad for Boots cosmetics,

Face the world

face is both a verb and a noun, linking 'the front of one's head' (the noun) to 'confronting the world confidently' (the verb). In most languages, words serving different functions will have different endings, so there will be no pun, but in English this kind of ambiguity between word classes is common.

With these homonyms, we recognise that the two meanings are related only by chance, not naturally as an attribute of the product, and enjoy the way this chance link is brought out.

Far more common than homonymy is the use of related meanings of the same word. Linguists call this *polysemy*, and dictionary makers show it by putting several numbered senses under one headword in dark type. For instance, almost all names for parts of the body have metaphorical meanings as well – *head* can be head of the body or head of the table or head of department or head of a phrase. *Mouth* can be mouth of the body or mouth of a river. These plays on meaning will be less surprising, but they will also seem more natural, as if the pun was waiting there all along and wasn't just coincidence. So for instance, US television ads for a company selling bonds tell heart-warming human stories and end with the slogan

Nuveen. The Human Bond.

Bond here is both the link of affection and commitment between humans, and the financial instrument, which they are claiming is humanised by their company. A viewer may either come to see the financial instrument in terms of their familial links, or throw a shoe at the television to express their disgust that all human relationships were being reduced to a financial investment. (I threw a shoe.)

Common polysemic puns involve words like *bright, naturally, clearly*, where the advertiser will want both meanings. This headline ran above a picture of sheep:

Take it from the manufacturer.
Wool. It's worth more. Naturally. (American Wool Council, 1980)

Here the pun is a way of attributing wool, not to a manufacturing industry, but to nature. The more interesting ads, for me, are those that expect us to get one meaning of the phrase first, and then switch to another, prompted by the picture or the product name or some other clue.

America's favorite cigarette break.
(Benson and Hedges, 1971; ran with pictures of the longer cigarette accidentally broken by, for instance, a windscreen)
Come to us when you want to talk rubbish
(a local ad for skip rental; shown on the side of a skip)
All the reasons for buying a tumble dryer summed up in one line
(Dry Electric; a washing line against a dark cloudy sky)

This switch is particularly effective where the advertiser wants to make us reflect on our reasons for our own first response, as in many ads for charities.

An ad for Shelter shows a snapshot of a young woman. The headline reads

When Emma told us she'd been abused, we put her into a special home.

Her own.

This works because of the pun and a carefully placed full stop. At the end of the first sentence, referring to a social problem, we might interpret *home* to mean 'an institution for residential care'. After the full stop we are told that it means 'family home'. So again, the point is not to arrive at a clear and unambiguous meaning – the advertiser may want us to go through the work of trying to interpret.

Strategic waffle

So far we can see two or more definite meanings in the examples, and we switch between them. Linguists call this *ambiguity*. It is worth distinguishing this from another indeterminate use of meaning, in which no definite meanings can be pinned down, creating a vague and undefinable aura around the word. Linguists call this *vagueness*. Consider the italicised words in this ad for a hotel in New York:

AS *PREFERRED* AS PARK AVENUE

Located in one of the world's most *exclusive* neighbourhoods, it promises an enclave of quiet *elegance*. Here are *superb* accommodations, a restaurant, lounge, fitness center, and *select* meeting facilities . . . and, of course, *uncompromising* service.

The picture tells us no more about the hotel itself than does this copy: it shows a uniformed doorman standing by a Mercedes-Benz, an elegant couple coming out the door and two kids in school uniforms passing by, a bit of a tree, and a flag fluttering above the entrance way. The aim of words and pictures is not to claim any particular advantage for the hotel, but to mark it vaguely as set apart from the threatening city.

Vagueness is often suggested by favourite advertising words like *quality, excellence, style, incomparable*. Look how they are used in these examples:

74 years ago, the language acquired a new word to indicate the ultimate in *luxury* and *elegance*. It remains the last word to this day. (The Ritz, 1980)

Grace space pace (Jaguar, 1960)

Quality in an age of change. (Famous Grouse)

Vibrant, Rich, and Extremely Well-Balanced. (Cinzano)

The vagueness of the adjectives in the Cinzano ad is shown in a witty way by the juxtaposition of the product bottle and some Italian shoes – the words can apply to either. It is pointless to ask what any of these words mean, exactly. It is interesting that all my examples come from luxury goods and services. A more practical product may make a specific claim in relation to its competitors, but these ads are solely concerned with an image.

In some ads, the vagueness may be required by taboos. This is true, for instance, in ads for feminine hygiene products (tampons, pads and liners) called 'sanpro' by the advertisers (I can't seem to find a non-euphemistic general term).

The cleaner drier feeling of Always. Plus extra protection.

The vague word here is *protection*. No ad actually says pads are to keep blood off your pants. (It's been pointed out to me that sanpro ads avoid red, as well.) The same vagueness arises in some AIDS ads (see Chapter 12).

In all these examples, the vagueness results from one word. Vagueness can also be a matter of relation within the sentence. For instance, ads very often make comparisons that are vague because they don't say what the product is being compared to: *better, smoother, richer, more, longer.* Surprisingly, very precise numbers can also be vague in a similar way:

Ultraviolet rays and free radicals can cause as much as 80% of premature ageing.
Use it Nightly.
While you sleep, it enhances cellular repair by 95% – to keep your skin looking healthier, younger.
The proof is in the testing. After ten weeks you could see a 40% reduction in appearance of little lines; 84% increase in moisturisation. (Estée Lauder Advanced Night Repair)

The copy floors you with specific measurements that it offers as proof. But as long as *premature ageing, cellular repair, little lines,* and *moisturisation* remain undefined, it doesn't matter whether the increase is 84% or 48%. Academics have been known to be vague in the same way, giving immense precision to undefined measurements like 'readability level' or 'intelligence' or 'complexity'.

Beyond the dictionary: associative meanings

These last examples show that it is not just the dictionary definitions of words that are used in ads. If advertisers were only concerned with conveying information from them to us, they could choose the correct words to carry the senses they required. But they are trying to place their product in a shifting system of meanings, to give it an image. To do that, they need to draw on associations we have with the words. If you are marketing a soap for men, you have a range of words that all refer to the people you want to use the product:

men, gentlemen, males, boys, lads, guys, blokes, les hommes.

None of these choices is neutral in effect, not even the biological term *male*. Dictionaries, which are a good guide to distinct meanings, are not always helpful with these associations; these meanings require us to follow a word through its uses, by different people, to different people, in different situations.

It helps to divide up the kinds of associative meanings so that we can see how they work. I will consider associations with the things referred to, with the speaker, with the attitude towards the hearer, and with links to other words.

Referent associations

Referent associations arise from social attitudes towards the thing referred to; linguists call these associations *connotations*. So when the cigarette company chose the name *Bachelor* cigarettes, they weren't meaning they shouldn't be smoked by married men, or by people who didn't have undergraduate degrees. One Bachelor ad from 1962 shows a man leaned back in a deck chair, hat at a rakish angle, and says

The tip that's setting the trend.

The picture and headline suggest that the name *Bachelor* is meant to carry connotations of the freedom and pleasures of a single life. Note that this also conveys social assumptions – I doubt if there were any *Spinster* cigarettes. The dictionary definitions of the two words should be similar, but against the background of a patriarchal society, an unmarried man is free while an unmarried woman is undesirable.

The associations with referents are not entirely fixed, though some are hard to shake, such as the association in European culture between white and innocence, red and passion, black and death or evil. (These are not universal: to wear white at a Chinese wedding would be bad luck, while red is preferred for good luck). A television ad for Bianco chocolate both invokes and denies the associations of its name. A woman eats the product and imagines doing such subversive things as letting her annoying young nephew be carried off by a kite to land on her annoying suitor. The slogan is

Who says white is innocent.

This leads us through complex associations. First there is the use of an Italian name for an English product. There is a statement that white is said to be innocent, and that the activities of this chocolate eater are not innocent. The aim seems to be to associate the brand of chocolate, not with innocent children's treats (a huge but saturated market), but with the wickedness, and therefore adults.

The search for product names with effective connotations is so much taken for granted by sceptical consumers that an ad can draw attention to a name that was not so carefully chosen:

An appealing name is said to be crucial to the success of a brand.

So where did we go right? (Wild Turkey)

Compare this to the ad for Famous Grouse that I used as an example of vagueness:

Quality in an age of change.

Both whiskeys have potentially silly names, birds that are considered stupid, easy targets for hunters. Both ads are claiming that their whiskey stands outside the image-making of marketing. Famous Grouse does this by presenting the bottle with an oil painting of a grouse, associating their product with an imagined traditional time before advertisement. The Wild Turkey ad foregrounds the oddity of their name, as an indication that it has no need of its hype. Compare the slogan for a US line of preserves:

With a name like Smuckers, we have to be good.

It is interesting to compare brand names to place names and the associations they may call up. In the UK, place names seem to be a matter of tradition, their origins buried in now superseded languages. No committee thought up names like those around the university where I teach: Goosnargh, Chorley, Clitheroe, Wirral, Flookburgh, Coniston Cold. In the western US, on the other hand, names were given just as developers who got the land from the railroads began to use marketing techniques, so there are Pleasant Valleys and Richlands and Lakeviews and Sunnysides. A town in south-west Idaho was first called Rattlesnake Station, an accurately descriptive name as it happens; when people began selling real estate there it became Mountain Home, which has better connotations. Dickens' hero in *Martin Chuzzlewit* expresses outrage at this sort of American technique – for him place names should be place names, not advertisements.

Attitude associations

The examples I have just given show taken for granted social assumptions about the referent. Others choices show the attitude of an individual towards the referent (what Geoffrey Leech calls *affective meanings*). For instance:

house, home, residence, bungalow

job, career, position, employment opportunity

rural area, countryside, the sticks, isolated, middle of nowhere

You might reflect on the range of affective words for *women, men, dogs, films*. The importance of such choices in advertising is shown in estate agents' ads. You would see:

A superb family detached home, close to amenities, full of character.

Compare this to:

A house that is separate from others and near shops.

I'm not sure what equivalents I would use for *full of character*: it could well be synonymous with *full of damp patches and strange wallpaper*.

Speaker associations

Let's go back to my list of terms for males. If I call someone a *guy*, it may not tell you much about them, but it tells you about me – unless the man I am talking about is stuffed and on top of a bonfire: I must be a North American, or trying to sound like one. (The term has crept into business talk in the UK like many Americanisms). Advertisers often use words that carry meanings because of who is supposed to use them (Geoffrey Leech calls these *social meanings*). For instance, the name of a record store in Lancaster, '*Ear 'Ere*, indicates solidarity with a social group that does not pronounce the initial *h* (a very common pronunciation, but one stigmatised in schools). *Hear* and *here* are homophones, soundalikes, as is *ear* in the h-less pronunciation. So this name is both 'hear it here', and the parliamentary call to order 'here here'. I discuss the uses of varieties of English in Chapter 7.

A poster campaign for Regal Blue cigarettes exploits these speaker associations. Apparently they were trying to distinguish their brand from the elegant, sophisticated associations of the highly cerebral Silk Cut and Benson and Hedges ads. One campaign just had pairs of pictures, for instance, on the left, against a green background, a portable phone, and on the right, against a blue background, a 10p piece, with no indication of what was advertised except the government health warning at the bottom. This puzzled me. About the tenth time I passed the poster, I figured out that the portable phone was to be associated with the prats smoking other cigarettes, and the

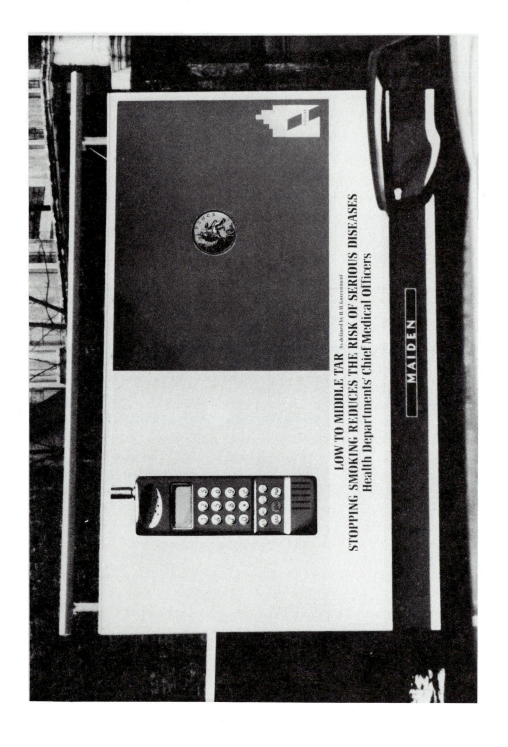

10p piece was to be used in a pay phone, which is associated with the normal folk who smoke Regal Blue cigarettes. Another, less puzzling poster had on one side engraved script reading, 'Jolly good to see you old bean', while on the other side, against a blue background, was a hand making a thumbs up sign. We are to take the two messages as equivalent, but one is associated with a pompous old chap, and the other with, well, regular blokes. (It is also a sign in British Sign Language, but I doubt if many passers-by noticed that.)

Word link associations

Some meanings carry over from other senses of the word, usually taboo senses; Geoffrey Leech calls these *reflective*. In general, advertisers try to avoid these associations, not always successfully. For example, I imagine there has been some worry at the company that makes AYDS (an antacid); a long-established trade name gets associated with a terrible disease. A television ad for Jacob's Cream Crackers recently fell foul of a reflective meaning. In it, a prawn sang about how the biscuit lets the taste of the food come through:

> Don't knacker it, cracker it.

Apparently the advertisers didn't realise that *knackers* is slang in Yorkshire for 'testicles'. (I didn't know this either). But as soon as the ad ran, hundreds of Yorkshiremen and Yorkshirewomen were phoning up to complain. The lesson, said *Campaign*, was that creative departments should make sure they hire at least a few token northerners.

Some advertisers take advantage of these associations, as in the famous Castlemaine XXXX lager campaign

> Australians wouldn't give a XXXX for anything else.

Here the slogan depends on the reflected meaning that comes from XXXX, the product name, also being used as a print substitute for a spoken obscenity. The reflected meaning works well for the image of tough and blunt-spoken masculinity that the brand tries to project.

These reflective meanings arise because they remind us of other meanings of the same word. A word also gets associations from the way it is associated with other words in familiar phrases. We tend to build our talk and writing out of pre-fabricated bits. A *collocation* is any group of words that tends to be associated together in one of these bits: a proverb, an idiom, a cliché, a slogan, a title. You'll notice familiar collocations in the names of rock groups: The Rolling Stones, Curiosity Killed the Cat, Simple Minds, Big Country, Nomeansno.

Many of the puns in ads involve a fractured collocation, with one word replaced, or a collocation used in a new context. An Ever Ready bike light poster, seen beside highways, draws on a collocation from a road sign:

ROAD FLOODED AHEAD [the letters are in the beam of light spreading in front of a bike onto a dark road]

Here we realise it is flooded with light, not with water. Other ads make us do a double take by taking a phrase literally.

The average cost of a wedding is now £7,359. And they still call it *giving the bride away.* (Halifax Building Society)

The difference between enjoying time on the road and *doing time* there. (Acura cars)

These are puns too. But they make us think about associations a word carries because of its place in a collocation.

Another way a word may take on associations is by evoking a certain specialised use of language, a *register*: examples would be medical language, football language, auto language, classical music. Ads may do this with collocations, as in the examples just given, or they may just use enough words associated with a register throughout the copy to evoke those specialised meanings. This travel ad draws on the register of fashion:

Tailor-made beaches with *off the peg* sunshine. (Spain)

This is, I believe, from snooker:

William dropped by, so *we left the black and sunk the yellow.* (Grant's Scotch)

The yellow here can be either a ball or the golden liquid prominent in the picture. An ad for VO5 hot oil treatment shows various damaging hair treatments on the left, with the heading:

The Crime.

On the right is small sized package of the product, with the heading

The Trial.

At the bottom, before the logo, it says

The Verdict.

It is not always clear that the advertiser wants all the associations that the register calls up: a scotch may want to be associated with the relaxation and skill of snooker, but there is no particular advantage to a resort in being associated with clothes. What is clear is that the headings don't make sense unless one recognises all the puns as drawing on one register.

One of my favourite radio ads is a splendid tour-de-force of plays on the meanings of *light* and *heavy*. It begins with a female singer talking about DHL picking up a package, and then doing what seems to be the spoken introduction to an R and B song:

Honey, this relationship is getting heavy

So here, *heavy* is both the weight of the package and the seriousness of a relationship. After the song, the spoken patter slips into several overlapping registers:

So if you're worried about your weight
petrified about putting on pounds
scared of being substantial

Here, along with the alliteration in each line (consistent with it being song lyrics), there are evocations of dieting (the euphemism 'substantial' for 'overweight') applied to package delivery. Meanwhile, the chorus of Atlantic R & B vocals in the background repeats 'Ain't No Mountain High Enough, Ain't No Valley Deep Enough', language from gospel music. So we have four different sets of meanings here:

- the heavy relationship signalled at the beginning

- heavy in the sense of overweight human body

- a heavy parcel

- heavy as opposed to light (with *light* taken in the sense of *speed of light*)

What these more complex examples suggest is that we cannot separate the dictionary meaning from the associative meanings. There is no plain language that doesn't carry associations, because even the plainest language signals the desire to be plain.

Conclusion

Puns have a bad reputation, as a low form of humour. People groan when you make them. That is because they seem so unreasonable – they depend on chance similarities, and undermine the logical relationships of language. You know how annoying this can be if people ever joked on your name (it is pure coincidence that my surname sounds like the word for *bog*). They also require more work to process. Despite this low reputation, some of the greatest writers of English are also the greatest users of puns – Shakespeare, Thoreau, Joyce, Nabakov. Puns appeal to just those writers who delight in language for its own sake. They signal a non-serious kind of discourse. That may be why we find them in recent ads, but not earlier ones, and in British ads more than those in the US, and on headlines on sports pages of newspapers more than on the front pages. In these contexts, the extra work to process them is part of the appeal. Advertisers want you to look twice, and so do many authors. If it is a bad pun, one that tells us nothing about the product, or one that plays no part in the structure of the literary work, there is a sense of trick, because we have devoted so much work for so little reward. I return to visual puns in Chapter 10.

The second part of the chapter emphasised that there are several different kinds of associative meanings. The lesson for advertising is clear. Critics who focus on the literal meanings of ads, as do most regulatory bodies, miss the point. Their power is in what is not said, what is implicit. Some of these meanings can be pinned down. But others have complex social meanings that can vary from group to group. A man may find a Silk Cut image witty while a woman may find it threatening. One of the most important ideas in current literary theory is that all language comes to us used, shaped by its earlier uses. This is as true of ads as it is of novels. I will consider this diversity of readings in Chapter 13.

Further reading
Puns and associative meanings

There is a good section on verbal play in Geoffrey Leech, *English in Advertising*. Guy Cook, *The Discourse of Advertising*, has a good section on the links between visual and verbal puns, pp. 42–43.

My outline of associative meanings, in the second part of the chapter, follows another book by Leech, *Semantics*, (2nd edition) with a chart on p. 23. For an especially readable consideration of word meaning and collocation, see Ronald Carter, *Vocabulary*. On the distinction between ambiguity and vagueness, see Ruth Kempson, *Semantic Theory*, Chapter 5, a fairly advanced but clear textbook. For more detailed descriptive treatment, see Joanna Channell, *Vague Language*. On puns in literature, see Jonathan Culler (ed.) *Puns* for a very heavy collection of essays. For comments on puns in ads, see Robert Goldman, *Reading Ads Socially*, p. 131.

The associative and literal meanings of place names, touched on briefly here, are discussed in Brian Friel's play about Ireland and language, *Translations*.

6

'You in the shocking pink shellsuit'
Pronouns and Address

Adshel, a company that puts posters on bus shelters, ran four ads recently in *Campaign* showing media buyers the effectiveness of their medium. Each shows a bus shelter on a street that suggests a distinctive social class, and a poster addressing a particular person of that class. For instance, one poster on a Knightsbridge street just has elegant white on blue script reading:

> Pardon me, Madam. That's right, madam with the pearls, the Asprey bag and the beautiful, deep winter holiday tan.

Another poster with blue on pink sans-serif print, set outside a new mall, says,

> Excuse me darlin'. Yes you in the shocking pink shellsuit with the 'Big Shopper' bag getting out of the 4WD Suzuki.

A third, outside an off licence, reads, in yellow on red:

> OI MUSH! THE BLOKE WITH THE PAINT SPATTERED OVERALLS AND THE FAG BEHIND YOUR EAR COMING OUT OF THE BOOKIES.

Each ad shows blurred passers-by, but not the woman with the pearls, or the woman in the shellsuit, or the man with the overalls. That spot, apparently, is reserved for the imaginary person looking at the poster, who is singled out in this personal and direct way, and recognises that 'Pardon me, madam' or 'Excuse me darlin'' or 'OI MUSH' is addressed to them.

What Adshel says it can deliver is the dream of the advertisers, and the nightmare of the media audience: the single salesperson facing the single customer, personally, but put everywhere, reproduced by the medium a thousand times over. In some cultures most things are still sold face to face, and in our culture it is still a way to sell double glazing, time-share properties, or insurance (assisted perhaps by banks of telephones dialling automatically). But in our distribution system it is not a practical way to sell soap or chocolate bars or loo paper. The copywriter John E. Kennedy promised the clients of Lord and Thomas at the turn of the century that ads would give them 'Salesmanship-on-paper', not just an informative notice. To sell like a salesperson, ads have to *seem* to address us personally, even when they address millions of us at once. And in being personal, they offer us versions of what it is to be a person.

At first glance print or broadcast ads seem to be a remarkably inefficient medium for addressing individuals, because they cannot pick out particular people the way the Adshel poster claims to do. Instead they seem to make wild guesses about the person reading or watching the ad.

> Your children don't stop growing just because you're dithering about what camcorder to buy. (Panasonic)
>
> Get tough with your cellulite (Babyliss)
>
> Truly, madly, deeply in love? Tell the world. Not your Mum and Dad.
> (British Telecom; poster shows a girl in a pay telephone)
>
> Who taught you to shave your legs?
> (television commercial for Soft Sense Shave Gel)
>
> Shamed by Your English? (a correspondence course)
>
> You have the Bible. But do you have the other testament of Jesus Christ?
> (TV commercial for the Church of Jesus Christ of Latter-Day Saints)

Reproduced this way, these messages seem to assume that you, the reader of this book, have children, cellulite, a boyfriend, smooth legs, faulty English, *and* the Bible. Do you? If not, your first thought might be that these advertisers were missing their mark and wasting their budgets. Your second thought might be that they were assuming that everyone must be or should be as they assume, and you may well resent this assumption.

I will argue that the process of advertisers addressing readers, and the process of readers finding themselves in ads, are more complicated than that. Ads can create a sense of addressing a person whether they are on target in that particular case or not. To make sense of the Adshel poster that shouts at me 'OI MUSH', I have to construct not just a person but a social world in which this kind of language goes with paint-splattered overalls, with a cigarette behind the ear, and with the bookies. As it happens, I don't recognise myself in this stereotype, and I doubt that anyone does. But for some ads I do step into the position offered – for instance, being a parent I may feel a twinge of regret reading the camcorder ad, even if I do not buy a camcorder as my way of dealing with regret at time passing. The address in ads can also be effective when I don't step in. Just by understanding the question 'Shamed by your English?', by recognising that some people could or should be ashamed, I am accepting the advertiser's view of language as a commodity that can be sold by mail, and as a personal attribute like halitosis. Pronouns like *you* are powerful forms, that can carry assumptions about gender, class, and nation. But as we will see, it is not just pronouns that have this effect, but the whole way a text is interpreted as personal address.

Who is you ?

My old copy-writing textbook tells me to make copy personal:

> Most valuable are names of people and personal pronouns that center upon people. All first and second-person pronouns are personal, but your copy should be made up predominantly of the latter. Usually the pronoun 'you' should occur with the greatest frequency. (Merrill De Voe, *Effective Advertising Copy*, 1956).

This is good practical advice, but it contains a contradiction, one suggested by the examples of *you* that we have seen so far; *you* works because it suggests a one-to-one relationship, but it is used in ads just because the advertisers cannot know whom they are reaching.

Contrary to what Adshel says, the *you* of ads is powerful because it is slippery, not because it picks out just one person. We can see the different ways of using *you* by comparing two famous recruiting posters from World War I. One has Uncle Sam pointing out of the picture and saying

I WANT YOU FOR THE U.S. ARMY

(The original, British version has General Kitchener and says 'Your country needs you.') Here the *you* is not specified by the ad. It would seem to be anyone who passed in front of the poster. But I place myself in it if I recognise the *I* as a personification of the nation, and the *you* as me, and the *want* as a call on draft age men.

Compare this *you* to that in a famous British World War I recruiting poster that shows a middle-aged man sitting in an armchair, a boy on the floor playing with toy soldiers, and a girl on the man's lap asking

Daddy, what did you do in the Great War?

Unlike 'I WANT *YOU* FOR THE U.S. ARMY', this ad does not tell us what to do. Literally, the *you* is the daddy of the little girl, not us. It has its effect entirely by allowing the reader to see himself (and it must be *him*self) in this position, not as a male of draftable age but as a father of the future. He joins, not because his country tells him to, but because of the threat of a very private shame. The ad let the reader do the work of including himself in the *you*. With this poster, the army moved from the first of the periods of advertising I described in Chapter 2, focusing on claims, to the second, focusing on substitution of associated meanings for commodities.

There is a special poignancy to the ways these recruiting posters address us, for many of those who responded to these calls were killed. But the strategies continue in ads for ordinary commodities, either invoking a very general and empty *you* , into which the readers may slot themselves, or defining a very specific *you* in the text. Even the general *you* may draw on assumptions of a particular place or time; that's one of the reasons ads date so quickly. During the Second World War, almost every ad in *The Picture Post* (the British equivalent of *Life*) was tied in some way to the war effort, like this one for Kay's Linseed Compound:

DON'T LET COUGHS KEEP YOU OFF DUTY

Guard your health. It has no more insidious enemy than cough or cold, which leads to greater troubles. So get rid of coughs and colds – quickly. Kay's, with its thirteen ingredients, works like magic. From all chemists.

The assumption that makes this make sense is that you, whoever you are, have a duty, so that your health is a public matter, and a pharmaceutical company can address you in the terms used by government information notices.

Ads like 'What did you do in the Great War' define who is saying *you*, sometimes in a comically specific manner. An ad for Nationwide Building Society shows a newspaper clipping on mortgage rates, torn out as if left on the kitchen table as a hint for someone. The headline says:

We agree with your wife. You can afford a new house.

Here the advertisement seems to know all about *you* already, and to intervene in a marital argument. Even if you haven't had this argument – even if you aren't married or aren't male – you have to make assumptions about married people and typical gender roles to interpret the ad, to figure out what the heading has to do with the clipping. For instance, you assume that ('of course') a wife is socially ambitious and a husband is financially cautious, and that this leads to arguments. Then a building society can mediate.

In this ad the person speaking is invisible. In others, like the 'I Want You', the speaker looks out at us. One ad in the much admired (though not ulti-mately successful) campaign to keep the Conservative government of Margaret Thatcher from abolishing the Greater London Council shows its Labour leader Ken Livingston ('Red Ken') looking out at us. The headline has him saying, in quotation marks:

'If you want me out you should have the right to vote me out.'

The cleverness of the ad is that it positions *you* as one of Livingston's oppo-nents, and then presents the abolition as the personal loss of the chance to vote him out democratically, a loss even for those Conservatives and others most opposed to the GLC. Like the Uncle Sam ad, it establishes a personal relation between the speaker and the interpreter of the ad.

This personal relation does not require that the *you* be us, in the first instance; we can watch as the ad picks out its audience before us. In a Laurentian Life ad, four black and white pictures of a famous model in a slinky black dress and high heels are spread across the tops of two pages. She is striking various poses seated on a starkly geometrical contemporary chair. The captions read:

What if you hate the words 'life insurance' [She strokes her feet]

[She looks at her legs]

But really . . . [She sits thoughtfully]

. . . You'd like a more sensible way of planning your life.

[She looks out at us]

The basic pitch seems to be to get young single employed women, as well as those with families, to worry about insurance. In the copy, it is presented as an investment, rather than as protection; it shows one is 'sensible'. We watch this model responding to the life insurance pitch. Life insurance is notori-ously supposed to make people uncomfortable (in *Take the Money and Run*, the Woody Allen character is punished, not by solitary confinement, but by being locked in a cell with an insurance agent). But here our squirming is dis-placed onto her, and in the end she looks out at us.

We: with you and without you

We is always tricky, because it can be used in both exclusive and inclusive senses, that is, either not including or including the person who is spoken to. In ads, one use produces a sense of solidarity with the customer, the other projects the image of the company as personal. An example of inclusive *we* is another ad used during the blitz:

WE ARE CONSTANTLY BEING ATTACKED

Not by the Blitzkrieg, which we can and will face – but by hosts of insidious foes in the shape of germs (Yestamin, 1941)

It takes considerable chutzpah to tell people who are being bombed that the real threat is germs, and to imply that your yeast vitamin product is playing the role of the RAF. It can only work because the advertisers present themselves as part of the threatened group. Advertisers seek this sort of solidarity when they talk about the environment, or identify with the nation.

The more common use is for *we* to refer to the advertiser, not including the audience.

Everything we do is driven by you. (Ford)

At McDonald's, we do it all for you.

We have to try harder. We're only Number 2. (Avis)

We just thought people might appreciate beauty that lasts for years. (Mazda)

This exclusive *we* form personalises huge and impersonal corporations, (especially when delivered in a folksy voice as in the last example, part of a series of commercials).

A striking use of the exclusive *we* that dominates a whole ad campaign is in a US ad for MCI long distance telephone services, in its battle with AT&T. Rather surprisingly, it shows no customers at all, but instead focuses on a sales meeting in which the MCI salespeople exclaim enthusiastically about 'Proof Positive', a programme that is said to demonstrate savings when a business switches to MCI. The style is important – black and white, with the framing not horizontal, the camera zooming in an out, very short sound bites, the sound boom and the camera sometimes visible, all suggesting broadcast-news-like realism. Electronic rhythms add to the sense of urgency. At the beginning, the sales manager begins in an empty room, as if informally telling early arrivals or an interviewer what is to come:

What I was thinking of talking about was what the customers were telling us and how we came up with the ideal solution.

Salespeople come in and introduce themselves. They talk about customers

They're overwhelmed by choice.

Their business isn't telecommunications.

Then they picture themselves reassuring customers with this new programme, and the *they* becomes *you*:

You made the right decision. You can stop thinking about long distance.

They finish with salespeople asserting the bond between them and their customers:

One salesman: Time and time again my customers say, 'Can you back it up.' Now we are.

Another salesman: The way we do business is: This is who we are as people and this is what we are as a company.

It would seem to be an off-putting approach to show the salespeople congratulating themselves. But in the ferocious competition over business telephone services, all three major contenders stepped back from addressing customers directly in their ads – perhaps there was too much scepticism for that. Instead MCI seems to open up its own internal workings, to show the enthusiasm of its own people for this programme, to show itself to other business as another business. That is where the informality and realism of the style comes in. We are then to believe that if these individual people are candid and convinced, then 'Proof Positive' is genuinely for the benefit of the customer.

I and the paradox of the individual

In the MCI ad, *I* is used for the salespeople. Usually, though, *I* speaks as the potential consumer, the endorser or the sceptic.

If I can do it, trust me, you can
(Shari Belafonte in a Slim Fast television commercial)

But it raises a paradox. Many ads call on the consumer to become an individual. In a commodity system, as I said in Chapter 2, we are defined by work over which we have no control, in which we have no sense of being identified with what we can make or do. Ads offering consumption of one commodity or another seem to offer an alternative way of defining ourselves: if we buy, say, a car, we will be distinctive individuals. It is a paradox because, of course, the advertiser addresses thousands or millions of people with the same message at the same time, and always hopes that more than one of them will buy the car. (If I really wanted to be different from other people, I wouldn't buy a car at all.) The trick is to be different *like* other people.

The strategies for defining ourselves as in some way different are strongly tied to gender; few of these *I* ads will work the same for men and women. In a Suzuki ad we see a man in expensive glasses, a tie and a striped shirt looking off into middle distance and saying defiantly:

It's Not Everyone's Choice of Company Car But It's Mine.

I don't know exactly how an investment banker convinces the personnel department that an off-road vehicle is a company car. But here we are supposed to recognise him (and the thousands of other London business people following the fashion for 4WD) as independent (and perhaps suggesting he has a home in the country where he can use it, and not just a flat in Fulham).

A similar assertion of individuality works both against and with femininity in an ad for Champion athletic clothes. It breaks with the usual conventions of gender display – a young male is flopped back in the passive position, while a woman is perched and tensed on top of a sofa. She is wearing athletic shorts and top and seems to be contemplating her running shoes.

He's my comfort, my inspiration, my life. But I am captain of my soul.

She gains this autonomy from the male by buying this product; it is not taken for granted. Try reversing the gender in this ad; could a man stand above a woman and assert that running shorts allowed him to be captain of his soul? The example shows that the positions an ad offers, though open, are by no means empty or entirely free.

The position offered by an ad may be at the intersection of a number of identities, linked by the text. Here is an ad in a fairly traditional format, that of an apparently private document (such as a letter or a note on a bulletin board); this shows a list of New Year's Resolutions, written on a January 1989 calendar page. There is no *I* here, but we recognise a person from a collection of details. I won't tell you the name of the advertiser until the conclusion to this chapter, so that you can guess just what the position sketched here might lead to.

2 Monday
1. Won't feel guilty about owning a Filofax.
2. Will argue for the broadest possible alliances to defeat Thatcherism.
3. Rejoin CND and Anti-Apartheid.
4. Stop using aerosols.

3 Tuesday
5. Book that trip to the USSR!
6. Give up eggs.
7. Ignore all those loud and macho paper-sellers.
8. Read some Gramsci, and catch up on the debate on post-Fordism.

4 Wednesday

9. Scrub that racist graffiti from the wall down our street

New Year's resolutions are by their nature supposed to be personal, individual, to pick out the reader out of the crowd. But as we read down the list, we build up a type – a politically active yuppie, aware of the stereotypes around this role, but not defensive about them (keeping his or her Filofax). Of course the ad is not just addressed to real people who do, or wish they did, all these things. But it suggests that these things can go together without inconsistency. Again, to say *I* is to say what can make a person individual.

Shared knowledge: he and she

The pronouns *I*, *we*, and *you* remind us of the basic communicative situation of the speaker (what linguists call the first person) and the hearer (the second). We might think third person pronouns (*he, she, it, they*) would be straightforward, because they don't involve either of the two parties to the communication. But they too can be used to set up positions. *He* and *she* typically refer to someone known to the reader, either known through the ad, as with the person in the picture, or known because taken for granted as part of the reader's life. An ad from the Department for Education, trying to win parents' support for the new national exams for all 7-year-old children, shows the chubby legs of a girl in a school uniform, with one knee sock fitting properly, labelled 'English Technology Science', the other sliding down, labelled 'Maths'. The headline says

> The sooner you can spot where she's falling down, the sooner you can lend a hand.

The pronoun alone suggests a personal bond even more than 'your child', because it assumes that the addresser and addressee must both be able to tell who is being referred to.

The old copy writing textbook I have been quoting gives this advice about *he* and *she*:

> Words that have masculine or feminine natural gender are personal. . . But common gender words like 'customer' and 'solicitor' are less appealing. (De Voe, p. 657).

This follows from what we saw with the pronoun *I*: the textbook implies that when people are addressed in terms of their gender, they see the message as addressed personally to them, or to individuals, in a way it can't be without this gender marking. In this view, the marking of what is appropriate for each gender is not the advertiser's main aim; the ad does it in the course of making the message personal.

Where better to see the uses of pronouns to construct gender than in the magazine called simply: *She*:

> Is he looking at your melting brown eyes, your silky smooth skin, or the spot just under your left nostril? (Valderma: Tough on Spots. Gentle on Skin. The picture is a close-up of a man's eyes).
>
> She gave me a son and I gave her the stars. (Diamonds. The picture shows a ring against a black background)
>
> Five minutes ago he was demolishing the house. (Farley's bedtimers. The picture shows a toddler asleep on a chair)

All three ads build familiarity by using a pronoun rather than, say, *that man* or *my wife* or *our son*. But in addition, the first *he* takes for granted that the male gaze defines the woman; the *she* of the diamonds ad assumes dynastic relations in patriarchy. Even the toddler ad would probably be different with *she* rather than *he*; though girls can make just as big a mess (I know), it is boys who are considered comically destructive in the Dennis the Menace style. An ad for *SHE* itself stresses that the pronoun offers many roles, not one.

> SHE is a woman and a lover
>
> SHE is a worker and a mother
>
> SHE is the magazine for women who juggle their lives

The ad suggests that these are contradictory roles that can be reconciled in the mystical femininity suggested by the pronoun.

Sometimes there is a rhetorical reason for using *he* or *she* rather than *you* to refer to the audience, especially where the pitch implies something unfavourable about the person referred to. I mentioned in Chapter 4 Shirley Polyakoff's slogan for Clairol hair colour:

> Does she or doesn't she? Only her hairdresser knows for sure.

If we take there to have been at least a mild taboo on dying one's hair, then the use of *she* for the user of hair colour, placing the reader as an observer, would make sense as displacing the possible threat. Another example is in sanpro ads. As we have seen, these ads have a problem – they have a mass market product to sell, but can't talk about what it does. It seems to be too touchy even to mention directly that the woman reading the ad might have periods. The first company to breach the taboo on advertising, Kotex, made a bundle in the 1920s with indirect ads that showed successful women had confidence, and using indirect pitches of that sort.

> 8 out of 10 of the better class of women (1928)

The same strategy was picked up by their competitors.

Socially alert women use Tampax (1941)

And it continues today.

For inner peace, she uses Tampax (1992)

The aim is to create an image of a woman associated with the product, without directly addressing the reader. The picture is the key here – it introduces a woman who can then be referred to as having desirable qualities. Ads warning of risks of AIDS are typically in third person (*he* rather than *you* or *we*) for similar reasons; there is such a strong taboo that to say *you* might be at risk could lead the reader to turn off. I will return to these ads in Chapter 12.

They is tricky in ads, just because it is not personal; it usually refers to the great undistinguished mass that fails to use the product. But it can also define a new and as yet nameless class of people to which the consumer will want to belong. A Diet Coke television commercial has images of young people doing exciting activities or in exotic places, the camera swooping around them dramatically. Words drift across the screen independently, forming phrases that suggest the people pictured break with stereotypes.

Ministers who surf
Surgeons who sculpt
Insurance agents who speed
Some people live life as an exclamation!
They're tasting it all in one awesome calorie
Taste it all

The images draw on stereotypes (ministers), break them (who surf), and set them up again in the new category of people who 'live their lives as an exclamation'. The spatial disorientation of the visuals is, I think, part of this message. We are not told that we are like these people, but the movement of the camera identifies us with their point of view, perched on a cliff or zooming around the racetrack. By buying the product, we can step out of our assigned places, into this free-floating fulfilment.

Conclusion

The choice of pronouns carries significance in a wide range of texts that represent some sort of interaction. For instance, when I write comments on students' essays, it makes all the difference whether I say 'you' or 'this paper'. (Generally I say 'you' to heighten praise and 'this paper' to soften criticism.) You will hear pronouns used strategically by all great orators (think of the

Gettysburg Address, or one of Churchill's speeches), by university presidents and vice-chancellors, by parents, and by pop lyricists.

I have looked at pronouns to raise questions about the construction of audience. When I recognise myself in the *you*, I am stepping into a position and taking on the other assumptions that make the ad make sense to me, that make the parts fit together and make it purposeful. Many of the academic analyses of ads that I list in the 'Further Reading' sections have focused on this process, and have asked how we can resist it. Earlier studies tended to try to make people sceptical of the sales pitch itself, so that we could resist the pressure to buy. But studies over the past 20 years or so have focused more on the other assumptions we take on when we interpret, on how we are positioned by the ad. Even if we don't buy the product, we may for a moment buy a view of the world.

Recent work has focused, not on the texts of the ads themselves, but on ways people play with the roles they are offered, stepping into and out of them. Let's return to the New Year's Resolution ad that I discussed at the end of the *I* section, to see how multiple readings remain possible. The last resolution on the list, the one that brings together all the others, is:

10. Join the Communist Party.

I assume that it comes as a surprise to find the Communist Party advertising in this way at all; we associate them with banners saying 'Workers of the World Unite', not with lifestyle ads about Filofaxes. The ad appeared in the once excellent and now defunct journal *Marxism Today*, which was associated with the Communist Party of Great Britain, but which led debates attracting interest from a wide range of readers on the left, not just party members. The point of the ad is to convince the reader that Communist Party members do not fit the stereotype, that joining the party might be just one of a portfolio of political activities. Some of these activities are predictable – reading the latest leftist theory or visiting a country that was then still communist. Others are not – the Filofax suggests a professional, not a manual worker, and the giving up eggs refers to the salmonella scare current at the time, and thus to a consumerism that was not typical of Marxism.

That, at any rate, is my reading. But if we want to know if the list worked, we have to look at the diverse ways readers could interpret these fragments. Some yuppies may have recognised parts of it, but not others ('Post-Fordism? What the hell is that?'). Members of rival socialist parties might have singled out the remark about loud macho newspaper sellers as directed at them, while people unfamiliar with these rivalries may have thought it was some reference to *The Sun*. Some older Communists might have been disgusted by the approach of the ad, and taken the fact that the Party advertised at all as a sign of its approaching capitulation to the market. Some people might note that feminist issues don't get a look in ('Typical'). Some might just laugh.

The dream/nightmare of the Adshel poster, in which we are singled out on the street, has not arrived. Ads position readers, but the position they construct is not *the* position. They act as occasions for trying out a number of positions. When a poster says 'You in the shocking pink shell suit', it does not dress me in a pink shellsuit. Some criticism of ads assumes that I have only two choices, to turn around in response to this form of address or not. But the Adshel poster, like the Communist Party ad, allows for a number of positions. How can they all be there in one text? One mistake made both by some advertisers and by some critics of advertising is to assume that ads work on each person in isolation. This makes positions seem more sharply determined than they are. In fact, people talk about ads with each other, they read ads with other ads and other texts. It is closer to the complexity of this process if we imagine audiences talking back. I will be exploring audiences further in chapter 13.

Further reading
Addressing audiences

For a highly influential and much more advanced study of how ads position readers, see chapter 2 of Judith Williamson, *Decoding Advertisements*. The 'Daddy, what did you do in the Great War' ad is analysed in Gillian Dyer, *Advertising as Communication*. On 'she', see Robert Goldman, *Reading Ads Socially*, Ch. 6, 'Commodity Feminism'. The GLC campaign is perceptively analysed by Kathy Myers in *Understains*. My brief mention of postures of men and women is based on Erving Goffman, *Gender Advertisements*. Kathy Winship, *Inside Women's Magazines*, has a sophisticated analysis of the way women are addressed.

On the social significance of pronouns, see Peter Muhlhausler and Rom Harré, *Pronouns and People* ; and Roger Brown and Albert Gilman, 'Pronouns of Power and Solidarity'.

7

Bread wi' nowt taken out

Languages and Varieties as Signs

In the broadcast of the 1993 All-Star baseball game, Nike showed a commercial calling the Dominican Republic 'La Tierra de Mediocampistas', the 'Land of Shortstops'. The commercial had a voice-over in Spanish, with English sub-titles. Actually, *Campaign* tells us, the ad was originally planned to be in English; the idea of Spanish voiceover came later, and they got their location driver to do the talking. The network CBS objected before the ad was run, and did not run it after the first showing. What's the big deal? After all, Spanish-speaking people make up a large part of the US population and the CBS audience, and they buy a lot of Nikes. One can get Spanish channels (and ads) in many big cities. But this was different, one of the three main networks. The problem was not that English speakers who didn't know Spanish wouldn't understand; the sub-titles were clear enough. Clearly it was perceived as threatening to switch to the first language of a large minority of the population (and a good number of the All-Stars playing), even for just 60 seconds. Quite apart from what the ad said, the choice of language meant something. That choice is part of what I will be considering in this chapter.

An ad need not go as far as Spanish to mark a switch in language; varieties of English can also come with clusters of associations. So, for instance, Allinson Bread has the slogan

Bread wi' nowt taken out.

This stands out as a switch because it is a written version of a spoken dialect; it comes with associations of Yorkshire and the past, like the bewhiskered gentleman on the bread wrapper. Ridley Scott's beautifully nostalgic Yorkshire commercials for Hovis evoked the same sort of associations in amber-tinted visual terms; people still remember them 15 years after they were shown. Accents (varieties that differ in pronunciation) and dialects (varieties that differ in grammar and words) can suggest geography, class, or historical period. The choice is not simple; it is not a matter of northern accents for northerners. Accents are part of the meaning, like choosing a Handel oratorio or a brass band or Screaming Jay Hawkins for the soundtrack.

On one level the issues of language varieties and language switching are narrowly linguistic; they have to do with when and how one can switch, and how one describes the result. On another level, they are broad cultural questions, about how we construct difference, how we build up meanings around other nations, regions, and classes. One way of describing these clusters of meanings is suggested by the French cultural theorist Roland Barthes' analysis of myth, in the last and rather difficult essay in his very readable book *Mythologies*. In that essay, he explains myth as a kind of second order system of signs, drawing on the meanings we get from our interpretations of pictures and words.

> I am at the barber's, and a copy of *Paris-Match* is offered to me. On the cover, a young Negro in a French uniform is saluting, with his eyes uplifted, probably fixed on a fold of the tricolour. All this is the *meaning* of the picture. But, whether naively or not, I see very well what it *signifies* to me: that France is a great Empire, that all her sons, without any colour discrimination, faithfully serve under her flag, and that there is no better answer to the detractors of an alleged colonialism than the zeal shown by this Negro in serving his so-called oppressors. I am therefore again faced with a greater semiological system: there is a signifier, itself already formed with a previous system (*a black soldier is giving the French salute*); there is a signified (it is here a purposeful mixture of Frenchness and militariness); finally, there is a presence of the signified through the signifier. (p. 116)

So in this example, we have one level of signs on which we figure out that this is a picture of a young man saluting a flag. That in itself is not a trivial matter of processing: how do we know he is saluting and not just shading his eyes? But then that whole 'picture of a young man saluting' functions to evoke a more deeply buried concept having to do with French imperialism. The complex terminology is useful because it reminds us that the picture is not, itself, imperialism. It is dangerous to think that these associations are simple, or that they are just there.

In the same way, the examples I will analyse are first of all written words, voices, and pictures, signifiers to which we attach a signified. The Allinson slogan tells us that the bread has had nothing removed, and that it is said by a Yorkshireman. But then we treat that signified as itself a sign in another system, telling us about the nation or group that uses those words. The Yorkshireman comes to stand for an older, simpler life, resistance to modernity, and therefore healthy, unprocessed food. (The same associations can work for beer, and beer ads also have lots of exaggerated Yorkshire accents.) That cluster of meanings, a second level of interpretation, is what Barthes calls 'myth'. National stereotypes – the Italians, the Swiss, the Chinese, and of course the French – provide some of his favourite examples. After looking at some of the evocations of national stereotypes by switches in language, we can understand better some of the switches between varieties within English and the associations on which they might play.

English/Anglaise/Engels

The first thing we notice about the use of other languages in English ads is that they are generally restricted to a few products, a few effects, and a very few languages. They use the minimum possible switch to call up the desired stereotypes. Here's a typical instance:

Say magnifique

[then a picture of a rocky cove]

Say superbe

[then a picture of two men in chef's toques behind a lavish spread of food]

C'est Jersey

Here the product is vacation travel, and the reader is encouraged to think of Jersey as being like France. The intended effect is suggested by the lower picture; chefs are stereotypically French in the British (and French) imagination. The non-English spellings work because the advertiser can assume that the British (or at least those they wish to attract to Jersey) know a little French. But even if they don't, the words are cognates, that is, they are very similar in French and English. So the only bit of knowledge required is the pronunciation of *c'est*, and you don't need A level French for that. In fact, it works better if your French accent (like mine) isn't very good, so that *say* and *c'est* sound exactly the same. That keeps the code-switching as a reference to Frenchness (*Gallicité?*), not really as a message in French.

French is the most accessible of foreign languages to British readers, as Spanish is to most Americans. And the language here is just part of the effect, like the golden photos in the print ads for wine, or the accordion music in broadcast ads for cross-channel tours. It is the France of berets, bicycles, striped shirts, moustaches, baguettes, the Eiffel Tower, a glass of wine, an auberge. It is not the France of, say, the nuclear power industry, motorways, chemical production, depressed industrial cities, the TGV, hypermarkets, the grandes écoles, the National Front, *Libération*.

The best-known use of German in an ad is Audi's

Vorschprung Durch Technik.

This is not a phrase familiar to beginners, though it has an apparent cognate (technik/technique). And German is not much known in Britain, even by those who might admire German cars. The strangeness is part of the effect. I am told that the full effect comes when this German slogan is pronounced with an atrociously English accent.

In ads for imported beers and other luxury items, foreignness can suggest exclusivity. A bizarre evocation of foreignness occurs in the bus poster campaign for Oranjeboom, a beer from the Netherlands, which uses a string of Dutch words which, if spoken aloud, will sound like an English sentence:

De woord onder bus es Oranjeboom.

The last line of all the ads is

Not everyone will get it.

So the puzzle-like difficulty of the ad and its foreignness are supposed to suggest the exclusivity of the drink. But those people in London who do speak Dutch must have been especially puzzled, because for them the words strung together like this were meaningless.

For languages that use different writing systems, only a few characters are needed to evoke a whole myth, and these characters need not be used correctly. A Toyota ad, headed in English, 'Eight journalists were completely carried away', has in its lower left hand corner a calligram, and the translation,

Inner peace requires inner space.

For nearly all British readers, this is just an attractive decoration. I've had to check with some of the Japanese students to see that the character had some relation to the English underneath (they said it could indeed be translated as something like 'peace'). They could surely get away with putting Japanese characters for RUST or BREAKDOWN and not many British readers would be the wiser. (The same is not true in reverse: the Japanese equivalent of *Cosmopolitan* has lots of English in the ads for fashion and cosmetics.)

Again, the point is that Japanese characters suggest Japaneseness, an abstract concept, here associated with classical serenity, not that they actually introduce the culture of Japan.

A similar point could be made of Cyrillic characters in ads suggesting Russian. The Russian of ads just requires reversing the *R*s and *N*s, to make it look strange. But those letters do not in fact go with *R* and *N* sounds in Russian. An ad for Peugeot has the headline

ALMOST ANYONE CAN ACHIEVE POWER,
THE TRICK IS STAYING IN CONTROL.

The picture has a bright red car, with a grey urban background in which we dimly see a toppled statue of Lenin. It is an example of a current visual cliché of references to the former Soviet Union. A Russian-speaking colleague pointed out that the statue doesn't actually say *Lenin* in Russian; it has backwards *N*s where the Russian spelling has a letter that looks like an *H*, and a right angle letter with a /g/ sound where the Russian has a letter that looks like a backwards N, so that it says something like /leigi/. The spelling used, though wrong, looks more 'Russian'.

Languages beyond those of Western Europe are treated jocularly, as exotic, possibly made up. This ad for Air New Zealand is dominated by a wooden mask:

'Tino pai tenei.'
(As the Maoris say, Wow, what a deal.)

The grin of the mask and the colloquial translation suggest the jokiness. Now what is New Zealandicity? In my mind, following the tourist ads, it's a sort of Scotland/Norway/Australia. Here they are trying to modify it, linking it to the South Sea paradise. They do not go far, though, in presenting it as multicultural (no Maori translation of the airline's name).

All that I have said so far applies just as much to the switch to English in ads in other languages. Though English has become very widespread, even imperialistic, in some discourses, such as that of pop music, in advertising it is restricted to some products, some kinds of associations, and a few popular phrases. In the Spanish magazine, *Muy interesante*, we can see an ad that shows technical engine specifications over a close-up of the bum of a woman wearing Levi's. The next page has a picture of a car and says

PONTELO
[more specifications]
Renault 5

BLUE JEANS [written like a Levi's label]
Serie limitada

Here the English goes with the jeans, which goes with American youth culture associations. The rest of the ad can be in Spanish. Other ads in the same magazine, for Italian, Dutch, and even Spanish products, are sprinkled with English words:

Campari. It's fantasy. Con tonica naranja o soda

[picture of a man, a woman, and a city skyline]

. . . Con el Bazooka vas a arrasar con todo.
RADIO CASSETTE BAZOOKA - MOVING SOUND - PHILIPS

[picture of young men with a portable cassette player]

Made in Spain.

Una empresa española sitúa sus productos en órbita. . . . Alcatel
Standard Eléctrica, S. A. [picture of a satellite antenna]

Here the English can convey links to urban sophistication, youth culture, or international trade. Another ad in the same magazine, for Fiat Tipo, can make links to London with no English at all – just pictures of punks on the pavement, and a Union Jack behind the car. English words in these ads can do the same sort of cultural shorthand as the flag and punks.

English serves different functions in different national contexts. In the Netherlands, a large part of the educated population speaks English – so much so that it has been seriously suggested that English be the language of all higher education. English is found especially in ads aimed at the young. On the cover of a brochure for young people's accounts from ABN AMRO bank, there is the English phrase

LOOK OUT!

A poster for Kangaroo running shoes on a railway platform says

Speed 4 your feet

which assumes English good enough to catch the homophone of *4* / *for*. In both these ads, English is the language of street cred.

We should not assume that English words have exactly the same effect when they are read in a non-English speaking country. A British agency ran an ad in a German style magazine (something like *The Face* or *Blitz*) with a condom over a middle finger extended from a fist, and the words

FUCK
AIDS

Could such an ad appear in any British magazine? Somehow the shock may be softened when it is used in a non-English country, just as when we hear an obscenity in a language we don't know well, we may translate it more or less accurately but miss the visceral effect.

In a way all this switching is not too surprising. The elite of educated Britons have always been bilingual or trilingual, filling their speech with French or before that Latin tags. Pop songs have often thrown in bits of French, and may now get in some German. What is different today is the widespread circulation of these phrases, taken out of any context. They are like the bits of a symphony that might turn up these days on a dance record. Stripped of their naturalness as communication, in this new context, they become a new sort of sign, not reducible just to a translation. In this they act more like pictures or music than like text.

Accents and varieties of English: talking Manchester/talking posh

The camera tracks across a marble floor, passing a bottle of perfume and a sunken bathtub. A woman wearing a black evening gown and high heels walks to a dressing table where she applies cream to her face, murmuring 'soft, rich'. A man in a dinner jacket enters from behind a curtain at the rear, and says:

> By 'eck petal, you smell gorgeous tonight

This is in what is supposed to be a Manchester accent . We then see that the cream she is applying is the foam off the top of a pint of beer. He takes a quick sip before helping her with her jacket, and wipes his lip with his sleeve. The ad is for Boddington's bitter; it's a pun on their slogan 'The Cream of Manchester'.

There is ferocious disagreement among Mancunians about whether this is really a Manchester accent, or is what some Londoners think a Manchester accent sounds like, but there is agreement that it is funny, that this way of talking is entirely out of keeping with the elegant and sophisticated surroundings, as much as the pint of bitter is out of keeping with the dressing table and elegant surroundings. A Manchester (or exaggerated Northern) accent can convey many things, but not continental sophistication.

All broadcast ads are in one accent or another; there is no variety that can be said to have no accent. But some foreground the accent as part of their meaning. When I go to the market and ask for

> A half pound of Lancashire tasty, please

I am telling the cheese stall clerk that I want cheese. I am also, inevitably, telling them that I am American (or perhaps they will think Canadian). But for everyday purposes, that is not part of the message I intend to convey; I am only reminded of it when people respond by asking me where I am from (and when I am going back). Were the same utterance to occur in a British ad, it would be *meant* to say that the speaker was American. For instance, a radio ad for Levi's, a speaker with an American accent talks casually and at length about his old Leica. Then it ends:

> I mean, I could buy any of a hundred of cameras on the market today. But I grew up with this one.
>
> [African American male voice]:
> Levi's. The more you wear them, the better they fit.

The words of the ad praise a (German) camera. Only the voice at the end tells us to draw an analogy to a pair of jeans. But both voices also signify that this is an archetypically American product. The accent works like the Blues guitarist in the Budweiser ads.

Accent is used to evoke associations much more in British ads than in US ads. Britain has a wide range of geographical accents. But there is also a class element in the variation, because the accents of middle class people vary less with region than do those of working class people. There can also be an element of nostalgia for the stable solidarity of a working class culture that people associate with some accents. The most prestigious accent, spoken by only a tiny percentage of the population, is popularly called BBC English or Oxbridge English, but is given by linguists the more neutral name of 'Received Pronunciation' or RP. The simplest uses of accent, those you might expect knowing British prejudices, equate RP with wealth and power, and any other accent with provinciality and stupidity. An ad for Fairclough Homes uses a woman's voice that you could imagine was the Queen's:

> Step up to the Fairclough standard of quality

The use of Pachelbel's canon (the most popular bit of baroque music) as background suggests the effect of wealth and refinement the accent is supposed to have. A move into one of these homes is a move into a higher class, where they talk posh. They are imagining an audience of people who live in terraces and admire ensemble bathroom suites and UPVC double glazing. I can't imagine anyone falls for this.

But the more complex and interesting ads use accent to assert solidarity within class groups, as well as to divide them. The audience need not have any particular accent to respond emotionally to the use of an identifiable accent to signify ordinariness or genuineness. One British commercial, part of a series for N&P Building Society, has a young woman recounting her feelings on moving. The home movie effect of the jerky black and white photographs at the beginning suggests genuineness and nostalgia. (I imagine that using black and white in the colour world of TV was the original idea behind the series, and everything else followed from that.) The Northern accent of the voice (sorry, I can't place it better with my American ear) suggests genuineness in the same way. The father keeps pigeons, a hobby that seems to have clear class associations in Britain.

> When I was a girl, I used to worry when we moved. Would the pigeons get lost? My father told me it would be all right. Now I'm grown up, I know you need someone to turn to for advice . .

Many companies are trying to convince us that financial advice is not just for the rich, but for the mass of people who, we are told by the government, have bought their council houses and invested in privatised stocks. Here the secure advice of the company is linked to the solidity of the father. Financial advice is made a part of the normal course of life, just those events that are common to most people.

I've mentioned the use of specific local associations with the Allinson's bread slogan. Authenticity in general is invoked by use of a specific regional accent, emphasised by its strangeness in print. The same device is used in a headline of an ad for Highland Spring, in which a lass looks at her reflection in the water:

> 'Yuvgoat taethinko' yerinsides aswell.'

For those who miss the fact that this is supposed to be Scottish, the quotation marks are in tartan. Here the association with Scotland is an important selling point of the water. The advertiser, Highland Spring, notes that 'the literal spelling out of the accent is intended, in a lighthearted way, to appeal to Scots and Brits alike and reinforces the water's Scottish heritage, implying quality and purity'.

Each of the national varieties of English (such as English, Scottish, Irish, US, Australian, Canadian, South African, Indian, Hong Kong . . .) has markers that can be used or exaggerated to foreground the variety as part of the meaning. Here is an example from South Africa, for Brooks running shoes. It shows a naked man, his groin covered by pictures of shoes. The text says

> 'I feel naked without my Brooks.' Mark Page

This works as a pun only in South Africa, where *brooks* is borrowed from Afrikaans, as slang for shorts. As is typical of such borrowing from a language

'Yuvgoat taethinko' yerinsides aswell

Reflect a moment. On all the nasty things you put inside your body. Then flush them all out, with pure Highland Spring. You'll be glad to know it will show.

HIGHLAND SPRING

NATURAL MINERAL WATER

IT COULDN'T BE
CLEARER

with different grammar, the Afrikaans word is stripped of the ending and article it would have in Afrikaans – it is made into an English word. It can then suggest the colloquial and the uniquely South African, while also being a pun on the shorts and the shoes.

US ads use accent much less. That's partly because US accents are harder to place, with a few exceptions; the historical shift and present mobility of the population mean broad areas of the country have similar ways of speaking. If American readers want to imagine British ads, they must think of a world in which the accent of Chicago is very different from that of Cleveland or Minneapolis, and is even different from that of Gary, and yet the upper class speaks the same accent around the country. And geographical accent is not tied to social class the way it is in the UK; a southerner or Bostonian does not abandon his or her accent at university. (Think of the diversity of accents among recent US presidents, compared to the uniform RP of recent British prime ministers.) I'm sure someone with a better ear can hear differences in US accents, but they are not useful in evoking a whole world of associations the way they are in UK ads.

Accents on US television tend towards a bland folksy uniformity. But some ads (in the western states at least) exaggerate the folksiness with a kind of drawl one might hear from a caricature westerner. Here is a local television commercial from Boise, filmed mostly in the parking lot of the works:

> Hi, Tom from Western Sidings. You know most replacement windows are made in cookie cutter factories, but not Alumax replacement windows. They're made right here in town. It's like having a Larry at the factory! There's Larry, expertly welding the vinyl master frames [continues tour of the works, which I'll spare you] Alumax replacement windows from the Larrys and Toms at Western Siding. Order your custom set today.

Of course you can't hear the folksiness here in the lengthened vowels and the heightened intonation, but you can guess it from the greeting 'Hi, Tom,' the 'you know', and the 'right here' (see Chapter 8, on everyday talk). To my ear it is an exaggerated western US accent. The folksiness goes with the pitch: these windows can be trusted because they are made locally. A minute or two later the same channel advertises carpets with a rather implausible British accent and water colours to suggest luxury and refinement.

I will describe one UK ad in some detail to show how the choice of accent can be related to the message and to the visual style. It is a government ad urging people to take up disability benefits. Disability benefits are complex, and they change often, and applications for them involve quite a bit of intrusion. So they are not always taken up. The image they don't want here is of the well-meaning but bossy social worker. Instead, they want the plainest possible image that says, 'disabled'. They have the rock star Ian Dury in a black jumper against a grey background that focuses attention on the face and the wheelchair, talking in what I am told is a London accent.

If someone owed me money I'd be a mug not to collect it. . .

The script goes with the tough talking, assertive but not aggressive image suggested by the voice. At then end, the telephone number to call flashes on the screen, then goes off.

Oi!

he shouts, and points at the place the number was, until it returns. The speaker sets himself up in opposition to the producers of the commercial – they are rushing on, while he is on the side of the people at home scrambling around looking for a pen. The ad shifts the point of view from that of the government, trying to administer regulations, to the plain talking world of everyday life.

But there is another language in this ad; in a box in the upper left there is interpretation in British Sign Language. This too is a choice of language. The deaf are among the groups categorised as disabled for these purposes (though I should note that they do not always categorise themselves this way). To reach them, the easiest thing for the producers would have been subtitles. But subtitles are not the language of the deaf; they would have come across with the wrong associations, as something tacked on, and besides they are rather wearing to follow. So the advertisers have used a sign interpreter, a female rather than a male, but wearing the same dull grey as Ian Dury. There is another distinction here, for with sign, as with speech, there are varieties. The variety many hearing people learn, Sign Supported English, which closely follows English grammar, would have the wrong associations for this message. Among deaf people themselves, it is more common to use BSL, a language with its own grammar, recognisably different from English. As far as I can tell, the advertisers have chosen to use BSL here. Just as the man's speech signals straight talk, the use of BSL suggests deaf person to deaf person communication. It evokes an even stronger feeling of shared community than do spoken accents.

This ad, like the other shifts of language or language variety I have discussed in this chapter foreground language, make it a symbol like the cowboy hat or the baguette. Each of these concepts – Texanness, Frenchness, Deafness – can have many signs attached to it. Now if these concepts were pure, that would be the end of our analysis: we could give a dictionary of signs and meanings. But Barthes points out their instability.

> The knowledge contained in a mythical concept is confused, made of yielding, shapeless associations. One must firmly stress this open character of the concept; it is not at all an abstract, purified essence; it is a formless, unstable, nebulous condensation, whose unity and coherence are above all due to its function. (*Myth Today*, p. 119).

The function in this case is the brief of the ad: to sell bread as wholesome and traditional, or jeans as hip and authentic. We sort out these images, find the American meant here, or the Yorkshire meant here, by referring back to the apparent intention of the ad, as well as to the images and accents. This instability is important. It is our ability to shuffle around such concepts into new shapes that enables us to reuse them with new products and new associations. It also means that none of these clusters of associations, none of these *myths* as Barthes calls them, is impervious to change or reworking. Germany can call up associations of the Third Reich or High Technology, 'Lebensraum' or 'Vorschprung durch Technik'. The Fairclough Homes ad may make you associate the overly posh accent with the rootlessness of brand-new, tree-less, empty estates. To see the ways associations can change, you need only look at older ads, which offer stereotypes we no longer take for granted, such as wide Cockney lads and smiling black servants.

Barthes points out something similar. The making of a myth – whether precise Germans or cheerful Maoris or bluff and healthy Yorkshiremen – requires us to strip away the history and context of the sign, and replace it with a different history and context. His essay is devoted to making us see that process. The critical reading, then, asks how the sign came to be produced as a sign, and traces it back to its previous context. One way is to look closely at the specific language used and how it gets there. Why can just those phrases be embedded in an English text, and just those languages? What are the cultural processes that give them an apparent transparency? Package tours, pop music, O level French, the distinctions made about who learns what language and how far. Similarly, with varieties of English, which specific features of an accent mark it? How did the associations with Brummie or Geordie accents arise? How did RP get standardised? The critical reading does not just mock the posh voice in the Fairclough Homes ad. It also asks how the bluff, no-nonsense voice of the disabled benefits ad or the N&P home movie get their uncritically positive associations.

Conclusion

Most speakers of English are so sensitive to slight variations in English, and have so many stereotypes to draw on with English and other languages, that we don't think about the mechanics of language switching. I have looked at just how the switches are done to learn about how we build up these associations. Here are some points that have applied to many of the ads I have discussed:

1. Language choice, which usually goes unnoticed, is foregrounded by the contrast made in switching (as in a switch to a more prestigious accent at the end of a radio ad).

2. Choices of accents and languages can also be foregrounded by their appearance in print (as in the misuse of the Russian alphabet, or the spelling out of a Scottish accent).

3. The associations with language switches are often made by references to other texts or types of texts (such as westerns or home movies or ads for other products).

4. The associations with a language choice, which can go in many directions, can be constrained by or conflict with the visuals presented with the words (as in the picture of a chef, or a city skyline, or an elegant bathroom).

5. The clusters of associations are a second level of interpretation, a myth, that can draw on words, music, and images .

6. These myths are not fixed. They change with different contexts, and different functions to which they are put.

In a way, this whole chapter is about the uses of the exotic – foreign languages, and varieties of English marked as strange and evocative. The next chapter is about an opposite but equally important use of language, as part of the everyday.

Further reading
Language switching

I've drawn here on writings by Roland Barthes; the short early essays in *Mythologies* are delightful reading, though the longer essay I have quoted, 'Myth Today', is harder. His later essay, 'The Rhetoric of the Image' in *Image–Music–Text* has important comments on the creation of a national stereotype in an ad for Italian pasta sauce, but it is much more difficult going; I return to it in Chapter 10.

What I have called 'language switching' is usually called 'code switching' by linguists. A good introduction, with references, is John Gumperz, *Discourse Strategies*.

Robert McCrum's BBC book and television series *The Story of English* gives some of the social background of various varieties in a popular and illustrated form. For a more technical description of British regional accents, see J. D. O'Connor, *Phonetics*. For a brief and accessible guide to standard varieties of English (US, Scottish, Australian, Indian . . .), see Peter Trudgill and Jean Hannah, *International English*. For academic surveys on varieties other than those of the UK and US, see Jenny Cheshire, ed., *English Around the World*. Phillipson has produced a critique of the world-wide spread of English in *Linguistic Imperialism*.

Of the many books on sociolinguistics, three of the best are Martin Montgomery, *Introduction to Language in Society*, which is relevant to this and the next chapter; Richard Hudson, *Sociolinguistics*; and Ronald Wardhaugh, *Language in Society*. On the relationship between social power and varieties of English, see Dick Leith, *A Social History of English*; John Milroy and Lesley Milroy, *Authority in Language*; and for comments on its place in education see Norman Fairclough, ed., *Critical Language Awareness*.

For the globalisation of advertising, see Armand Matellart, *Advertising International*. But he does not deal with the way specific ads are adapted for different countries; for that you could see many articles in *Campaign*, such as the special section in the 21 September 1993 issue on 'Global Advertising'.

8

'Do we have time for a coffee?'
Conversations and Everyday Life

There is a kind of ad that tells us they don't need advertising; a car ad might say, paradoxically, that it is word of mouth and not television advertising that sells the car. But if that is the case, why pay for the television ads? Clearly, everyday talk is assumed to have a persuasiveness that advertising talk can never have. Advertising copywriters make a similar distinction. In *Campaign,* a creative director criticises a Prudential poster from a rival agency (the one that says, 'I want to be ready for whatever life throws at me'), saying:

> I'd like to see some of the headlines using language which is closer to conversation than strategic statements.

Copywriters have been taught since the beginning of the profession that advertising should sound like conversation. But it is quite a trick to get the conversational sound while also getting in all the product information demanded by the client. If it works, the conversation can evoke a kind of ordinariness, of everyday life, that is paradoxically effective in persuasion.

To understand the importance of everyday life in ads, and the difficulty of evoking it, we need to think of 'everyday life' with quotation marks around it, as a specialised academic term, like 'Romanticism' or 'proletariat' or 'momentum'. It refers to a special place and time with its own special characteristics, a sort of science fiction alternative world. This world is set apart from bosses and employees and buying and work – and salespeople. It is a world of immediate time and place and actions, that we take for granted and do not think about. The sociologist Harvey Sacks suggests we try to think of all the details that go into making ordinariness. 'An initial shift is not think of 'an ordinary person' as some person, but as somebody having as one's job, as one's constant preoccupation, doing 'being ordinary'.'

In fact, that is just what advertisers must do, think out all the details and assumptions that make something ordinary, everyday. My argument is that conversation plays an important part in marking that world. So an advertiser wants language that sounds like conversation, not the kind of language that might be used, say, in a sales talk or a political speech. The first part of this chapter is about *why* advertisers want to suggest everyday life, and the second is about *how* they use conversation to do it.

Why ads use everyday talk

Picture an ad selling margarine. It might say something like:

Use Stork.

It's so soft that even a child can spread it.

Now compare this way of presenting the same strategic message. We can use this ad to show what I mean by treating 'everyday life' in quotation marks.

The opening title says

STORK TALK ON PELHAM STREET

[There is a crowded, noisy living room with many women in small groups drinking coffee, other clusters of women visible but out of focus in the background.]

Woman 1: When my son was learning to make sandwiches, the good thing about Stork is it was so manageable for him. You know, the cheese wasn't, but the Stork was.

Woman 2: The kids think it's great because they can just slap it on, make their own sandwiches, put them together.

Woman 3: One day his brother did it for him, he went to school and when they came home my son said to me, Mum he said, what did I have in my sandwiches today? I said I don't know, your brother made them for you. What have you got? And he said, I didn't put anything else in it, just Stork.

[Stork logo]

One of the things that this ad is trying to do is to emphasise the ordinary, everyday nature of this conversation. How does it do this?

1. It is located at a particular place – Pelham Street. The specificity is important. Space in everyday life is just what is immediate. That doesn't mean it is limited to one house or one street, but that we think of it in terms of here, or that over there, in relation to me rather than placed on a map.

2. But space is also taken to be universal. It is unnecessary to tell us where this Pelham Street is, Bristol or Bognor Regis or Bolsover. This place can stand for all places – or at least all British places. Everyday life is indivisible, and goes on beyond what we can see. The same sense of both particularity and endless expanse is created on the first page of any realist novel.

3. The sense of an outside to the particular conversation is important. So we hear other voices murmuring in the background. That murmur is part of what gives the coffee morning its sense of realism, while the clear and uninterfered with sound of a studio would undermine it. Here they are talking about margarine, while over there they are talking about the weather, or clothes, or bus timetables.

4. Time here is seen as cyclical. That is why the phrase *everyday* gets extended to mean *ordinary*. Here they talk about the processes of children growing up and learning to make sandwiches, the daily routine of school, the routine of the coffee morning itself. There is no need to give a particular date, because one day is like another, every Monday is a Monday. The only variation is the 'one day' that signals the beginning of a story, as it does here.

5. The conversation assumes shared knowledge. The speakers do not introduce themselves or name their children. The story, to be funny, requires us to see something definitely odd about making a sandwich with just margarine in it.

6. Everyday life is gendered. In a sexist society, women are assigned to lives tied to the cyclical, the immediate, the family, while men are more often assumed to live lives in a wider, historical, public world. Even where this distinction is violated in ads (men chatting about washing powder, women at board meetings), the violation is taken as something surprising.

All this may make more sense if we contrast it with what everyday life is not. Everyday life is not institutional – not politics, or church services, or courts. It is not transcendent – not paradise, fame, history, the globe. More important, for our purposes, it is not the world of advertising. Advertising is strategic; it is trying to get us to do something, and everyone is ultimately either a buyer and seller. Talk in everyday life is man to man, or woman to woman, or woman to man or whatever – here they relate as mothers. We can tell there is still a sharp line between everyday talk and advertising language, because it probably sounds odd to almost everyone that these women insist on referring to the margarine by its brand name, Stork. That is the essential bit of sales talk that has come in.

Ads often invoke the superior believability of everyday talk where the advertiser has a problem, either because of taboos around the product, or because of the established suspicions on the part of the audience.

> [picture of a young woman in jeans, reading a magazine, with one knee up, and a hand to her forehead]
>
> IF YOU THINK YOU'RE PREGNANT,
> DON'T BELIEVE EVERYTHING YOU READ.
>
> You're period's late. You feel a bit different, and you want to find out why. Quickly, and without a lot of fuss and bother. So what can you do?
>
> Ask your friends. Ask your pharmacist. They'll tell you that while some pregnancy tests say they're simple, they're actually more like chemistry sets . . .
>
> That's why most people will tell you that . . .
>
> [Clear Blue pregnancy test]

Here the headline makes an explicit distinction between the written – here the world of advertising – and the spoken words of friends and pharmacists. Paradoxically, the ad presents itself on the side of personal address, against print ads. The first paragraph is the sort of address to *you* that we looked at in Chapter 6. Then it turns to tell you to ask your friends. None of the selling is done by the ad itself – it is all attributed to what they tell you is word of mouth. But something more complicated is going on here. This happens to be a product that people may not talk about. The ad is talking about a moment when a woman may not discuss her hopes or worries with anyone. So the ad is providing everyday talk to replace the missing advice. Exactly the same tactic – saying that your friends and even your mother might not be able to tell you – was used in the 1920s to sell Lysol disinfectant as a contraceptive. (Don't try it – I've heard Lysol isn't very effective for that.)

The invocation of the everyday in the text may be limited to just a gesture before the sales talk begins. An ad in the *New Yorker* for the US lumber company Georgia Pacific has the headline,

> 'Who's going to make sure the trees will be here tomorrow?'

On the right is a picture of two figures perched on a rock before a vista of hills covered with rather uniform conifers (and no signs of clear-cutting). The text continues with the context for the headline.

'Not an easy question.
But that's what my son
asked the other day.
He's thinking about it.
Just like everybody.
He wants to know if the
trees will still be
around when he grows
up. Well, working for
Georgia-Pacific like I do,
I can tell him we're
doing our part. Planting . . '

It ends with the signature of 'Steve Delfs, Forester', and the Georgia Pacific logo. As we saw with 'What did you do in the Great War, Daddy?' in Chapter 6, there is a long history of ads using the child who raises a guilt-making question. The ad replaces the huge corporation defending itself against public outcry with a father out on a hike justifying himself and his work to his son. The everydayness is signalled by the quotation marks, and the conversational quality suggested by the *well* that marks the transition from family talk to corporate publicity.

Even the layout contributes to the effect of a personal rather than a corporate statement. A picture above, with a text below, would signal the kind of serious message often used in corporate advertising. A broad horizontal panorama of identical trees would have emphasised extensive ownership ('Someday, son, all this will be yours.'), which might look good in a corporate report but not here. Here the text occupies a narrow vertical band (as I have reproduced it) running on the left alongside a narrow, vertically oriented photograph that links father/son and trees.

As this ad shows, it may take just a quoted headline and a photograph to suggest everyday talk, even when the body copy is a straight sales pitch. A British ad, promoting an employment training booklet, shows a similar mixture of the everyday and the strategic. The everyday is suggested by the headline and the black and white photograph of two young women sitting on steps, one leaning forward to the other, talking, smiling, and gesturing, the other on the left looking off into middle distance. The 'Page 8' refers the reader from this everyday talk to the relevant page of the booklet.

'I saw an advisor.
Together we sorted out a
Back to Work plan.'
PAGE 8

Here the ad is addressed from the government to unemployed young people. But one characteristic of this target audience is that it will believe nothing the government says. So the message is put as one young woman telling another, not as an advertisement but as a story about her life, her day. Then the body copy of the ad goes into direct address to the reader.

When you're just out of work, a Back to Work plan sets out how you can help yourself – and how we can help you – to find the right job.

Here the client becomes *you*, and the bureaucracy becomes *we*. Even the title of the booklet – 'Just the Job' – suggests in its idiomatic form an everyday relationship quite different from what would be suggested by a title like 'Employment Training Procedures Revised Edition'.

Of course, once people have heard enough 'real people' ads, they get suspicious of them. So there is a genre of ads that reassures you that 'real people' are 'real people'. To do this they have to sound extraordinarily ordinary. You may have heard such ads on the radio. It is hard to convey in print just how dull such people sound. The flatness of intonation is part of what makes them seem like 'genuine people'. They may talk as if responding to earlier turns, as if somebody had just said something we had missed. At the end, there is nearly always the voice of an announcer, which comes in with its wider range of intonation and rich timbre, as a contrast to the realness of the people. This reminds us that everyday talk is created out of a contrast with advertising talk.

How ads make talk ordinary

Let us look more closely now at the features of talk that make it sound ordinary, not like the sales talk of announcers or the printed copy with the coupon in the corner. A good place to start would be with radio, where there are many ads that rely entirely on such talk. Here is a typical example from a local commercial radio station.

A: According to the paper, that film's on *again* tonight.
B: [in breath] Great, pass me the scissors, will you?
A: Why, what's the matter?

"I saw an adviser. Together we sorted out a Back to Work plan."

PAGE 8

When you're just out of work, a Back to Work plan sets out how you can help yourself – and how we can help you – to find the right job.

Sensible, practical ideas like this are on all 30 pages of the new Just The Job booklet.

It adds up to more help than ever before. In fact we help thousands of people back to work every week.

So why not you?

JUST THE JOB.

MORE HELP THAN EVER BEFORE IN YOUR SEARCH FOR THE RIGHT JOB.

Ask for the booklet at your Jobcentre, or fill in the coupon, or phone free on 0800-250 200.

Post to: Just The Job, FREEPOST CV1037, Stratford-upon-Avon, CV37 9BR.

Name (Mr/Mrs/Miss/Ms)

Address

Postcode   RT1

EMPLOYMENT DEPARTMENT

B: Look, here in tonight's paper. One of Normid's £2 Gold Dividend vouchers.

A: Oh yeah, saw one of those in the paper the other night. Bet they don't *really* give you £2.

B: [laughs] No convincing *you*, is there. Listen, all you do is hand in the voucher at the checkout, show them your Golden Dividend card, and provided you spend £20 or more, they'll add £2 to your savings.

A: What savings?

B: The savings you make every time you shop at Normid with your Golden Dividend card. In fact, I've started saving for 1992 now, and I'm looking forward to my Golden Dividend payment at the beginning of December – just in time for Christmas.

[Male voice] Golden dividend. Only at Normid superstores . . .

Here the two characters are engaged in an activity that has nothing to do with the product – they are looking at the paper to decide on a movie to see. It is important that the topic of the advertised product come up as if by accident.

We need to step back from this talk to see the features that make it seem more like conversation and less like scripted advertising talk.

1. To begin with there is *turn taking* – one person talks and then another, one of the defining features of conversation. *Turn* is the term used by conversation analysts for each person's utterance. In turn-taking, one turn usually ties to the next. So 'Bet they don't really give you £2" only makes sense as a response to the pointing out of the coupon. In other ads we might also find interruptions, pauses, hesitations, *uh-huh*s and *mmm*s, which mark how the participants are responding to each other.

2. But this cannot be all there is to creating a conversational feel, because we recognise the way each turn is *packaged to address another person*, even when we don't know what comes before or after. Here there are interjections in almost every turn (*great, look, oh yeah*), words that make sense only as a response to another remark or immediate action. There are also tag questions (that is, short questions following statements): *will you? is there?* The simplest way to make something sound conversational is to use one of the words that marks a turn as a response, such as *well* or *okay* or *anyway*. Again, this works even when we don't know what the other person is supposed to have said. The turns are marked as packaged for a present and listening audience.

3. The relationships of the characters are marked by their *mutual knowledge* – such as the name of 'that film'. And it is assumed that the first

woman is habitually sceptical; then the 'No convincing you' makes sense as a response. Note how these turns create the first woman as a sceptic, as someone who always responds like this. She then stands for us, the kind of person who doesn't cut the coupons out of the paper, who doesn't have a Normid account. Other ads might get this effect by mentioning names of partners or children, or referring to work. Listening to this is like overhearing two people on the train.

4. I have focused on words, but people in conversation don't just say things, they say things in a certain way. Linguists usually study the utterance of sounds that make up words – linguistic features. But they also recognise the influence of pace, pitch, timbre, grouping, intonation, aspects they lump together as *paralinguistic features*. Here for instance there is a very wide range of intonation. 'They don't REALly give you £2.' What they can't do on radio is display the kind of gaze and movement characteristic of everyday conversations.

These four kinds of features – turn-taking, turn packaging, indications of mutual knowledge, and paralinguistic features – can be seen in print ads as well as in broadcasts. For instance, the *well* in the Georgia Pacific ad is used in conversation to mark an unexpected turn or a change in topic. Its effect can be rather complicated, but in this ad the effect is to give the impression of conversational informality, while also signalling the shift from the man's son's question to his answer. Other print ads might arrange the people in the pictures to suggest how they are oriented towards each other, as we saw in the Employment Department ad, or underline a word to suggest intonation.

I have started with a radio ad because the whole effect is based on the conversational sound. You only have to hear an inept local ad to realise how hard it is to create this effect. Television ads are more complex, because the talk takes place in a visual context. People participate in conversation with their whole bodies. In this fairly typical instance of everyday conversation on television, a teenage boy in a letterman's jacket is slouching in a chair and looking away, while a younger girl circles around him, and grabs a basketball to seize his attention.

Boy: So what's a little dandruff?

Girl: Okay big brother, imagine, you're at the social event of the year, and your dream girl says helloooo, just as you do this [brushes shoulder]. Her first impression, what a hunk, and only a few flakes.

Boy: [laughs] Give me a break.

Girl: The breaks are that you never get a second chance to make a first impression.

Boy: So?

Girl: So if ordinary shampoos don't fix your problem, try this. *[reaches into gym bag]*

Boy: Head and Shoulders. You don't have dandruff.

Girl: Tu-dahhh. *[She leans her head forward]*

[Head and Shoulders bottle covers the screen]

Male voice: Head and Shoulders. Because you never get a second chance to make a first impression.

The strategic marketing problem, I imagine, is how to sell the shampoo to boys, who are just as likely to have dandruff, but who are not supposed to be as concerned with appearance as girls. A direct appeal might seem to associate the product with a feminine concern for appearance and social success. So the advertiser has a confidential advisor recommend the product to a sceptical consumer (we saw this earlier with the Employment Training ad). The twist here is that it is the younger sister, rather than the father, mother, or friend, giving the advice; she announces her relationship the first time she speaks. It allows the concern with looks and social success to be identified with a girl, but still to apply to a boy.

Now what makes this seem like everyday conversation? The features of turn-taking in the Normid ad are here again. There is also the determinedly colloquial language, used especially in appeals from old advertisers to young audiences: 'what a hunk'. Each turn is in a form to show it is responding to the previous turn, as in the repetition of 'break' in the sense of relief (his use), or in the sense of a lucky chance (her use). There is also evidence of packaging for conversation in the way she tells a story, with reported speech, and a moral, 'you never get a second chance'. His initial resistance – also readable as masculine embarrassment with matters of appearance – is suggested mainly by his posture and gaze.

Note that the product is not mentioned until the end of their everyday dialogue. She just gives him what is supposed to be her shampoo. Then the announcer comes in at the end to do the sales pitch, with a different voice and a different sort of language and over a huge picture of the bottle. Only at this point did I realise that her earlier proverb –

you never get a second chance to make a first impression

– was to be taken as quoted from the Head and Shoulders slogan.

One other point this ad illustrates is that everyday discourse may draw on ads, just as ads draw on everyday discourse. Let's look at her

Tu-dahhh!

Out of context, this is puzzling. It is said in response to his

You don't have dandruff.

In previous Head and Shoulders ads, which had a number other examples of advice given in everyday conversation, someone usually says,

Head and Shoulders. I didn't know you had dandruff.

The response then is

I don't.

suggesting the product has eliminated the problem, so that they need no longer feel embarrassed about being associated with the product. We are to believe that the line has now become so common that he can say this as if ironically, and then she responds by displaying hair as if playing in an ad. That is, even though she realises this is the sort of thing people say in ads, she will still say it. While this particular example may seem far-fetched, ads have become so much a part of our language that people may quote them, usually jokingly, in all sorts of conversations.

So far we have been talking about how the everyday can enter into ads. But as the Head and Shoulders ad suggests, it also works the other way, and ads can enter into everyday talk. This has happened with one of the most famous series of recent UK television ads, for Nescafe Gold Blend. This particular ad is one part of a story that has been going on for four years, in which two yuppies meet, get to know each other, get jealous, break off, and meet again, all over cups of instant coffee. (In this transcription, I'll use (.) to show pauses, which are important to the meaning).

[doorbell rings]
[first woman] Hi.
[man] Laura.
[first woman] You always did stay up late.
[man] How long have you been back?
[first woman] About a day and a half. I was just (.) passing by.
[man] At this time of night?
[first woman] Are you alone? *[turns around]*
Yes (.) er (.) No (.) Look, I'm expecting someone.
[first woman] At this time of night?
[man] It's (.) a neighbour.
[first woman] Well, do we have time for a coffee?
[Male announcer's voice] GOLDEN ROASTED RICHER SMOOTHER

NESCAFE GOLD BLEND
[doorbell rings again]
[second woman] Hope I didn't get you out of bed.
[first woman] This coffee tastes good.
[man] *[sighs]*
[second woman] [astonished gaze towards camera/first woman]

You might think that this ad depends on knowing earlier ads in the series with these characters. But it isn't really necessary. Note how their status, not just as lovers but as ex-lovers, is established quickly. The 'Laura' with a very high rise in pitch on the first syllable, and fall on the second, shows he is surprised to see her, and she invokes mutual knowledge of his having stayed up late in the past. Then he refers to her being back, which assumes mutual knowledge of her having been away.

The exchange also depends on turn-taking. The opening depends on the bell as a summons, and on the way greetings are exchanged. Note the ironic effect from the repetition of 'At this time of night?' His comment implies that she could not have just been passing by, while her use of the same words implies that his visitor could not be a casual one. He then responds, 'It's a neighbour,' the implication being that a neighbour might drop by innocently long after others could. These interpretations depend, not on what was said, but the way each turn relates to what was said before.

The ending has no turns exchanged. The second woman says 'Hope I didn't get you out of bed.' The first woman comments on the coffee. The joke is that these two statements are unrelated. Or are they? The first woman, by holding out for coffee, has discomfited the second woman. The second woman's comment is delivered as late night, private talk, which was not intended to be overheard, while the first woman's comment on the coffee can work just because it is self-consciously casual, out of keeping with the tense situation. The man's only comment is a sigh. The last turn in the ad is the gaze of the second woman, a nice example of the way gaze (directed as this one is) can substitute for speech.

As in the Head and Shoulders ad, the two worlds of brand promotion and everyday talk are separated textually and visually. So the characters only talk about a generic coffee – real people don't ask for coffee by brand name. What I can't figure is the effect of how she does say 'coffee', in 'Do we have time for a coffee?' I think it is lower in pitch and slower than the rest of the sentence. Also, the *well* suggests that it is an unexpected and perhaps unwanted turn following his previous statement that someone was coming over. The effect is to suggest that we are talking about more than coffee here.

The brand name is introduced in an inset that also stands for time passing in the world of the story. It includes no whole sentences, just words describing Nescafe.

Golden roasted Richer Smoother Nescafe Gold Blend

The picture here is also a world apart. It isn't a representation of a kitchen, with him (or her) spooning out the coffee. Instead we see an abstracted essence of coffeeness, beans falling past a golden light. This sales pitch is kept quite separate from the everyday story.

What makes this ad remarkable is the way people talk about it. There have been many examples in the past of advertising lines entering colloquial language:

Does she or doesn't she?

I can't believe I ate the whole thing.

Where's the beef?

Been there. Done that.

What is different here is the interest in the cliff-hanging plot of the ads, played out in 60-second episodes over years. His proposal made front page headlines, and there has even been a novelisation, as with hit movies. A McCann Erickson ad in *Campaign* says of this campaign that it costs less to run now than when it began, because it gets talked about, it gets covered in the editorial content of media (and they could have mentioned, it gets taken up in textbooks).

This takes us back to the argument about whether this blurring of the boundary between private and public discourse is a good or bad thing. Dating agency ads may seem to be a commercialisation of romance, while the Gold Blend ad is a romanticisation of commercials. But we must remember that the realm of romantic love is not virgin territory, which advertisements entered and defiled. It is already heavily colonised. People have obtained their sexual ideas from the church, from problem pages, from conduct books, novels, songs, cartoons, magazines, soap operas, and even their parents. It is not a natural realm, already there, but one shaped by the way we talk about it. Ads are part of that talk.

The peculiar success of the Nescafe ad shows that audiences do not just adopt the view of the world embodied in ads. They can step back from them, play with them, talk about them, treat them as they would other cultural objects, a new pop song or a new situation comedy. The Nescafe ads take the tired genre of romantic ads, and tie them to the equally tired genre of soap operas, providing a perspective on both that is seen as witty and sophisticated. There is no claim here that the coffee will make your love life better – if it did, the story would have been over long ago. Instead, the story works just because they don't sit around talking about Nescafe Gold Blend. The coffee sneaks in as an ordinary part of their daily (and nightly) lives.

Conclusion

This chapter has dealt with both the effect of everyday life, and the linguistic features associated with everyday talk. The main points are:

1. Advertising discourse often tries to place itself in a world of everyday life, with the following characteristics:
   - Space in everyday life is immediate.
   - Space is also universal.
   - Time is cyclical.
   - Everyday talk assumes mutual knowledge.
   - Everyday talk is not institutional.
   - Everyday talk is not selling anything.
   -The everyday world is gendered, masculine or feminine.
2. Ads may themselves refer to everyday talk as a more reliable source of information on products.
3. The effect of ordinary conversation is based mainly on features that suggest turn taking, such as
   - turn-taking, interruptions, pauses, uh-huhs
   - turns packaged for a listening audience, with stories, interjections, tag questions
   - mutual knowledge
   - paralinguistic features (intonation and gesture, or representation of intonation in print).
4. Ads may themselves enter into everyday talk.

I have used mainly broadcast ads as examples. But many of the features of turn-taking, mutual knowledge, story-telling, and design of a turn with a listener in mind can be seen in many print ads.

I have included one last example, an ad for First Response pregnancy test that appeared in *She*, to show how print can take on features of everyday talk. The photograph suggests intimate talk; the headline plays on hearing from the test, and hearing noises from the womb. Apart from this and the slogan, all the copy is in dialogue, with the functioning of the product and the claims for accuracy worked in. It has examples of turn-taking (such as questions and answers), packaging (such as *well*), and mutual knowledge.

YOU HEARD IT FIRST FROM US.

 "I'll never forget your reaction."

"You'll never let me."

"You didn't believe me when I said I was pregnant, did you?"

"It was pretty unbelievable."

"Can you remember what you said?"

"Where's the bubbly, I think."

"No, before that, when I said I must be. It's gone pink."

"Oh yes. I said does that mean it's a girl. Yes I remember."

"Idiot."

"I admit I wasn't much of an expert in those days."

"And you said why don't you do the second test just to make sure."

"Well I didn't know how accurate they were."

"You can't get much more accurate than 99%."

"That's true."

"Still, you'll know better next time won't you?"

"What next time?"

FIRST RESPONSE
1-Minute Pregnancy Test

THERE'S LIVING PROOF IT WORKS.

'I'll never forget your reaction.'
'You'll never let me.'
'You didn't believe me when I said I was pregnant, did you?'
'It was pretty unbelievable.'
'Can you remember what you said?'
'Where's the bubbly, I think.'
'No, before that, when I said I must be. It's gone pink.'
'Oh yes. I said does that mean it's a girl. Yes I remember.'
'Idiot.'
'I admit I wasn't much of an expert in those days.'
'And you said why don't you do the second test just to make sure.'
'Well I didn't know how accurate they were.'
'You can't get much more accurate than 99%.'
'That's true.'
'Still, you'll know better next time, won't you?'
'What next time?'

Further reading

Talk and everyday life

Readable introductions to conversation can be found in Deborah Tannen's academic books, *Conversational Style* or *Talking Voices*, and in her other more popular books, *That's Not What I Meant!* and *You Don't Understand Me!* Textbooks include Geoff Beattie, *Talk*, which is mostly psycholinguistic; Margaret McLaughlin, *Conversation: How Talk is Organised*; and Ronald Wardhaugh, *How Conversation Works*, which is an accessible but sometimes simplistic account that focuses on the social effects of talk. Martin Montgomery, *Introduction to Language in Society*, has one chapter on conversation.

More advanced treatments of conversation analysis can be found in Stephen Levinson, *Pragmatics* , Ch. 6, and in the introductions to such collections as J. Max Atkinson and John Heritage, eds., *Structures of Social Action*; Deirdre Boden and Don Zimmerman, eds., *Talk and Social Structure*; or Paul Drew and John Heritage, eds., *Talk at Work*, though all these collections are rather specialised and technical. Paddy Scannell, ed., *Broadcast Talk*, is an excellent collection, but surprisingly has nothing on advertisements.

There are good treatments of the literary representation of speech (that is, how it is quoted and changed in print) in Geoff Leech and Mick Short, *Style in Fiction* , in Michael Stubbs, *Discourse Analysis* , and in Paul Simpson, *Language, Ideology, and Point of View.*

My opening remarks on everyday life draw on Harvey Sacks, 'On Doing 'Being Ordinary''. For a treatment of 'everyday life' from a Marxist perspective see Agnes Heller, *Everyday Life* . Here is a sample:

> When someone says to someone else, 'I'm going to talk to you, man to man,' what this means is that in this particular contact both parties are going to be abstracted from the positions they hold in the social division of labour, and from observance of the prescriptive customs which delineate their contacts on the social average. (Heller, p. 217)

A feminist treatment of these issues is in Dorothy E. Smith, *The Everyday World as Problematic: A Feminist Sociology* ; she gives a much more detailed analysis of ways in which everyday life is gendered, a point I have just mentioned in passing. All three studies are fairly hard-going for those new to sociology.

The quotation on the Prudential ad at the beginning of the chapter is from Bill Thompson, 'Private View', *Campaign* (6 March 1992).

9

Shall I compare thee to a pint of bitter?
Metaphor

Shall I compare thee to a summer's day?
Thou art more lovely and more temperate *[Sonnet 18]*

Shakespeare picks up this comparison and then, as he often does in the Sonnets, rejects it as flawed or clichéed. In Sonnet 18 he says the comparison does not work because the summer is sometimes too hot, sometimes cloudy, and always declines into autumn and winter, and the poet denies this of the loved one, who will live on in his verse. Such comparisons are absolutely typical of love poetry, whether sonnets or Top 40 lyrics: love is compared to a rose, or to sunshine, or to a sinking ship, or to a steam roller. But Sonnet 18 reminds us that while these comparisons work to bring out some similarities, they also require us to forget some differences, so that even the simplest comparison can have differing interpretations. As Shakespeare points out, his comparison to summer could remind us, not of sun, but of the imminence of autumn.

In Chapter 7, I mentioned a campaign for beer based on the slogan, 'Boddington's: The Cream of Manchester'. Each of the posters for this campaign, which we see on bus shelters all over town, shows a glowing, golden pint of beer made in the shape of some dairy product, such as a wedge of cheese or an ice cream cone, or with an ice cream scoop, or some other sign to suggest cream. The slogan suggests that we are to make a comparison, perhaps seeing that Boddington's is the best thing about Manchester, as the cream is taken to be the best part of the milk. But as with the comparison to a summer's day, this comparison could carry unwanted associations. Is Boddington's fattening? Does it go off after a few days in the fridge? Is it good on strawberries?

If I say 'You are a summer's day' or 'Boddington's is the cream,' I am using a metaphor. The term *metaphor* comes from the Greek for *carry over* – we are supposed to carry some meanings over from *summer's day* to *you*. Some X (you) is described in terms of Y (a summer's day). Metaphor is one type of *figurative language*, language that means more than what it literally says (you are not in fact a summer's day, and Boddington's is not in fact a dairy product). For centuries the study of figurative language was restricted to poetry and speeches. But we find metaphors in ads, as well in poems. As we saw in Chapter 2, we would expect soap to be described in terms of ivory, sunlight, caresses, doves; in fact, we would expect soap to be described in terms of anything but soap. Similarly, Exxon gasoline compares itself to a tiger, and Miller beer compares itself to champagne.

We use metaphors in every discourse, even when we aren't being tricky or arty. I have chosen, more or less at random, the opening of the leader to an article in *Campaign*, the weekly newspaper of the UK advertising business. Don't worry about what it is literally about (the way ad agencies charge their clients). Just note how often they use metaphorical expressions.

THE *BELLS SHOULD TOLL* FOR THE COMMISSION SYSTEM

For the first time since Campaign began its billings *league tables*, the Top 300 Report with this issue has *wrung* the admission from many agencies that their business was worse in 1991 than it was the previous year. No one doubts that this was the case, but it is a striking indication of the *depth* of the recession that an industry renowned for *putting a brave face* on any situation could not *muster* even an approach to parity with 1990.

In the circumstances, it is remarkable how few agencies have actually *gone to the wall . . .*

There are some clear examples of figurative speech here. *Bells toll* when someone dies, so this system should die, or be ended. The list is like the *tables* set up in the football league. The admission was obtained as if *wrung* through torture. The agencies are compared to people putting on faces, and the *muster* suggests the calling up of troops. I don't know where the *gone to the wall* metaphor comes from, but it certainly isn't literal. There are also many other words that could be interpreted metaphorically, that we don't even think of as metaphors because they are so common. The *depth* of the recession is an

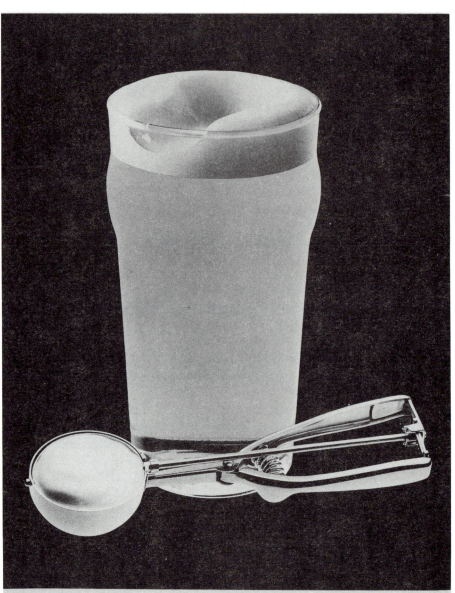

 BODDINGTONS. THE CREAM OF MANCHESTER.

Boddingtons Draught Bitter. Brewed at the Strangeways Brewery since 1778.

example of a dead or dormant metaphor, and some analysts would say we never really think of it as meaning that the recession is like a hole. But I will be assuming that metaphors never really die – they keep carrying their meanings, potentially, in them. We know this because an ad can bring the deadest of metaphors back to life in the right circumstances.

Types of figurative language

The critic Wayne Booth has said that metaphor is defined in so many ways that there is no expression that couldn't be metaphorical in *someone's* definition. Sometimes the term refers to all figurative language, and sometimes it refers to very specific types. Here are some types that often come up in discussions of ads; they are worth distinguishing because they can have subtlely different effects.

Metaphor

Metaphor sets up a relation of similarity between two referents, as if they were the same thing. X is described in terms of Y. For instance, an ad for gin says

BOMBAY SAPPHIRE
POUR SOMETHING PRICELESS

The picture shows the bottle being poured into a martini glass; the liquid splashing out takes on the shape of cut gems. Usually the interpretation of the metaphor is suggested by the name or copy, but sometimes the visuals do more of the work, as with the Boddington's posters.

Simile

A simile (from Latin for *like* – pronounced 'simalee') does the same thing as a metaphor, but with a *like* or *as if* in the wording to show that it is not literal. This makes a big difference to philosophers and literary critics, because it does not require the reader or hearer to reject a literal meaning. I remember Anita Bryant saying this for Florida citrus growers:

Breakfast without orange juice is *like* a day without sunshine.

Though simile is common in poetry, I didn't find it much in ads. It could be that similes are a bit insistent – they don't let the audience make the connection and select the features to be compared themselves. Or it could be that similes are too hesitant in their claims. Try rewriting this beer slogan:

Miller: The Champagne of Bottled Beers

as

BOMBAY SAPPHIRE
POUR SOMETHING PRICELESS.

Miller beer is like champagne.

The simile (the second version) both insists too much on the similarity (Miller is not really a grape product) and suggests doubt (it's only a little like champagne).

Synecdoche

In synecdoche (Greek *receive jointly* – pronounced 'sinEKdoeKEE'), the name of a part of something is used to refer to the whole thing. When you say you need a *hand* with the washing up (you really want a whole person to help), or when you call someone a *prick* (you are referring to the whole person, not just the organ), you are using common examples of synecdoche. A doctor uses this synecdoche in describing a patient in terms of an ailment:

> I hightailed it to the school surgery, leaving the scleral haemorrhage putting on her coat in my examination room. *(Barry Brewster, The Doctor).*

Visually, it is very common for ads to show a part to represent the whole – think of all the car ads where the dashboard instruments are made to stand for the car. A US TV commercial for Lexus combines synecdoche with metaphor. It shows people dressed in business suits on the Tower of Pisa, dropping their car keys (keys as synecdoche for car ownership; falling keys as metaphor for falling prices). Then they bring out a difference; Galileo asserted that all objects (including keys) fall at the same rate, but the price of this car falls slower.

A particularly witty ad for Brooks Brothers, an expensive traditional clothing shop, shows a button with the label '$395'. The text says:

> The Brooks Brothers Wardrobe Suit Collection
>
> [42 regular]
>
> As far as we know, the only thing that fits the 'average' man perfectly on a 42 regular suit is the buttons.

Even Brooks Brothers does not charge $395 for a button. We are to read this as standing for the whole suit. The text explains that the rest cannot be shown because it is not a standard size, but must be fitted. The black and white ad, little picture and lots of text, suggests the kind of understatement for which *New Yorker* advertisers strive.

Metonymy

Metonymy (Greek: *change name*) involves taking something related (rather than a part, as with synecdoche) to stand for the whole thing. We use it when we refer to the Queen as the Crown, or if I say a Volvo lives next door. One kind of metonymy is found in many ads, where the product is associated with some person or surroundings: a car in a country club drive, or a drink in the hands of a beautiful woman. The metonymy is in saying this car *is* this country club life, or to drink this drink *is* to be this woman. An ad for Cutty Sark scotch suggests understatement much as the Brooks Brothers ad does. It shows, not the bottle or a glass of whiskey, but a photograph of a cocktail napkin with the ring left by a glass.

> Some people order certain drinks to be cool, others to be trendy.
> But this is the only impression you leave when you order Cutty
> Sark. And if that's all right with you, you're probably pretty impres-
> sive already.

Strictly speaking, there is metonymy here; the drink is described in terms of the ring it leaves. This is then the occasion for a pun on *impression* as the mark of a glass and as the response of other people to a personality. The ad works because nearly all other ads for expensive spirits (such as single malt whiskeys) suggest metonymically that by drinking the drink one participates in a larger world (grouse shoots, men's clubs, yachts, horse races, country houses) of which it is a part. This ad suggests, paradoxically, that those who have highest status need not project an image through consumer choices. Or more exactly, they choose a whiskey to show that they do not need to choose a whiskey to show anything. But it uses the same device of visual metonymy as the image ads.

Some literary theorists have argued that the effect of metonymy is quite different from that of metaphor. In a realistic fiction, we think of some detail of clothing or setting as standing for that whole world. Similarly, in a metonymic ad, we think of the product and its surroundings as naturally associated. Metaphors, on the other hand, are foregrounded; they only make sense if the audience sees the violation of expectation and makes the interpretative leap. The person waiting for the bus who thinks that Boddington's is advertising cream has missed the point.

You may have noticed that some examples of figurative language that I have given depend on more complex examples than just talking about X in terms of Y, which is how I defined metaphor. For instance, the slogan for Miller:

> The Champagne of Bottled Beers.

sets up an analogy like this:

> Miller (W) is to other bottled beers (X) as champagne (Y) is to other
> wines (Z).

The thing compared is not stated. And we are left to guess in what ways Miller is like champagne. The advertiser would like us to see it as a luxury item. But other associations – with colour and fizz – are also supposed to carry across; otherwise they could say

Miller, the Margaux 1983 of bottled beers

which compares it to an equally expensive wine, but doesn't work as well. On the other hand, we are supposed to suppress some comparisons; for instance, Miller does not cost $20 a bottle, and the top of a Miller bottle does not pop off into one's eye when it is opened.

One we have introduced the possibility of these more complicated comparisons, we can also see *extended analogies*, in which the relationship of W to X is compared to the relationship of Y to Z, not just in one aspect, but on a long list of points. We see such metaphors in the poetry of the seventeenth century, and admire the skill and artifice with which Donne or Marvell draw out the comparisons to more and more unlikely features. In ads too, the effect of an extended metaphor may be comic. In a Shell ad, men in overalls come into a laundrette. They are sitting on the floor scrubbing engine parts, and loading other parts into a machine.

First man: Just look at all that ground in grime. I can't see anything shifting that.

Second man: Don't tell me, these stubborn stains are impossible. It just never gets deep down clean, does it.

After they leave, the women who have been watching say the men should have known about Shell's detergent gasoline. Among the many plays going on here is an elaborate extended analogy:

Shell petrol cleans engines

as advertised detergents clean clothes

The joke comes because of the juxtaposition of two worlds, and more important, two kinds of texts: the petrol ad and the detergent ad. The men are in a situation appropriate to a petrol ad (worrying about engine maintenance), but are using language familiar from detergent ads ('ground in grime', 'deep down clean'), in a setting of a detergent ad, and even with the visual clichés (a shot from inside the machine) found in such ads. Just as Shakespeare expects us to recognise the language of other love poems, and how it is twisted, Shell expects us to recognise the language of other ads, and the incongruity of its use here.

On one level, then, the ad is saying that the petrol cleans like a detergent. But that is not all that is going on; we are seeing how the world is in terms of gender, as we saw with address (Chapter 6) and with everyday talk (Chapter 8). The joke depends on our seeing the juxtaposition of the petrol station and the laundrette as incongruous, and this incongruity arises because one is marked as a man's world and the other as a woman's world. This joke is followed out at the end, as the reassembly of the engine is compared to the sorting of clothes that ends a trip to the laundrette. A man sitting on the floor holds up an engine part and appeals to a woman for information.

Do you know where this goes?

Having crossed the line into the women's world, the men are left helpless on the floor, unable either to do laundry or mechanics. One reading of the ad would be that it ironicises gender roles (women knowing more than men about engines). Another would be that it shows the boundaries between the worlds of men and women to be absolute. But the ad is not about laundrettes, it is about other ads, about the language used to address men and women. The joke is that the men have taken the metaphor of washing an engine literally. The women know that the washing of an engine is a metaphor for the action of the petrol.

Some terminology is required in most discussions of figurative language for sorting out the X and Y. The two parts of the equation in a metaphor are not treated in the same way; one of them is taken for granted, to tell us about the other. The critic I. A. Richards referred to these two parts as the *tenor* and the *vehicle*. The tenor is the thing compared, the thing we want to describe. And the vehicle is the thing it is compared to, the thing we know about that contributes some of its features.

I have stressed that the complexity of interpretation arises because the ads require us to find some features equivalent, while keeping others distinct. Let's go back to the Bombay Gin ad. How is this gin like sapphires?

It is priceless

It is clear

It is solid

It is sharp-edged

It can be worn in a pendant around your neck

It must be locked up in a safe place

As this list shows, the metaphor can be made absurd by stressing the dissimilarities that have been suppressed, or denying the similarities that have been foregrounded, or by reversing the metaphor, reversing the tenor and vehicle, so that we say that sapphires are like gin. So the interpretation of a metaphor is very fragile, leaving lots of room for appropriation by the audience. Metaphors are powerful, but they can easily get out of the advertisers' control.

The blue Earth

So far I have been finding one meaning each for a range of metaphors. Let us look now at a complex image that has become particularly common in ads today, to see how it brings together a number of possible interpretations. The image of the blue and green globe floating in space has been used in a number of different, perhaps conflicting, metaphors. Of course the image of the globe has been a symbol for a long time. Habsburg palaces are crowned with figures holding golden globes, and Charlie Chaplin as Hitler in *The Great Dictator* plays ball with a large inflatable globe. The globe has often been used to suggest the widespread activities of a corporation, putting the Kodak logo on it, or showing it with the slogan of a paint company:

Sherwin-Williams covers the earth.

These globes typically have lines on them – they are the human-mapped globe of schoolrooms and offices.

The image of Earth seen from space is different. We can trace it to a definite time – the moonshots of the late 1960s. It can be used to suggest that the Earth is a closed and fragile system. It can also be used to suggest the technological triumph that allowed such a point of view, far out of our world, unattached to anything. As a round object, it can be a ball, a balloon, a face. But it is also a map; any blue globe must put some part of the world to the front. So we see the world as centred on Europe, or America, or Africa. But what is most important is that these readings can coexist, brought together in an image.

At the end of a Colgate television ad, the toothpaste draws a mouth on the world, which smiles. One meaning is that Colgate is sold all over the world, and it makes people smile. But it also establishes a similarity between a round face and the round world. This is important, because some environmental rhetoric depends on us thinking of the earth as a person. If we extend the metaphor, we might think of it as having feelings and being capable of action, like a person. Very often, this person is female. Or it may be, as here, of indeterminate gender, indeterminate because it is just a round face.

A German magazine ad, for IBM, says simply

OFFEN [Open]

with the O as a globe. Here the globe is not a person, it is a crystal ball, a toy to be taken (by buying the new computers). There is similar imagery in a Nintendo television commercial. In it, people in red or blue are looking up, fists raised, chanting 'Mario, Mario'. It is an alarming sight that reminds me of Leni Reifenstahl's propaganda film, *Triumph of the Will*. But as the camera draws back, we see the people in their colours are arranged to form the shape of the familiar Mario. Then as we draw back further, through the clouds, we see that Mario is filling a continent on the blue globe. This is a bit unnerving – Mario conquers the world.

The globe can be used to make an explicitly environmental message. In a recent public information campaign to get us to conserve energy, child-like drawings of animals and of environmental catastrophe are shown with a boy's voice saying what his dad tells him about the Greenhouse Effect. The blue globe appears first as the eye of a terrified monkey, then shown in a green-house – the metaphor is taken as literal, the way a child might think of it. The earth is shown as an extension of our houses. Thus environmental action is a matter of extending our everyday actions, such as turning off taps. It becomes a matter of domestic manners. (I look at such environmental messages fur-ther in Chapter 11.)

The blue globe image is so arresting that it can be used to advertise almost anything. In an ad in *Nature* for Applied Biosystems, the world is just part of cliché:

> When you need custom peptides, the personal touch makes a world of difference.

The picture of a hand tossing the blue globe combines the two metaphors of the heading – the personal touch and the world of difference. Is there perhaps any relevance in biotechnology firms using this imagery? It is associated at once with the technological triumph of space travel, and the protection of the environment.

A particularly spectacular British Airways ad draws on the blue globe as a unifying image at the end of a dazzling sequence of signs. It has massed crowds in blue, red, or white clothes moving in choreographed steps or strokes across landscapes and water, with the strains of a jazzed up aria from *Lacmé* in the background. These shots from great distances are intercut with extreme close-ups of an eye, or lips. Then we see that each massed crowd forms in its shape a part of a face: eye, lips, ear. Once this pattern is estab-lished, we cut to faces against the background of the Union Jack. They greet each other and embrace, guided by a uniformed flight attendant and a pilot. At the end, the eye, lips, and ear meet on a desert plateau to form the face just suggested earlier. The only words to help us interpret this are:

> Every year the world's favourite airline brings 24 million people together.

There are two meanings to the words 'brings people together': the literal unit-ing of separate people, and the metaphorical assembly of the face. At the end of the ad, the face in the desert winks and then turns to an image of the blue globe, with the roar of the jet behind it.

I have seen this ad dozens of times and I must confess I find it very beautiful. Where is the emotional charge coming from? The visuals show us a highly disturbing image of a shattered face and regimented movement. The peoples of the world are shown as one person that has become dispersed across threatening terrain. Then, thanks to these wonderful uniformed people and this wonderful flag, they are brought together, leaping and hugging. The image at then end makes a whole face, a whole person, a whole globe. The only suggestion of what an airline literally does (pick people up and take them somewhere else) is at the end, in the roar of the jet engine, and the vast view from above. (A recent Christmas version of the same ad ends with a view from space in which the blue globe is orbited by a Christmas pudding moon. No, I don't know what to make of it either.)

We keep seeing the blue globe in ads because it can carry a complex of meanings that we have not yet worked out. It is just because of its potential ambiguity that it is useful.

Earth is a person to be cared for

Earth is a home to be managed

Earth is a ball to be played with

Earth is a pad for space-ships

Earth is an eye watching us

It is like other metaphors in that the meanings cannot be pinned down. What readers carry over from vehicle to tenor, Y to X, depends on their own situated reading. And they can carry over several meanings at once, without untangling them (Is global warming like domestic heating? Is jet travel good for the environment? Do custom peptides lead to world power?) The blue globe, like the summer's day or the Boddington's ice cream cone or the gin gems, can carry radically opposed meanings.

Let me summarise the key points I have made about metaphor:

1. Metaphor occurs in nearly all uses of language.

2. It always involves highlighting some comparisons while suppressing others.

3. It can be done through pictures as well as words.

4. Different kinds of figurative language have different effects, depending on the degree of surprise in the link they make.

5. The effect of most metaphors depends on intertextuality, on reminding us of other texts that make similar or opposite comparisons.

6. The same image, in words or pictures, can carry a number of inter-twined metaphorical readings.

Further reading
Metaphor and metonymy

For metaphor in ads, see Guy Cook *The Discourse of Advertising*, pp. 54–55 or 104–109. For an elaborate classification of advertising metaphors, following classical rhetoric, with lots of illustrations, see J. Durand, 'Rhetorical Figures in the Advertising Image'. The most accessible discussion of metaphor and metonymy is a parody of Judith Williamson in David Lodge's satirical novel about academics, *Nice Work*. It's meant to show the academic talking over the head of a bluff, commonsensical manager, as they drive along the motorway, but it's not a bad explanation. For more on metaphors in ads, see the references in the next chapter, many of which deal with visual metaphors.

There are many theories of metaphor. Wayne Booth jokes that if studies of metaphor keep growing a their present rate, by 2039 there will be more researchers studying metaphor than there will be people on the earth. Just type METAPHOR into a library computer under the title search and you'll see what he means. I have listed a few of these studies that might interest you if you are studying literature or art, but you can find book length bibliographies. Some of these studies, especially in philosophy, have been concerned with separating literal from figurative language. I have been assuming, in contrast, that language is inherently metaphorical.

Three fairly accessible introductions to figurative language are Chapter 9 of Geoffrey Leech, *A Linguistic Guide to English Poetry* ; Terence Hawkes, *Metaphor*, which is one of an excellent series of very short, clear guides to literary terms; and George Lakoff and Mark Johnson, *Metaphors We Live By* , a linguistic and philosophical study which has been popular and influential in a range of disciplines. I have drawn particularly on two classic statements: I. A. Richards, *The Philosophy of Rhetoric* from 1936, and Roman Jakobson, 'Two Aspects of Language and Two Types of Aphasic Disturbances', from 1956, which is reprinted in his *Language in Literature* and elsewhere. As you might guess from Jakobson's title, it is not an easy read.

There are many collections of studies on metaphor, which might be a good place to start. One of the best is: Sheldon Sacks, ed., *On Metaphor* (Chicago, University of Chicago Press, 1979). For a nice, commonsensical introduction, see Wayne Booth, 'Metaphor as Rhetoric: The Problem of Evaluation', in this collection (it is the article from which I have quoted). For very difficult but influential philosophical approaches, see Paul de Man and Paul Ricoeur in the same collection.

10

See above, see above, see above . . .
Words and Pictures

Why pictures?

Almost all the advertisements we have looked at so far involve some pictures. But in most cases I have just looked at the words, and referred to the picture as if it were secondary, a way of illustrating and clarifying the words. Of course that isn't the case – advertisers and their audience devote at least as much attention to the art as to the copy. The production of these visuals, and the traditions of interpretation of these visuals, are matters beyond the scope of this book. But some of the issues we have considered in reading the words are also relevant to reading the pictures, and the ways the words and pictures are related. People tend to take pictures, especially photographs, as having a simple and obvious meaning: 'It shows a car' or 'It shows a gay man'. Our analysis so far can get us to think and talk about *how* they have their effects.

Advertisers themselves have long stressed the superiority of pictures over words – the preference is not a recent cultural change. One argument has been that 'pictures do not lie', that the audience will believe what it sees illustrated, especially if it is a photograph. My favourite of this genre is a print ad that shows a Volvo suspended dangerously over a man, with the text:

If the welding isn't strong enough, the car will fall on the writer.

Campaign tells us that the copy-writer himself, David Abbot, appears in the photograph, showing a commendable faith in the client's product claims.

But even the least sophisticated people in our society know that pictures, including photographs, *can* lie. The boot of that car won't look quite so big, the watch won't glimmer like a spaceship, the sky over the resort won't be so blue. A stronger and more interesting argument for using pictures in ads is that people can't argue with them. Roland Barthes says something like this in his famous essay 'The Rhetoric of the Image', when he says that photographs don't seem to have a code. Language does have a code, and you know something about it, and you can tell sometimes when someone is trying to put something over on you. Any statement in words provokes an answer back, in words, but a picture does not evoke such a clear rational response. We would laugh at an ad that said 'Buy our car and you will never get stuck in traffic', but we don't laugh at the typical picture of a car out on the empty open road. We would laugh at the claim that a soap would make anyone beautiful, if this claim were put in words, but if it is implied by a picture of a beautiful woman holding the soap, our sceptical faculties are not invoked.

Ads often play explicitly on this relationship of words to picture, as a relationship of non-rational and rational faculties. For instance, an ad for Chrysler heads the picture of the car (strangely lit and seen in profile, off the road) as 'The emotion' and the text about its features as 'The logic'. That, I am saying, is how the advertisers themselves see it. There is another nice example of this division in another car ad, for the Citroen BX. Following a standard layout, the top three-quarters of the page is taken up with a picture of the car. The heading is

The sudden popularity of diesel fully explained.

The space below is filled with text, which would usually be 'reason why' copy describing the engine, interior, braking system, and standard features. Here the text fills out the same sort of space with the words 'See above, see above' repeated in the shape of sentences and paragraphs. This suggests that the picture of such an attractive car is itself an irrefutable argument, that further words are unnecessary.

Both these reasons for using visuals – pictures do not lie, pictures are non-rational – treat the audience as passive. Following the view of the audience I have taken throughout this book, I would suggest a third reason for the dominance of pictures. Pictures involve the audience in constructing for themselves a range of messages. The relationship of picture to text is never simply one of illustration, never simply a supplement to make the ad look prettier or more informative. Even in the most banal ad, with a claim and a picture of the product package, the picture leads us off in a number of different directions. Let's take an example so complex it baffled me for a while. This ad has a black and white photograph of a runner sitting on the ground.

The text, which takes up the right hand third of a double-page spread, says:

Tina Shanur.
Order clerk, parts department, Kenwood USA.
10 km runner.
Personal best, 57 minutes, 26 seconds.
Today, 59.15.
Damn, damn, damn.

The only clue to what is being advertised is the Kenwood logo in the lower right, with the slogan 'It's the people who make it'. Here we must somehow find the relevance of this image to the audio components that Kenwood manufactures. The image comes first in my reading. We go back and forth between the text and the image. A number of different readings are possible. The text tells us only that she is a runner. It gives us the times, but we have to figure out that the time she has run today is not her personal best. The 'Damn, damn, damn' serves as a commentary on the dejected figure. Since she works at Kenwood, she will apply the same high standards and determination there. This, I must say, took me minutes of time to come up with. But it comes to me as my own construction, my own discovery, so I do not ignore or challenge it as I might with an ad saying in words, 'Every Kenwood employee strives for personal excellence even when they are relaxing from work, so our components are better.'

Linking words and pictures

If we are going to consider words and pictures together, we need to think about ads at the most abstract level. One way of looking at this is to consider the pictures and words as *signs*. That is a very general way of saying they are physical forms (called *signifiers*) carrying meanings (called *signifieds*). Signs are the subject matter of an academic field known as *semiotics*, a field which had its origins with the American philosopher C. S. Pierce at the beginning of the century, and which had an enormous vogue in literature, film, anthropology, and cultural studies in the 1960s and 1970s. Semiotics has influenced many academic writers on advertisements through the work of Roland Barthes and Judith Williamson.

Pierce and others pointed out that signs carry meanings in three different ways. Let's take a simple example, a poster used on bus shelters around town. It shows a can of Coca Cola that almost fills the whole frame, and below it has the single word,

Thirsty?

We read the picture of the can of Coke as meaning 'a can' because it looks like one, it is perceived through our complex processes of image processing (which are not my concern here) as smooth and cylindrical and shiny. Of course we know that it is not actually a can – the poster is flat and paper and five feet high – but a sign representing a can. That is what semioticians call an *iconic* relationship of signifier and signified, a relationship of resemblance.

We also know the can is cold, because of the droplets of water on the side. The relationship between the signifier 'droplets' and the signified 'cold' is not one of resemblance; the droplets are caused by the cold. This relationship is said to be *indexical*; other examples in which the signifier results from or is associated with the signified are tyre tracks signifying a car, or an uneven walk signifying drunkenness, or the ring on a napkin signifying a glass. It is worth making this distinction between the iconic and the indexical, because indexical signs are often read as more real, less tricky and questionable.

Now what about the word 'Thirsty?' Here the signifier consists of eight letter shapes that neither look like thirst nor result from it. They are associated with the meaning 'needing a drink' only by a convention of English speakers. As with most words in all languages, the connection is arbitrary; any other set of sounds or letters would do as well. These conventional signs are called *symbols*, and they include not just what we usually think of as symbols (a cross for a hospital, red lights for stop) but all written and spoken language. While we realise that symbols can be understood only by those who share our culture, we tend to take iconic and indexical signs as somehow naturally connected to the thing they represent. But they are still signs. A picture is not the thing itself. It is always open to multiple interpretations.

Layout

Ads never show pictures by themselves; our reading of the picture is crucially affected by layout, the positioning of the picture on the page, and in a television ad, the editing. Gunther Kress and Theo van Leeuwen have some very perceptive comments on the arrangement on the page, based on the temporal progress of the reader through the composition. Their comments echo those of advertising layout books. In one standard layout of an ad, with the picture making up the top two-thirds, they would see the top/bottom split as having a meaning; it could be a split between ideal and real, for instance, or before and after. Ads usually end with the product or logo in the lower right hand corner, the last thing read and the answer to what is posed above.

Kress and van Leeuwen offer a more complex reading of the arrangement of layouts split between left and right. Linguists talk about a distinction in sentences between what is *given* – what the hearer already knows about – and the *new* – what this sentence is adding. So if I say

Elena is a lecturer

I am assuming you know who *she* is from the earlier part of our conversation, but that I am adding the information about her employment. If I say

The lecturer is Elena

I am assuming you know the lecturer I am referring to (perhaps she is standing in front of us) and that what is new to you is her name. Typically, in English sentences, the given is near the beginning, and the new near the end. We tend to read ads from left to right, so Kress and van Leeuwen suggest the layout may be following a pattern similar to that of a sentence. This generalisation works surprisingly well in ads in which a picture on the left is followed by a text on the right, or the expectation on the left is followed by the surprise on the right. For instance, a Volkswagen ad says on the left page:

Is it the best car in its class?

with a picture of the car in a spotlight. On the right is an empty spotlight, and the words

We may never know.

(The text explains that there is no other car in its class).

Once we think of layout as a way of guiding the movement of our reading in time, not just as an arrangement in space, we can apply to pictures the ideas of parallelism that I applied to texts in Chapter 4. That is, multi-picture ads may set up expectations by arranging several images in relation to each other. An ad for Moschino can serve as an example. Each ad in this series, which appeared in youth style magazines, consists of four pictures with the single word Moschino. For those of us who did not even know that this company made clothes, it was completely baffling. One approach was to try to relate the pictures as parallel in some way.

upper left: a skull and cross-bones with the words 'I [heart] drugs'
upper right: an photograph of old man sitting on a bench, with the words, '. . . and me?'
lower left: a romantic painting of a battle scene with the words 'No to violence'
lower right: a woodcut Indian saying 'Don't touch my plants'

The disparate visual styles are linked by a set of four statement that are parallel in addressing social issues. It is like a Benetton ad, cubed. I still have no clear reading to give you on how this relates to Moschino clothes (answers on a postcard please . . .) but I realised I was following conventions of reading that held for many other, less puzzling, ads.

Anchorage and relay

In all the examples so far, we have looked back and forth between words and pictures, looking for clues to interpretation. An influential essay by Roland Barthes, analysing in excruciating detail a single bog-standard ad for spaghetti sauce, describes this movement. For him the main relationship is *anchorage*. Barthes emphasises that words and sentences inherently have many meanings. The picture helps constrain, narrow down, the possible choices, though it cannot pin them down entirely. Like Barthes, I will take a simple example. A current Volvo ad has the headline,

Now this Volvo carries just as much as a Granada Estate.

Even such a straightforward text contains ambiguities. The 'carries just as much' suggests that the Granada holds more. The word *carries* has many interpretations. The possible readings of the text are constrained somewhat by the picture, which shows a man with a blowtorch who has apparently cut off the back quarter of the Volvo. Now our interpretation shifts – the Volvo doesn't hold 'as much' as the Granada – it holds more, and would have to be cut down to be the same. So the text is anchored by the picture.

Barthes sees a smaller role for another relationship, *relay*, in which text and picture work back and forth to carry the message. His example is comic strips. But in any real reading of these ads, we go back and forth repeatedly, as we did, for instance, with the picture of the runner in the Kenwood ad. This relationship is more common than he suggests, especially in television commercials. Let's try it with a poster that shows two babies and has the text:

One has full human rights

The other has cerebral palsy

The picture narrows down the possible readings, by telling us who the *one* and *the other* are. But that still doesn't provide us with a reading. We have to go back and forth between the statements, and between statements and picture, each carrying on the interpretation a step further. How are these two statements related? There are lots of possibilities. It could be informing us that people with cerebral palsy *are* less than human. Which baby is which? The context here includes the fact that it must be advertising something, and that the ad carries the logo of the Spastics Society. So one possible reading goes like this:

look at pictures of babies

read text

look back to picture to tell which is which

VOLVO

NOW THIS VOLVO CARRIES JUST AS MUCH AS A GRANADA ESTATE.

Them: Surely that can't be right?

Us: Yes, we thought that too. But according to Ford's figures their Granada carries 25% less shopping, suitcases, golf clubs (and trolleys), jet skis, hang gliders, inflatable rafts....

Them: Making it such a big car it's difficult to drive, right?

Us: Wrong. The Volvo has a smaller turning circle than the Ford Escort never mind the Granada. And with power steering even town driving becomes a pleasure. (Well, as much as it can be.)

Them: The Ford is available with a bigger engine though.

Us: True, but our 2.0L Turbo is quicker and more powerful than the 2.9L Ford. Do you want to talk about safety?

Them: Not really.

Us: We do. The 940 has SIPS (our unique Side Impact Protection System), 3 three-point seat belts, an integrated child seat, anti-lock brakes, seat belt pre-tensioners, a burst-proof fuel tank, a standard driver's side airbag, our legendary safety cage and crumple zones....

Them: Ok. Ok. Let's face it you pay for it though. Volvos are more expensive than Fords aren't they?

Us: Strangely enough the Volvo 940 starts at £16,895 and the Granada £18,670, a saving of £1,775. (Another sizeable difference.)

Them: Surely that can't be right?

Us: Yes, we thought that too. **THE VOLVO 940 ESTATE. A CAR YOU CAN BELIEVE IN.**

go back to text

realise we can't tell which is which

conclude that it is not right that one should have different rights than the other.

Well, you might say, you could do all that without reading Barthes on anchorage and relay. What he provides is way of talking about the problems involved. I think it is a good exercise to realise that the words and the pictures both could have multiple meanings, and to try to think how we use the picture and words together to arrive at our readings.

Checklist on the visual image

Let us look back to the Kenwood and Volvo ads to see how our study of language can help us describe pictures. In both ads, despite the verbal wit, the photograph is what first attracts our attention. I have already described them as 'a man with a blowtorch who has apparently cut off the back quarter of the Volvo' and 'a picture of a runner sitting on the ground'. But this gives no suggestion of why they have their striking effects, the emotion of the Kenwood picture and the understatement of the Volvo picture. As we looked first at foregrounding and deviation in language, let us look at how things stand out in pictures. As we looked at structure in sentences, we can look at framing and composition in pictures. As texts suggest an attitude, a point of view, and a form of address, so can pictures. And as words play with meanings and associations, so can pictures.

Foregrounding and deviation of basic elements

One way to make things stand out in a photograph is to put them in colour. But the Kenwood ad is in black and white, and the Volvo ad is in such muted greys that only the red of the tail light and the yellow of the side blinker tell us it is a colour picture at all. The runner stands out because of *definition*: she is in focus while the background is out of focus. The car stands out because of texture: it is gleaming while the background, in the same grey, is matte. The car is picked out by the gleam of reflected light, while the runner is mostly in shadow, outlined by the sun on her shoulders, arms, and hair. All this play with light, I am saying, is serving the function of plays with sound in language.

Framing

The structure of a picture is given by its frame, what it includes and excludes. Here there is no doubt; the runner in one and the car in the other virtually fill the frame. Only the shadows and blurred background of the runner picture

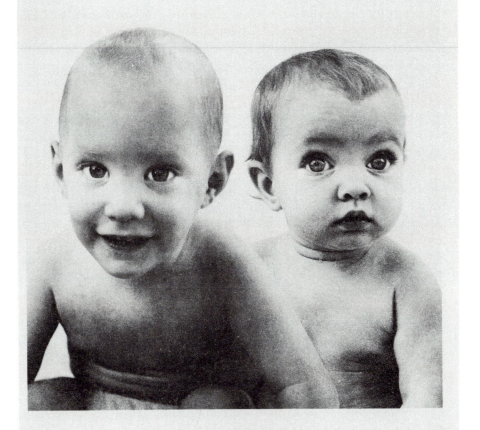

One has cerebral palsy.
The other has full human rights.

The baby on the left finds it hard to sit up.

In a month she might have the occasional spasm.

In a year she won't be walking because her legs will be taut one moment and floppy the next.

Then her problems will really begin. People will notice she's different. They'll start treating her differently.

Her rights to education, employment and housing will be out of her control because she can't control her limbs.

Entering society will be impossible because she won't be able to get into polling stations, public buildings or public transport.

In an ideal world, she'd turn to the law. In reality, she'll turn to The Spastics Society.

We might give her physiotherapy at one of our centres.

Work experience at one of our colleges. Or training to live in her own house. (We'll even pay for the house.) We can't cure cerebral palsy. But we can do our best to cure society's prejudice.

To this end, we need the means: your time, your money and your positive attitude.

If you value these rights yourself, isn't it wrong to deny them to others?

To: The Spastics Society, FREEPOST
PO Box 99, Liverpool L69 1TB.

I wish to donate £ .... by cheque/p.o.
I wish to pledge £ .... per month.
To donate by credit card call 051-624 4040.
Please send more information about The Spastics Society's work to help people with cerebral palsy. [SC]

Name
Address

40th Anniversary1992
THE SPASTICS SOCIETY
FOR PEOPLE WITH CEREBRAL PALSY

suggest a world continuing on outside (as realistic photographs usually do). Within the frame, the structure is largely given by vectors, lines of eye movement. The cut in the Volvo seems so dramatic because it interrupts a long horizontal line that dominates the picture. The erect posture of the man emphasises this break. The tension of the runner picture comes from the diagonals of her posture; a similar picture of her standing or lying down would not be the same. But her back, arms, and legs form a triangle with the long side down, suggesting stability, coming to rest.

Point of view and address

All pictures give us a point of view, the way pronouns do in language. Here, for instance, we are close to the runner, and at the level of her eyes, not looking down from above her, suggesting empathy rather than judgement. We are set back from the Volvo as if it were on a stage; we are at the level of its midline, so that the man with the torch rises above the horizon. Whenever there are human figures, their gaze and position are important as well as our own. Here, we do not see either person's eyes; the welder is masked, making him or her mysterious and robot-like, while the woman is looking down in a private moment. It is a crucial distinction in ads between those in which the characters (usually female) look out at us, and those (usually male) who keep to their own business.

There is a point of view in time as well as in space. Pictures suggest what happens before or after; in both these ads we are asked to imagine what has just happened, a race and a cut. They also carry *modality*, a suggestion of how much we are to take them as representations of reality. One crucial indicator of modality is the presence of gratuitous detail, more detail than we need to tell what it is a picture of. Thus, an outline drawing does not present itself as directly related to the thing and the moment, while a grainy black and white photograph does. Here, the plainness of the Volvo picture, with no distracting background, suggests it is a demonstration, an image set up to display one fact. The runner photograph, on the other hand, suggests with its background and detail that it is a moment snatched objectively. The choice of back and white carries further associations of immediacy, because we associate it with news photos.

Associative meanings

Just as part of the meaning of words comes from their associations, not just from their dictionary definitions, part of the meaning of pictures comes from associations with the image and style. In fact, we can find visual equivalents for the associative meanings we looked at in Chapter 5. So, for instance, the runner currently has favourable *referent associations* of self-discipline and determination, that can carry over from her leisure activities to her employer. What does the welder suggest? Because of the mask and still flaming blowtorch, I see it as a violent image, emphasising the excess (and thus the silliness) of what has been done to make the cars equivalent. As with associations with words, these meanings arise from changing associations with the things referred to, not from the form of the image.

Collocative meanings

Collocative meanings with words result from the other words that a word tends to go with. The same can happen with pictures, but we usually notice the expected combinations only when they are violated. I saw an example on a poster in the underground in Montreal, which had the Creation scene from Michelangelo's Sistine Chapel, with God handing Adam a bottle of wine with the appropriate brand name, La Vallée du Paradis. Someone had written 'blaspheme' on it – this member of the active audience had decided that the parody was making fun of God, not of Michelangelo.

Just as collocations of words sometimes become so predictable as to be clichés, so there are clichés in pictures; you should be able to find three or four in any magazine or commercial break: the car in front of a country house, the divided screen demonstration, the enormous product, or the mountain peak, which suggests some sort of cleanliness and freshness that applies from Coke to Alpen to mineral water. Cliché may be a matter of style rather than symbol. Many ads now take on the style of 1920s Soviet posters. (I know this is a cliché because the reviewer in *Campaign* says so.) I noticed this last year when NatWest and Cable tv and Cellnet phones all started to use socialist realism with some claim of revolution. There is probably an essay to be written on why this style is popular just as the communist regimes crumble, and why it is most popular with distinctly capitalist institutions like banks. Visual clichés, like verbal clichés, survive because they are useful in all sorts of situations. The images come to seem natural.

Reflected meanings

What about the last one on our list of associative meanings in Chapter 5, *reflected* meanings, meanings that connect to images because of associations with taboos? Many ads are sexually suggestive. Let me just take one famous recent example, because it is so over the top.

We find the fresh eggs in Häagen-Dazs provide delicate flavour

body [in huge type]

and

texture [in huge type]

Häagen-Dazs
Dedicated to pleasure

The imagery is soft core pornography, while the text plays on this by enlarging the two words *body* and *texture* in copy otherwise quite appropriate to ice cream. Now there are lots of ads that show women looking orgasmic using all sorts of products. What makes this one lewd is that it is photographed in the style of pornography, low angle and soft focus, with the ice cream dripping down her chest, the product located down by her crotch. It is just like the copy of the ad, playing on possible suggestions of the word *body* in other contexts.

So far I have been showing that one picture can have many associative meanings readable in it. But can pictures contain puns, double meanings? The Boddington's poster in Chapter 9 is one example; the Silk Cut ads are another. Consider this example of a double visual meaning. The headline says

New Volkswagen Extra Mild

and the text of the ad (which ran on National No Smoking Day) contains many puns on 'giving up smoking'. The picture appears to show lips and a cigarette, but on close examination it is the exhaust pipe of a Volkswagen, emerging from the bumper. (Note how it has to be in black and white, fairly grainy, and cropped like this to be readable with both meanings. A colour tail light could only be on a car, not a face). This is an unusually adept example, but many posters play on two possible meanings, requiring active interpretation from the viewer.

Conclusion

I have been stressing the interrelationship of words and pictures. You might object at this point that some of the most famous ads of the last few years use no words at all – like the famous Silk Cut or Benson and Hedges cigarette ads, or the notorious Benetton posters. There are two responses to the challenge of no-word ads. One, given by Barthes, is that the techniques used in analysing linguistic meaning apply to pictures as well, if one approaches them on a sufficiently abstract level. For him, the machinery of linguistics is a way of tearing us away from the self-evidence of pictures, making us look at them in very simple terms, asking questions like, 'What is this a picture of?' 'How could it be different?'

Another response to no-word ads is given by Trevor Pateman. He points out that ads that lack words entirely depend on our expectation that there will be words. Our interpretation starts with the lack of words, and asks why

New Volkswagen Extra Mild.

It isn't easy giving up smoking.

But, after numerous attempts, we think we've finally cracked it.

Enter the Umwelt, or 'Environment,' Diesel. You can't buy cleaner.

Available on the Golf, Passat and Vento, its cleanliness is down to two features. A turbo charger and a catalytic converter.

The turbo charger isn't there to add performance. It's there to pump more air into the engine. And the more air there is, the less smoke there is.

The catalytic converter further reduces toxic gases like carbon monoxide.

For passive motorists, it does something even more important. It reduces that dreaded diesel smell.

Not that this is the first time we've cut down on pollution.

Lead-free paint is already available across our range. Our cars are more recyclable than ever. Even our factory chimneys are fitted with catalytic converters.

Alright, so the road to a truly green car is a long one.

But until we finally get there, we'll continue introducing environmentally sound ideas.

We're already making a habit of it.

Umwelt Diesel

it lacks words. Let's take the example of the recent Clinique ads. While the ads for men's soaps, like that in Chapter 4, give us the hard sell, the ads for the more established women's products do nothing but show a very large picture of the product, in a kind of pinkish brown tint of a black and white photograph. How do we read this? There is no text, not even the product logo. All there is is the product. This would seem to be the simplest possible ad. And yet its effect is complex. That's because we respond first to what makes the ad different, the lack of text. Our first move must be to recognise this as an ad, as a text that intends to sell us something. We look at the product, which is open, being used, but which has no user pictured. There is no text. One possible implication is that no text is necessary. The product speaks for itself. But that is just what it doesn't do – it needs to be artfully presented so that we recognise it as intended to convey a meaning. Even ads with no words require detailed textual analysis, considering alternative interpretations and relations to other texts. Approaches to analysis of language can take us part of the way to this detailed analysis.

Further reading
Words and pictures

I have referred in the text to four studies of ads that give special attention to visual interpretation: Roland Barthes, 'The Rhetoric of the Image'; Trevor Pateman, 'How Do Ads Mean?'; Roland Marchand, *Advertising the American Dream: Making Way for Modernity*; and Erving Goffman, *Gender Advertisements*. In addition, Judith Williamson, *Decoding Advertisements*, and Robert Goldman, *Reading Ads Socially* are examples of semiotic interpretations that stress the visual. Guy Cook, *The Discourse of Advertising*, has excellent readings of visual texts, based on linguistic approaches.

Many analyses of imagery done by researchers in cultural studies take examples from advertising. Kathy Winship, 'Sexuality for Sale', is about hands in ads; a longer illustrated version is in R. Betterton, ed., *Looking On*. Mary Talbot has an extended analysis of two pages of advertorial in *Jackie*, 'The Construction of Gender in a Teenage Magazine'; Angela McRobbie also analyses *Jackie*. Donna Haraway's powerful and readable study *Primate Visions* includes several analyses of ads. Susan Bordo analyses the representation of women's bodies in ads in 'Reading the Slender Body'. Janelle Sue Taylor has a brilliant reading of one image in a Volvo ad, 'The Public Foetus and the Family Car: From Abortion Politics to a Volvo Advertisement'. It begins 'Not long ago, a foetus tried to sell me a car – or should I say, a car tried to sell me a foetus? In any case, I didn't buy it.' Greg Myers, 'The Double Helix as an Icon' applies the approach of this chapter to images of DNA.

For introductory books on reading visual texts, see Gunther Kress and Theo van Leeuwen, *Reading Images*; and John Berger, *Ways of Seeing*. David Bordwell and Kristin Thompson, *Film Art: An Introduction*, is a good and critically subtle introduction to visual techniques; and James Monaco, *How to Read a Film: The Art, Technology, Language, History, and Theory of Film and Media* , as the endless subtitle suggests, introduces a very wide range of critical issues with nicely chosen examples. For discussion of the theoretical issues involved in photography, one could follow the Barthes essay, and his *Camera Lucida*, with Susan Sontag's controversial and readable *On Photography*, and the collection edited by Victor Burgin, *Thinking Photography*. There is a fascinating range of rather difficult sociological studies in John Law, ed., *Picturing Power: Visual Depiction and Social Relations*.

A taste of the ways ad people talk about the visuals in ads can be seen each week in the sometimes catty comments in the 'Private View' pages of *Campaign*.

11

Concentrated Persil Supports Trees
Green Ads and Agency

Among the many leaflets and fliers pushed through our front door recently was an attractive pamphlet from Lancashire County Council that says at the top (in green of course)

GO GREEN FOR GOOD

The text begins

Do you want to save the world but don't know where to start?
This leaflet shows how you can do your bit in Lancashire to help save the planet.

A cartoon picture shows a boy holding a stethoscope roughly in the area of Lancashire on a blue and green globe as big as a room; he has lines from his head to show shock, and a dog looks on with similar signs of concern. On the next page there is a space for me to sign, pledging I will 'Go Green for Good', and saying:

The future of Lancashire's environment concerns all of us. The little things we do, added up, have a huge effect.

The suggestions range from recycling and turning down the central heating to building a pond in one's back yard and reporting property development to the Council Planning Department. At the end we are told to pass on the leaflet to three others, and to put their names in three more spaces.

GO GREEN
for GOOD

Do you want to save
the world but don't
know where to start?

This leaflet shows how
you can do your bit in
Lancashire to help
save the planet.

Lancashire
County
Council

Readers will recognise this as a fairly typical (if unusually well-produced) piece of environmental campaigning. It raises two general issues about the social effect of ads: how do they show who can do what? And how do they represent the environment? The first issue, who can do what, is discussed in the social sciences under the heading of *agency*. The 'Go Green for Good' leaflet tries to get us to recognise ourselves as agents, while also defining companies, the council, and lumber companies in developing countries as agents. One way of tracing these issues of agency is by looking at who or what does things in each sentence of a text, who or what is acted on, and which agents are left out entirely.

The second issue takes us back to our discussion of metaphor. The environment is represented in various images and (less obviously) phrases that encapsulate larger processes. The blue globe, as we have seen in Chapter 10, is one of these images. Here this globe is seen as being examined with a doctor's apparatus, implying it is sick. But it is being examined, not by a doctor, but by a boy in a baseball cap. So three different kinds of synecdoche and metonymy are going on in one picture: the globe could stand for the environment as a whole, the stethoscope could stand for doctors and by extension for disease, and the boy could stand for future generations. The symbols work by referring to their opposites – blue globe vs. sick earth, doctor vs. patient, boy vs. man. The reliance on oppositions makes apparently simple symbols very complex in their effects. In the same leaflet there are cooling towers, radiators, bottle banks, bicycles, washing up liquid, a frog in a pond, a rabbit fleeing a bulldozer. They are symbols, but we must not dismiss them as *just* symbols, for this is a part of the terrain on which environmental battles are lost and won. The interpretation of signs leads us away from the logic of cause and effect to the kinds of associative meanings we have considered with words (Chapter 5)and then with pictures (Chapter 10). For each green ad we need to ask, 'Green as opposed to what?'

Green ads raise crucial issues of agency because environmental problems are not primarily about relationships of individuals to nature, but about relationships of people to people in social networks. So, for instance, some people think that the relevant agents in environmental change are unions of Brazilian rubber workers, or pressure groups like Greenpeace, or government agencies, or corporations, or nations, or political parties, or transnational groups like the UN or the World Bank. But environmental damage keeps creating new groups. Imagine, for instance, the group of all people hurt by Chernobyl, from the Ukraine to Cumbria, or all the victims of asbestosis, or all the users of dry cell batteries. Can they be agents?

This is where ads come in. Ads ask us to imagine different kinds of agents and networks. I am going to argue that their main effect is not in their messages – buy this washing powder or that car – but in the way they extend or limit our ability to conceive of social agents, reducing agency to an individual consumer and personified company, or extending it along networks of circulation and exchange (for instance, asking where hardwood comes from, or where Third World debt goes). In this chapter I look at who is doing what, and what signs are used. I consider ads that propose four kinds of agents: nature itself, companies and consumers, and campaign organisations. Finally I will look at some ads that try to alter ideas of agency.

Nature and the individual

Many of the ads that use green imagery aren't about saving the environment – they're about nature saving us. For instance, two ads for sugar, one in the US and the other in the UK, both play on readers' established oppositions of the natural and healthy with the artificial and unhealthy. The US television ad has a man eating cereal in a field of sugar beets, as the camera draws back to reveal a vast green panorama. He says:

> The people who make sugar would like you to spend the next thirty seconds reading the back of your artificial sweetener packet. *[pause]* Interesting, huh?
>
> *[voiceover]* Pure natural sugar. A sweetener only nature could make.

The UK ad has a similar strategy in a print ad. It has the headline:

> If you thought sugar was made in manufacturing plants, you were right.

This leads us to expect that *plants* will refer to factories, drawing on our association of the unhealthy with the artificial. But the pictures flanking the two page spread show old-fashioned drawings of a sugar beet and sugar cane. The word *plants* is meant to evoke associations of naturalness, as the copy says:

> . . . Just as a bee gathers nectar from flowers and converts it into honey-comb food reserves, so we purify sugar for our own use . . . The question is, do you prefer your sweetener made from sodium saccharide, aspartic acid, aceto-acetic acid, and phenylalanine? Or sunshine, air, and water?

The ads reverse the associations promoted by healthy eating campaigns: sugar = processed = added = unhealthy, trying to get us to see sugar = pure = natural = healthy. (Parents find that a children's drink that says 'no artificial ingredients' contains sugar; one that says 'no added sugar' contains an artificial sweetener.)

If you thought sugar was made in manufacturing plants, you were right.

You're looking at two of Nature's sugar factories. And highly productive operations they are too.

On the left, *Saccharum officinarum*, or sugar cane. On the right, *Beta vulgaris*, or sugar beet.

They work every hour daylight sends seven days a week.

Their raw materials are sunshine, air and water. The finished products they turn out are sugars and starches.

Sugar cane was discovered in India more than two thousand years ago.

It grows best in rich soils and humid tropical climates, so its planted in countries like Mauritius and the West Indies.

Sugar beet, a large root vegetable, grows well in cool, temperate climates like our own. Napoleon first ordered it to be grown in Europe when the English naval blockades prevented the raw cane sugar ships getting through.

Between them these two plants supply most of the world's sugar.

At which point you might fairly ask, if sugar is made by Nature then what on earth do the sugar companies do?

The answer is, we extract, clean and crystallise.

Just as a bee gathers nectar from flowers and converts it into honey-comb food reserves, so we purify sugar for our own use. Though the individual treatments for beet and cane vary the results are just the same.

The washed plants are crushed or sliced into hot water, making a dirty brown juice.

This we filter, clean and boil down to a thick syrup, from which pure white sugar can be crystallised.

The dark, treacly molasses left behind is used to give brown sugars their characteristic colour and flavour.

And that's it. Brown or white, in plants or packets sugar is sugar.

It contains no colouring. No flavouring. And no preservatives.

Sugar can be extracted from many plants, though it seldom makes economic sense.

In Pakistan they use sweet, sticky dates. In the East, coconut palms. In America maize. The Canadians take maple syrup from the sap of the maple tree.

Of course, artificial sweeteners are also made in plants. But plants of a rather different kind.

The question is, do you prefer your sweetener made from sodium saccharide, aspartic acid, aceto-acetic acid and phenylalanine?

Or sunshine, air and water?

Sugar. The more you know about it, the sweeter it tastes.

Some cosmetics ads present nature both as an agent of harm (through environmental threats) and of rescue (through natural ingredients). A reader who sees the headline

Hydration-Plus
The New Response to ENVIRONMENTAL PROTECTION

might imagine that the product would protect the environment (the US government office charged with fighting pollution is the Environmental Protection Agency). A closer reading shows that the product is protecting the user from the environment, not the other way around.

Pollution. tobacco smoke, sun rays . . . They challenge the beauty of our skin. CLARINS *NEW* Hydration Plus Moisture Lotion pioneers effective countertactics to neutralise the dehydrating, sensitising aggressors that bombard skin daily.

We have switched from the language of ecology to the language of war. But there is still a use for traditional appeals to nature (the product is shown against a background or wet tropical leaves).

Concentrated with natural plant extracts and vitamins proven to soften fine lines, ensure daylong comfort. Key ingredients in CLARINS 'PLUS' Complex include reflective rice bran extract, skin-softening linden, ginseng, wheatgerm, and horse chestnut, Vitamins B, C, and E. The synergy of actions counteracts the visible effects of environmental aggressions/pollution.

The environment is both a source of comfort (with 'skin-softening linden') and of 'aggressions'. The reader can slide between the two meanings of 'environmental protection' because they are both clusters of possible associations, with nature as threat and as threatened.

What holds the threat and threatened together is a conception of the human developing as an individual alone in an almost human but sublimely powerful nature, a conception often traced to Romantic poets. A recent British Rail poster quotes Wordsworth:

Nature never did betray the heart that loved her.

Advertisers do love her. A cinema ad for British Nuclear Fuels Ltd. starts with helicopter shots of Cumbrian landscape, with a lone man perched on a fell top, and then cuts between such scenes and visitors peering at exhibits at the Sellafield nuclear reprocessing facility, which is on the coast near these fells. Opponents of Sellafield criticise it as a major source of radioactive emissions into the Irish Sea, but here nature and technology are brought together as part of a single tourist experience.

Companies and consumers

In most green ads, the personified company is the main agent of environmental repair, assisted by the individual consumer. We saw this in the ad for Georgia Pacific discussed in Chapter 8. This strategy foregrounds some signs of environmental action to stand for greenness in general. Let's take a typical sort of campaign, one of a series showing lovely photos of green grass, trees, blue skies, and maybe a cottage, an intense vision of rural England. In this particular ad, we see a line of washing supported between two trees, apparently reversing the message of the headline:

Concentrated Persil supports trees.

In case you're wondering how, the copy continues

Concentrated Persil Automatic comes in a small pack. It was developed to give you less to carry and less to store. As a result, less cardboard is used for packaging.

Better still, four-fifths of the cardboard has been recycled. And the rest of it comes only from those areas with strict reforestation policies. All of it is biodegradable.

Because the powder is concentrated, you need use only about half the amount for perfect Persil results. In all, it's a very happy outcome for the whites, the colours, and the greens.

What Persil has done is focus on one environmental signifier – waste packaging. The skillfully crafted matter-of-fact effect comes from developing this focus in four short sentences, so each sentence seems to take the claim further: there is less of it, most is recycled, the rest is reforested, and all is biodegradable. But there is nothing here about the effects of the detergents themselves; the end returns to traditional claims.

One company that has a very long history of environmental ads is Shell Oil. One features a picture of an idyllic landscape in North Wales with the heading:

Wouldn't you protest if Shell ran a pipeline through this beautiful countryside?

Then it tells you,

We already have.

It is assumed you see the company as a threat to the environment, but then shows it can be a healing force. (Note that it is a personalised *we*, here, not *Shell Oil.*) The national park landscape serves to classify the company as environmentally correct, so that there are no further questions about how the

Concentrated Persil supports trees.

Concentrated Persil Automatic comes in a small pack. It was developed to give you less to carry and less to store. As a result, less cardboard is used for packaging.

Better still, four fifths of the cardboard has been recycled. And the rest of it comes only from those areas with strict reforestation policies. All of it is biodegradable.

Because the powder is concentrated, you need use only about half the amount for perfect Persil results. In all, it's a very happy outcome for the whites, the colours and the greens.

product is produced before it gets into this pipeline or consumed after it gets out.

The ads for Shell and British Nuclear Fuels suggest that we are to expect green ads from what are in public opinion the least green companies, especially those associated with extracting raw materials or producing pollution. A television ad for Boise Cascade, shown in southern Idaho, presents the lumber company as the active guardian of the environment. Boise Cascade is not addressing us as consumers, as Persil is. It, like British Nuclear Fuels, is addressing us as citizens who could affect the regulatory framework in which it operates.

Visual	*Voiceover*	*Sound*
Aerial view of dead trees	Why so many dead and dying trees in Southwest Idaho's national forests?	Discordant chord
Black and white view of trees	Years of drought.	Chord
	Epidemics of insects that attack and kill the trees.	Chord
	Some activists say let the trees rot or burn up in wild fires.	
Man planting trees	Doesn't it make more sense to salvage the dying trees and avoid the waste?	Music
Close-up of hoe and seedling	Then start planting new trees immediately to breathe new life into the forest.	
Aerial view of live trees		
Black and white trees	Let dead or dying trees rot or burn?	
	What a waste.	
Text: Boise Cascade Idaho Region Operations		

Here nature causes the damage, with drought and epidemics and wild fires; even the natural process of decay is presented as wasteful rotting. Faced with this threat, activists are passive, and only the company can step in, with a Genesis like breath of life. The issue is presented in rhetorical questions, assuming that we can only agree with the salvage operation, and with the final exclamation.

Criticisms of green consumer ads have been publicised since the late 1980s by mock awards from the Friends of the Earth for the 'Green Con'. One famous example (which Steve Yearley has discussed) is the claim of some washing up liquids to be phosphate free. Well they might, because washing liquids have never had phosphates in them; phosphates are used in powders for clothes. The assumption was that the public had identified phosphates as the single sign of environmental damage. Environmental campaign organisations spent a lot of time pursuing these claims, showing that, for instance, a product that might claim to be environmentally friendly because it did not contain some pollutant, might cause great damage in other ways. The Advertising Standards Authority criticised Austin Rover for claiming that a car that ran on unleaded petrol was 'ozone friendly'. It would not put lead into the atmosphere, but it would put out plenty of other pollutants. 'Ozone friendly' was made an issue because of CFCs in propellants for aerosol cans; here it was carried over to another area of advertising. Recently there was controversy when the fur industry was given a Green Con award for claiming its products were environmentally sound because they were a natural and renewable resource. Well, they are natural and renewable. But the trapping and keeping of animals involves a different view of nature from that of environmental groups.

In a way the 'Green Con' charge is misleading, because like other critics of advertising, Friends of the Earth focus on the literal text of ads, requiring the texts to stick to the facts (see Chapter 13). The larger effect of ads is not in their information or misinformation, but in how they shape our notions of reality and of practical action. The 'Green Con' criticisms leave intact the symbols of green action and leave intact the idea that the main actors are corporations. Who can do what? In these ads, it is only big multinational companies that do things; we can act only by supporting them. Note also the verbs that go with these agents: they support, they purify, they prevent, they salvage. All these verbs contain an idea of protection. What signs are used? Chemicals and pipelines and dead trees are opposed to an idyllic rural world without any indication of human habitation.

Campaigns

Of course the actors relevant to the environment are not limited to companies, nature, and consumers; there are a number of highly visible campaigning groups, such as Greenpeace, the Sierra Club, and Friends of the Earth, that offer themselves as a means of collective action outside or against the commodity system. But they find themselves in a paradoxical situation, for to generate funds, to increase membership, or to highlight issues, they have to turn to ads very similar to those for commodities.

The problem for campaign groups entering the discourse of advertising is apparent in different responses to the Braer oil spill in January 1993. I have already discussed in Chapter 1 an example of the central icon of these ads: pictures of oily birds. Benetton used this image to raise awareness of environmental issues in general; in Benetton's view, awareness of social issues is, itself, enough. But the images are also used for other purposes. First there are the straight oily bird pictures encouraging us to give to the Royal Society for the Protection of Birds or the Royal Society for the Prevention of Cruelty to Animals, which would use the money to clean them. These were followed by later ads, such as this for the RSPCA, thanking people for giving and showing the effect of the clean-up they had paid for:

> This is an Eider Duck.
> (Last week it was a Blackbird).

This keeps the story from becoming too grim, and rewards the people who gave money.

Greenpeace took a different approach. It too had oily birds asking for contributions at first. Then it created a controversial ad in which a British Petroleum memo was leaked, saying that 'we should keep our heads down on this one'. The point of this memo was that BP had nothing to do directly with the spill, and wanted to avoid identification with it. The text of the memo is on top, with the words 'Oil Leak' scrawled across it in thick black paint. At the bottom is an inset picture of a seal looking out over the water with the caption, 'Unfortunately, 8000 seals can't keep their heads down'. The ad again asks for people to join Greenpeace, but it also suggests they call the BP chair directly; its aim was not just promoting the organisation, but focusing attention on a demonised actor. BP took legal action to keep Greenpeace from running the ad. As with earlier Greenpeace ads targeting specific companies, the legal action led to discussion in the press and had the effect of attracting attention to the ad when it was run. *Campaign* says that the attack was so successful that Greenpeace is now planning to spend more of its budget taking positions on issues, and less on encouraging membership.

Even this sort of directly anti-company campaigning leaves intact the assumptions about commodities underlying advertising. Ads can direct consumers to one kind of commodity or another, but it is hard to use them to attack the commodity system. One ad that tries appeared on German television recently (and was shown in an ITV programme on the Cannes Advertising Festival). It begins as a straightforward parody of two of the memorable BBH ads for Levi's, 'Laundrette' (in which a young man takes off his jeans to put them in the wash) and 'Bath' (in which a young man wears his jeans in the bath). The German ad has the same sensual photography, and the same use of a pop classic on the soundtrack, Sam Cooke singing 'Wonderful World', as the man slides into the bath. But at the end of the first line of the song there is a sudden flash of the oil tanker Braer breaking up on the rocks. The man shakes his head in shock, and then sinks back into his bath. As the bath and the song go on, and he puts his head under water, he gets flashes of oil and birds. When he reaches for the soap, he gets a flash of birds being held as the oil is scrubbed off them. Finally, as he turns on the tap, oil comes out, and the song ends with the romantic song lyrics commenting on how the world might become better.

Only then is the advertiser revealed to be a campaign group, with its slogan on the screen, as we hear a plaintive bird call:

. . . and how long can you ignore it? SOS

John Hegarty, whose agency made the Levi's ads, commented that SOS was just using the imagery they had created because it appealed to young people. But this is a strikingly obtuse interpretation of the ad, which has not chosen this imagery at random from some pop video. The ironic words of the song suggest a blinkered innocence. The man can ignore the large world because he is immersed in a culture of commodities. It is true that Levi's, as far as I know, is no environmental villain. But because it has become such a symbol of consumer desire in youth culture, it can stand for all the other products we take for granted. And campaign groups would argue that the assumption of continuing unbridled consumption is a greater environmental danger than any one company's actions.

So we have seen in response to the Braer incident four strategies:

- Benetton suggests that awareness, without any action, is praiseworthy.
- The RSPB says we can pay it to help clean up.
- Greenpeace says that a demonised corporation is the relevant agent.
- SOS attacks the commodity system in a parody ad.

At least some people find these strategies and aims are very similar. One letter to *The Independent*, after complaints about the Benetton duck, said, 'What I do find offensive is that charities such as Greenpeace and the Royal Society for the Protection of Birds are using the issue as a cynical recruitment campaign. Are they being any less exploitative?' (Max Barnes, 4 January 1993)

Images of action

Part of the usefulness of environmental discourse to advertisers is that it is ambiguously linked to other discourses; it becomes a resource for products that make no green claims. The environment can be a pitch like any other, like pitches based on status or nostalgia or sexual insecurity. An example of the way environmental concerns become merged with consumer images is an ad for a product that, as far as I know, is not specifically environmentally friendly – Tennant's lager. A man arrives by helicopter, people in the fishing port below travel in boats or walk through the village. In the pub, he looks at a picture of the harbour, and then covers it with plastic overlay showing the cooling towers of a power plant. He sits alone with his briefcase, observing the jovial regulars. When he throws the transparency in the real fire (no electric heat here), apparently withdrawing from participation in the plant, he is rewarded, not only with a pint, but with the companionship of the regulars.

In many ways this is typical of the 'A man's got to do what a man's got to do' genre of ads, a story showing how the product, plus moral courage, brings a man from isolation to companionship. The song in the background is saying something like that. The decision about the plant is presented as inherently personal; once again agency is placed at the level of the individual. Real environmental decisions are, of course, the result of more complex interactions of groups. It is paralysing to treat environmental action as the personal prerogative of powerful individuals, even if these actions are presented favourably. I'd like to think of a more complex version: when he gets his pint and joins the regulars, he finds that they are saying that they hope the new nuclear plant they have heard about will come there and bring a little work to this corner of the country so they won't have to move away to Aberdeen.

With such overlapping discourses, environmentalism can be just another style choice. Consider these nine pictures, in one ad (and take a guess about what is being advertised):

green wellies (with dirt on them)

toilet tissue (with the 'recycled' triangle on it)

a bunch of dirty carrots and a hand fork

a bottle bank bin

a plastic bottle of 'Green' washing up liquid

a button reading 'Save the Whales'

a petrol hose, green (for unleaded)

a bicycle

a bundle of newspapers

I am fairly confident that most readers can assign a fairly specific meaning to most of these signs. They relate to issues that might be seen to be quite separate – green wellies and gardening are not necessarily linked to environmental activism, and using unleaded petrol and bicycling are alternatives, not complementary. The headline presents them as having a single meaning:

After a hard day saving the world, the last thing you need is a wierdo health drink.

There is a kind of self-mockery here, for these are such limited measures to be described as 'saving the world'. The audience is supposed to identify itself with such environmental activities. But it is also supposed to be a bit ironic about them. The ad, it turns out, is for Lyons organic coffee and tea, so I'd guess that by 'wierdo health drinks' they mean herb teas. The advertisers assume that the market for organic products overlaps heavily with the market for green products. But there's no case made that organic products are better for the environment. The ad constructs a type, a bit of a stereotype, a bit of a joke, but still one in which the reader might want to see himself or herself.

It was only a matter of time before some advertisers for some audiences saw the advantages in playing with the language of environmentalism. An album by the heavy metal group Motorhead boasts

This album is ozone hostile.

Just as the last ad identified environmental activism with a particular type, other image can be defined against that type. Motorhead is still using environmentalism in consumer terms, but is assuming an audience already fed up with environmentalism, associating it with conventionality. Even companies that present themselves as environmentally friendly may play with this language. Down to Earth, a company that markets its products as environmentally friendly, has a headline,

At last a green cleaner that's tested on animals.

After this shock, a picture of rugby players in muddy kit tells us that the animals referred to are not laboratory rabbits. (In case we missed this, the copy reassures us, 'not real animals …'.)

Appeals to protect the environment are so common that an alternative advertising strategy, even one that is apparently ironic, can be shocking or puzzling. Here is the text of a jeans as in a style magazine. The picture shows a swaggering young man in jeans, a denim vest, and sunglasses, with a bare chest ornamented by a cross and a medallion. The background is entirely in flames, as in an oil well fire. The text is (I quote, really, you will have to believe me):

DIESEL JEANS AND WORKWEAR

HOW TO PLAY WITH FIRE (large type)

THE RAINFORESTS ARE SLOWLY DISAPPEARING. Too damn slowly!
So, why stick to logging crews and chain saws when you could
quite literally BURN THE F. . . out of the entire Amazon with just a
few thousand LOW COST barrels of highly inflammable gasoline!

Are You:

ALLERGIC TO ANIMALS? THRILL to the massacre of exotic birds
and monkeys.

A SELFISH BASTARD??? ROAR WITH LAUGHTER as unusual Indian
tribes are exterminated!!!

A SENSATION SEEKER?? OXYGEN-FREE AIR will give you a 'high'
you'll never come down from!

NOW *YOU TOO* CAN HAVE TOMORROW'S CATASTROPHE *TODAY!!!*

The irony here is very unstable. Try rereading it line by line. The initial joke
is based on our expecting appeals for the rain forest, so we can be shocked
when the speaker is annoyed, not by the disappearance, but by the slowness.
At what point do we read it as ironic? I'd say that the laughter at genocide
marks where I suspected we were to take this as meaning the opposite of what
it ways. The promise of 'oxygen-free air' confirms this. Yet the swagger of the
opening goes with the image of the product portrayed; rugged masculinity
here means a rejection of such conventional pieties as saving the rain forest.
Like the Benetton ads, it is unplaceable, shocking without coming to any
explicit statement. The last line, sending up advertising language, contributes
to the sense of an ironic reading. Environmental ads and anti-environment
ads like this one have similar imagery and language; both are about developing an image through consumption.

Redefining agency

One effect of green advertising is that we become aware of chains of agents
leading to environmental effects. The Co-operative Bank has a campaign that
traces links so that consumers can see that even banks can be polluters – or
can be agents for environmental change. The key to its effect is a complex
sentence, with all sorts of embedding – ways of putting one sentence within
another – like a children's nursery rhyme:

These are the trees
The Wilkinsons planted
With the interest accrued on their savings

These are the trees   The Wilkinsons planted

With interest accrued   Which their bank   To a chemical giant
on their savings   had lent

It happens.

But not at the Co-operative Bank.

Our customers know there are some things we will never invest in.

Such as companies whose activities are needlessly harmful to the environment.

Our policy is to lend to companies we believe to be as sound ethically as they are financially.

Of course, we still provide all the normal services you'd expect from a clearing bank, with assets of £2.8 billion, over 3,000 Link cash machines and a full telephone banking service.

The difference is that along with financial peace of mind our customers receive one other important benefit.

More peace of mind.

That ceaselessly spews   Toxic waste.

The CO-OPERATIVE BANK

Which their bank had lent
To a chemical giant
That ceaselessly spews
Toxic waste

The sentence is obviously complicated. For our purposes, you need only note that

These are the trees

is the main part of the sentence. The next bit is another embedded sentence that tells which *trees*. Then there is a prepositional phrase modifying *planted* and another sentence modifying *savings* and so on. For the effect they want, it must be *one* sentence, linked this way, to give us the sense that all these agents – family, bank, and 'chemical giant' – are linked in one chain of action that both plants and poisons trees. After this powerful illustration, the body copy moves on to a straight sell, with consumer advantages. But it comes back to the idea that it is offering its customers a view of themselves as agents for good. The style of the pictures supports this; the woodcut effect suggests something old-fashioned, perhaps a child's primer for teaching the basics. The Co-operative Bank ad, in linking trees to banks, may change our ideas of agency, drawing in banks as actors, and treating our personal financial decisions as environmental action, just as recycling or green consumption is action.

Conclusion

We should acknowledge that a great deal of the information people have about dangers to the environment – from CFCs, lead, greenhouse gases, phosphates, oil spills – comes from ads. As the 'Green Con' awards point out, there is a great deal of misinformation as well. But ads also define who we take as relevant agents in environmental change: groups, consumers, companies, or nature itself. In this respect, they overwhelmingly define action to be taken by individuals, by consuming. They make it hard to conceive any other types of agents, other alliances of people linked by environmental changes. The other effect they have is that they encapsulate complex networks in familiar signs. These signs then get removed as myths from history and historical circumstance – they become part of the world as it just is. Drummed into us constantly, these myths can make us buy things, they can make us angry or fearful, they can make us reject environmental concern with the rest of the conventional pieties.

In changing our ideas of agency and action, green ads may have effects unintended by the advertiser. Once the Co-operative Bank asks what it is to be ethical and environmentally sound in banking, we may question further the environmental consequences of finance. A B&Q leaflet that discusses difficulties of determining the source of wood for their products raises doubts that I never had before: what does it mean to be sustainable? A Sainsbury's leaflet that shows how green they are says that the massive lorry deliveries are made at night to avoid traffic. Without this reminder, would you have thought how much Sainsbury's contributes to motorway traffic and pollution? As with the other ads we have discussed, green ads can feed into other discourses, can feed off other discourses, and be read in unintended ways.

Further reading
Green ads

For a good readable introduction to the sociology of environmentalism, see Steve Yearley, *The Green Case*, which has extensive references. Nikolas Luhmann, *Environmental Communication*, is a profound but very difficult study of interlocking systems by an influential German sociologist. Jacqueline Burgess discusses oppositional readings of a BNFL ad in 'The Production and Consumption of Environmental Meanings in the Mass Media'. For a further study of environmental agency, related to this chapter, see Greg Myers, 'The Power is Yours: Plot and Agency in *Captain Planet*'.

12

AIDS, Ads and Us vs. Them

A sign on the door in the toilet of a local family centre says:

Have it on before you have it off.

How do people know what it means? The fact that the notice could leave out so much and still be understood suggests widespread awareness of AIDS and safer sex. On the other hand, the fact that the local health authority paid for the ad suggests this awareness has not always led to the change in behaviour it wants: the use of the condoms. Indeed, despite huge advertising and public health campaigns, there remains persistent ignorance about some basic facts about the transmission of the AIDS virus; this is indicated, for instance, by the bigotry towards HIV positive people.

There is a vast literature on AIDS and society (for a start, see the references at the end of this chapter). People have heard so much about AIDS that they may think they know all about it. It helps to make it strange again. One way of doing this is to look closely at the texts of AIDS ads. I will make two main points:

1. The way we talk about AIDS, in medical journals, in ads, and in every-day talk, structures ideas of AIDS, of what it is, who is affected, and what should be done.

2. AIDS structures ideas of society, the way we divide people into groups and relate them, who we consider 'at risk' and who consider as part of 'the general population', normal, neutral, unmarked.

To illustrate these points, I will look first at the choices of words we use to talk about AIDS, and then at some advertising campaigns that illustrate the ways different audiences are addressed, and that assume different views of society. Finally I will show how AIDS talk is used in ads for products that have nothing to do with AIDS, just as products that have nothing to do with saving the environment may be sold with environmental discourse.

Words for AIDS

One leaflet from the San Francisco AIDS Foundation is headed

> Straight Talk about Sex and HIV

The heading shows how thinking about and dealing with AIDS is tied up with language issues. First, it promises straight talk – frank information – about taboo matters. It also addresses a specific group: heterosexuals who might consider themselves safe from any risk. (Other booklets from the Foundation include *Man to Man, Condoms for Couples*, and *AIDS and Lesbians*). Also, the leaflet uses the abbreviation *HIV* throughout, rather than *AIDS*, and begins with a technical sounding definition:

> HIV stands for Human Immunodeficiency Virus. This virus damages the immune system and eventually causes AIDS.

Why so much care with terminology?

Names of epidemic diseases have always had social meanings; syphilis, for instance, was 'The French disease' in England and Germany (the French name said it came from Naples; Europeans traced it to the New World, while Americans said it came from Europe). Let's start with the name of AIDS itself (here I'm drawing on a good article, Jan Zita Grover's 'AIDS: Keywords'). AIDS was first called 'Gay Related Immune Deficiency' when it was diagnosed in 1981, because it was diagnosed in gay men. This had to be changed when it was found that haemophiliacs, intravenous drug users, and Haitians also had it. The name was changed in 1982 to AIDS (Acquired Immune Deficiency Syndrome), which was meant to be neutral, to avoid stigmatisation of victims.

AIDS activists point out the importance of the last letter of this name. AIDS is not a disease, it is a *syndrome*. People with AIDS are killed by various ailments that may be ubiquitous but that are kept under control by healthy immune systems. These illnesses differ in different parts of the world. The activists stress this because AIDS itself is not a disease like syphilis or hepatitis. What is transmitted is not the syndrome but the virus that attacks the immune system. People who test positive for the antibodies may take a long time to develop any of the AIDS diseases. But because of the stigma attached to AIDS, their lives will be treated as effectively over, even if they live without major health problems for years. This is why the leaflet I quoted talks about

HIV, and AIDS activists and official leaflets talk about HIV tests, or HIV virus, not about an AIDS virus. Some AIDS activists believe that changes in the words we use can change attitudes; they reject the popular term, 'AIDS victim' as implying helplessness, and they reject 'AIDS patient' because they are only occasionally under medical care. They prefer the term 'People with AIDS'. This is deliberately awkward. One can't say it without reminding oneself that they are people first, they have an identity separate from their medical condition.

Tabloids no longer refer to 'the gay plague', but the bigotry and fear remain in subtler forms. One key distinction made in many texts is between 'risk groups' and 'the general population'. The distinction as it is usually made assumes that the reader is heterosexual, monogamous, probably middle-aged, is European or North American, and doesn't inject drugs. That is defined as the 'general population', unmarked. Much of the discussion in the press is about whether or not it looks likely that the disease will spread from 'risk groups' to 'us'. The assumption underlying such worry (sometimes stated explicitly) is that it wouldn't matter much if AIDS just affected gay men, drug users, and Africans. Another assumption in talk about 'risk groups' is that these categories are definite and visible. For instance, when some doctors say that they will not treat people from risk groups, they are assuming there is some way of easily distinguishing 'them' from 'us'. The use of the phrase 'general population' constructs social barriers that dissolve when one thinks of specific cases.

The stigmatisation of gay people and other members of so-called 'risk groups', is, I believe, evil in itself. But it also has public health consequences, because it encourages people to believe that AIDS comes only to certain kinds of people, rather than stressing that it is transmitted through certain kinds of practices. Let me give you an example. One survey (by Mykol C. Hamilton) shows that a class of US university students thought lesbians a high risk group, just after male homosexuals, ahead of heterosexuals. Even some medical professionals share this belief: there were moves in California to block lesbians giving blood, and there was serious discussion of this issue in *The Lancet*, a British medical journal. A little thought about how HIV is transmitted would suggest that lesbians are a relatively low risk group (though not risk-free, as public health leaflets directed at them point out). This example shows how categories encoded in language shape our assumptions about reality. What seems to have happened is that straight students (and doctors) got in their minds that AIDS is a disease of stigmatised groups; lesbians were categorised in their minds with gay males, so they too must be 'high risk'. If people do not see themselves as members of these groups, they consider themselves safe, and anyone from a stigmatised group at risk.

Susan Sontag pointed out, in her book on AIDS, the way the metaphors around AIDS shape our perceptions of it. One of the metaphors that Sontag and others trace is that of AIDS as battle. The body has its defences; these are sabotaged from within, allowing invasion. This metaphor not just used of AIDS, it runs through the biomedical vocabulary of our time. When a friend of mine told me in a letter that he had cancer, he used the phrase 'I've been invaded.' This vocabulary helps explain to the patient why the treatment can be so brutal, as chemotherapy can be for cancer, and as AZT, a drug currently used, can be for AIDS. Powerful poisons can be justified as would the bombing of one of one's own cities in wartime. Sontag points out that this may be a dangerous way of thinking of one's own body, as a terrain divided between good and evil, defenders and enemy.

Another common metaphor has to do with what the press calls 'carriers': that is, people with the HIV virus who have not yet developed AIDS, so 'we' cannot recognise 'them'. A UK television ad showed a woman inviting a man to her flat for coffee. Below this apparently ordinary encounter between ordinary people, subtitles warned of AIDS. It is interesting that a parallel ad, showing an attractive man at a disco, had much less successful recall. Both ads assume that the audience is HIV negative, and incarnate the HIV positives as attractive and threatening, as agents of the disease (see Chapter 11). But the ad that made the man the threat had less effect. In fact there are far more cases of men transmitting to women than women transmitting to men. But given these paired ads, audiences response continued a long tradition that makes women the cause of venereal diseases like syphilis. As read by men, these ads again divide 'us' from 'them'.

One response to these metaphors of battle in the body or vampire-like carriers is to try to reject them and stick to the scientific facts. That is Susan Sontag's position, and she speaks with considerable authority, because when she was being treated for cancer she saw the brutal moral effect of the various metaphors on people who were already suffering from physical pain and grief. But AIDS activists who analyse culture have tended to take a different line; they say that there is no going beyond metaphors, that the scientific facts themselves are based on metaphors, and that activists should focus on the struggle to define which metaphors will circulate. They examine and criticise popular newspapers and media representations, and offer their own alternative metaphors and language.

AIDS ads and taboos

One reason AIDS ads attract so much attention is that official institutions – such as public health authorities – must often breach taboos in public use of language. Most public health ads are aimed at getting people to modify their practices so that the virus does not pass from one person to another – getting both gay and straight people to practice safer sex and getting drug users not to share needles. Earlier ads, which only talked vaguely about a threat, seem to have been very unsuccessful at getting people to change. In contrast, a very explicit campaign developed in and directed at the gay community led to very dramatic changes in behaviour.

In the British TV ads that most people remember best, there are two versions, one with a iceberg and one with a tombstone. The text at the end in both cases was the same:

AIDS: DON'T DIE OF IGNORANCE

Let's look a little closer at the iceberg message. It involves a metaphor, that of a lurking hidden threat. It is addressed at a 'general' audience, but this general audience is assumed to be unaffected (and ignorant) at the moment. There is no recognition of the diversity of audiences that make up the public. This ad has been much criticised because it emphasised the threat but gave no explicit information. Historians, public health officials, and advertising professionals have all pointed out that fear does not work well at changing behaviour. People have to have some sense of getting what they desire, not just of avoiding what they fear. (Think of how unsuccessful anti-smoking campaigns have been). There are some features of such ads that are specific to British culture – for instance, the rather abstract verbal/visual pun of the iceberg. But it does seem that the first wave of ads in almost every country involved both fear and vagueness, with very little information.

One difficulty in including any specific information about safer sex is that talk about condoms or masturbation or penetration or semen or vaginal fluids challenges taboos. For instance, a student group at my university protested about the inclusion of safer sex information in the handbook for new students; they said it was using public money to promote homosexuality. These taboos are rather flexibly defined: AIDS campaigners point out that great latitude is allowed in the pornography available at the newsagents W. H. Smith, or even in *Cosmopolitan*, but not in leaflets aimed at public health. The other interpretation of the vagueness of information is more subtle. Talk about safer sex focuses on what you do, not on who you are. Safer sex is the same for heterosexuals and homosexuals, drug users and non-users, men and women. For heterosexuals who feel they are far from the problem, such talk about specific practices denies the boundaries that make them feel safe.

The National AIDS Manual, a publication for UK professionals who deal with HIV and AIDS, stresses that plain language is crucial in addressing such personal behaviour. Both jargon and euphemism put off the intended audience. They make the advertiser or advisor sound like a distant authority. Their remarks recall some of the discussions earlier in this book about associative meanings (Chapter 5), forms of address (Chapter 6), and everyday talk (Chapter 8). The suggestions were made by public health workers, but they could have been made by experienced writers of advertising for any product.

> Language that is remote, too formal, or that sounds like scientific jargon tends to alienate most people. By contrast, language that is common and plain tends to involve most people and encourage their active participation. . . .
>
> – frankly, most people neither understand nor use terms like 'frottage,' 'digital intercourse,' 'brachioproctal stimulation,' 'fellatio,' 'cunnilingus' etc.
>
> –Terms like 'making love,' 'sexual intercourse,' 'sleeping together' are much too imprecise and fail to distinguish between safe and unsafe activities . . .
>
> –It's worth asking why Latin and Greek words are supposed to make something sound less offensive than plain English words? Because they misleadingly make the activities sound more remote . . .

To oppose these taboos, Simon Watney, who works with the Terrence Higgins Trust, insists on referring to *fucking*, not using any of the hundreds of possible euphemisms. But if one chooses to use colloquial words, one finds they are highly variable, and the choice of the wrong colloquial form is also likely to make the advisor seem remote. Consider this range of choices:

> prophylactic, condom, sheath, french letter, johnny, rubber.

It's clear that *prophylactic* is a word real people never use. But what of the others? Any choice risks sounding absurdly coy or dated, on the one side, or clinical and remote, on the other.

Dramatising condoms

The representation of condoms is a problem of taboo images that corresponds exactly to this problem of taboo language. Douglas Crimp mocks the coyness about condoms in ads for the mass media. 'An [advertising] industry that has used sexual desire to sell everything from cars to detergents suddenly finds itself at a loss for how to sell a condom.' The sales pitch is needed for condoms because there is apparently strong resistance by men to using them. One approach is to be clinical but informative. Leaflets for some public health agencies explain with diagrams how to put it on and take it off, and respond rationally to arguments that they make sex too conscious, or that they are too small, or too fragile. The people who make these leaflets argue that one must be explicit to respond to these fears.

The other approach to encouraging the use of condoms is to be coyly amusing about them. Until recently, condoms could only be shown in their wrappers in UK ads, but the ads from other countries in Jasper Carrott's annual reviews of television ads include an astonishing range of animated condoms jumping into holes, or being used to snap bums like elastics, or being blown up like balloons, or being stuck suggestively on fingers. An Australian ad has a woman breaking off an embrace and telling the man

It will be much better if I get my mates.

He looks hopefully at a photograph of her with her friends, but she is actually making the standard advertising pun, in which she mentions the name of the product (Mates™) rather than using the word to mean 'friends'.

The most recent UK television campaign just mentions HIV, and focuses instead on the condoms themselves, with older people talking about them in a matter of fact tone. The fact that the speakers are two generations older than the target audience suggests that these things can be talked about even by those the audience might expect to be more prudish. Both employ the sorts of indications of everyday talk that we saw in Chapter 8. In one, 'Fred Brewster, age 81' tells about the difficulties he faced with the tough reusable condom of his youth, which he called 'Geronimo'. The message is

If Mr Brewster put up with Geronimo, you can use a condom.

The other ad has a woman in her fifties or sixties sitting at a machine in a condom manufacturing plant. She says:

Of course, working here we were the first to notice the change in people's behaviour. We're making more of these things than ever before. Obviously it's down to AIDS and HIV. Young people can't afford to take chances these days. It seems they've got their heads screwed on though. After all, I've never been so busy.

The on-screen text at the end says, coyly,

KEEP MRS DAWSON BUSY

Sheila Dawson is identified as an ordinary person, talking to us as she might talk to friends. She talks about, but not to, young people; that's what makes her grandparental in her concern rather than nagging like a parent. She still remains euphemistic, talking about 'these things'. But the pictures make it clear enough what they are. Perhaps they show the testing machines to respond to the worries of women that they will leak, thus allowing a possible pregnancy, while incidentally demonstrating to men that a fairly large object will fit in them.

One effect of all this attention is that the taboos are challenged, whatever the ads actually say, just by putting the condoms on TV. And this is part of their aim; Chris Powell, Chief Executive of the ad agency responsible for the Health Education Authority AIDS campaign, says in defence of the ads:

> Advertising has played an important part in the process of the normalisation of condom usage. It has helped bring the subject out into the open and make it acceptable. This enables young people to talk about it, and take what can be socially difficult action. (*Campaign* 10/9/93, p. 31).

One strategy of familiarisation is apparent in a sticker apparently designed by a local campus entrepreneur, advertising a machine the dispenses 'Streetwise' brand fruit-flavoured condoms:

If you get lucky, get Streetwise.
Don't be silly, stick fruit on your willy.

This ad positions the reader as a sexually aggressive male. The breaking of language taboos and the ridiculous rhyme are part of this rude macho defiant image; condoms are treated as part of the kit, like beer at a football match.

Ads and audiences

I have argued that AIDS ads make assumptions about the audience as 'general public', and sometimes reinforce the 'us' vs. 'them' view of the disease. We can see the contrast by looking at some ads that challenge these divisions. Ads aimed at the gay community are particularly important because the British gay community is something of a public health success story; in the early years after the first diagnoses of AIDS, even before the isolation of the retrovirus, the gay community developed a very effective unofficial campaign, so that new cases among gay men in Britain after that point were much fewer than they might otherwise have been.

One ad from the Terrence Higgins Trust, a non-governmental AIDS information service, has a black and white picture of a young man pulling his jumper over his head, thus baring his torso. (The ad is a version of one produced by the Dutch public health service). The text reads:

SAFER SEX
KEEP IT UP
antibody positive & negative
– it's the same for all
The Terrence Higgins Trust
Helpline 01-242 1010

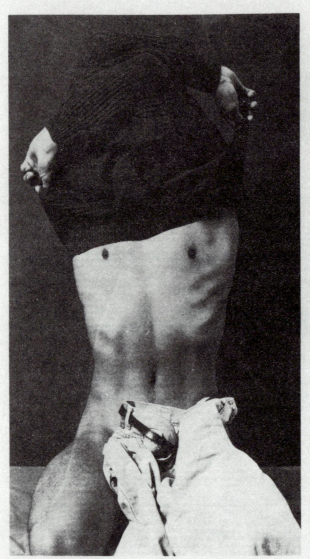

SAFER SEX KEEP IT UP!

antibody
positive
&
negative
- it's the same
for all

The Terrence Higgins *Trust*

HELPLINE
01-242 1010

DAILY
3.00 PM-10.00 PM

PHOTO: 1986 MARTIEN SLEÜTJES

18   MARXISM TODAY

As Simon Watney of the Terrence Higgins Trust points out in one of his articles, the emphasis in their ads is on desire: the picture is meant to be erotic. But it does not present the erotic as a threat; rather, it is an occasion for safer sex. The pun of the title, 'keep it up', refers both to an erection and to the gay community's efforts already. The audience is assumed not to be ignorant or foolish. Crucially, the ad addresses both antibody positive and negative people. Watney has argued that the strongest persuasion is to say that one must protect the people one loves; one assumes one might be affected oneself, and acts accordingly. That, he says, is stronger than threatening that any new sexual experience is deadly. There is no point is attacking casual sex, he says; many strong relationships were casual and uncertain at the beginning. This line of persuasion depends on there being a strong community in which people care about each other. So Watney and others argue that attacks on the gay community actually hinder the most effective public health campaign. As long as male gays are treated as total outcasts, already damned, there is no motivation for them practising safe sex. Changed behaviour emerges only from a sense of worth and trust.

It is interesting that almost all these features advocated by the Terrence Higgins Trust have been adopted in a recent HEA ad; the government-sponsored campaign is learning from the gay community's own campaign. Again there is a suggestive picture, an almost abstract close-up of two men's faces. It is suggestive because on the left we see the man looking over his shoulder, on the right we see the man much more closely than we could in casual encounter, and the men are looking aside as if glancing at each other. The text says:

THEY DON'T HAVE SAFER SEX JUST BECAUSE IT'S SAFER
Sex.
We all know how much we enjoy it.
So why should our attitudes change when it comes to safer sex?
After all, people were enjoying it long before the discovery of HIV or AIDS.
Safer sex means any activity where blood, semen, or vaginal fluid can't enter your body.
Mutual masturbation, fingering, massage or body rubbing are just a few examples you may have heard of.
But there are plenty of others you won't have, and half the fun is finding new ways to enjoy each other.
Anal sex, however, is still the highest risk activity and even using a condom won't make it completely safe.
If you'd like more information or advice, pick up a safer sex leaflet

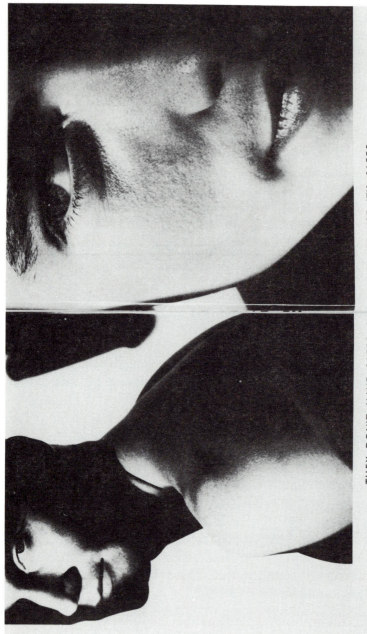

(available from gay bars and clubs), or ring your local helpline.

Alternatively call the National AIDS Helpline free of charge on 0800 567 123. It's open 24 hours a day and it's completely confidential.

The voice in the ad is 'we', identifying with the gay community. The information, unlike that in UK ads aimed at the 'general' population, is quite explicit about sexual practices. Safer sex is tied to erotic exploration (as in US ads developed by the gay community). If this health authority ad doesn't surprise you, ask yourself if five years ago you could have imagined the national government would pay for ads that encourage masturbation, or even for ads that use the word.

Ads for the London Lighthouse, which provides help for people with HIV and AIDS, are among the few I have seen that directly challenge stereotypes about HIV positive people, the way other campaigns challenge stereotypes about people with cancer or cerebral palsy. In one of their ads, the visual effect is plain, with black and white paintings of a phone, brushes, a cup of coffee, and a large headline saying:

HOW I SURVIVED AIDS

The copy again gives the effect of everyday talk, by referring to specifics and mutual knowledge, a cyclical conception of time, and a local sense of place.

At 9:37 am, on Monday the 8th of June (which also happened to be my birthday), my doctor told me I had AIDS. The first person I went to was my brother. I told him I was thinking of killing myself. 'Why bother,' he said, 'You already have.'

That was six years ago.

You see, the problem at that time was that on-one – not the doctors, nor their hospitals, not the media nor their public – really knew enough about HIV infection or AIDS. Or even if there was a difference. The only thing they were certain of was that if you caught it, you were dead.

One year later, I wasn't dead.

The ad goes on in this powerful, personal fashion, telling about his first call to the London Lighthouse. It is not just the choice of words that is informal; the form is directly addressed to some hearer:

I was amongst new friends (well let's face it, most of the old ones scarpered in the time it takes to say Acquired Immune Deficiency Syndrome).

This ad also illustrates the concern with language choices that I mentioned at the beginning of the chapter: the careful distinction of HIV and AIDS, the

HOW I SURVIVED AIDS.

At 9.37am, on Monday the 8th of June (which also happened to be my birthday), my doctor told me I had AIDS. The first person I went to was my brother. I told him I was thinking of killing myself. "Why bother?", he said, "You already have."

That was six years ago.

You see, the problem at that time was that no-one – not the doctors, nor their hospitals, not the media nor their public – really knew enough about HIV infection or AIDS. Or even if there was a difference. The only thing they were certain of was that if you caught it, in no time at all, you were dead.

One year later, I wasn't dead. It was around this time, that I first came into contact with the London Lighthouse. I remember the phone call vividly.

"I think I'm dying", I blurted down the receiver. "Don't worry", was the reply, "That's what I said when I first phoned."

Suddenly, I was back in reality. I wasn't the only person in the world with the virus.

A day later I was one of a dozen 'me's' perched on beanbags, drinking coffee and exorcising demons. I was amongst new friends (well let's face it, most of the old ones scarpered in the time it takes to say Acquired Immune Deficiency Syndrome). The difference with these people was that they were prepared to listen – really listen. With open hearts.

AIDS never hurt me maliciously. People did.

London Lighthouse restored my self-respect. I never thought I was much of an artist, but with a little encouragement from one of the painting therapists, I uncovered a hidden talent. Simple pastimes, like a night at the theatre or a game of monopoly (as long as I'm the 'Top Hat'), are pleasures I'd forgotten how to savour.

My renaissance is complete.

Yes, sometimes I get ill, but the challenge of AIDS has brought out the real person in me. More honest. More positive. More assertive. The Lighthouse worked miracles for me. Now I work for the Lighthouse. I've got a new career out in the community. Helping men and women affected by HIV and AIDS to face up to it like I did, not as a victim dying but as a person living. As for the future? Well, I've already paid for next year's holiday. I'm going to Cornwall to celebrate my birthday.

The London Lighthouse is never short of love and compassion. Money is another matter. Show your compassion. Make a donation.

NAME

ADDRESS

POSTCODE

I enclose my cheque/PO made payable to   FT 3/93
London Lighthouse for £

☐ Please debit my credit card Visa/MasterCard

Account number

Expiry date

Signature

☐ I would like to know more about the work of London Lighthouse. Please send me an information pack

Please return to: London Lighthouse, 111/117 Lancaster Road, London W11 1QT. Tel: 071-792 1200 Thank you for listening

London Lighthouse

A centre for people facing the challenge of AIDS

London Lighthouse is registered under the Data Protection Act 1984. Reg. Charity Number 295171 joking about the technical name, and later an insistence that the person faces AIDS

> not as a victim dying but as a person living.

Good copy-writing like this makes me wish the same issues of attitude change towards people with AIDS could be addressed on television, along-side the HEA prevention campaign.

Most countries in the world have some AIDS advertising campaign, some of them more extensive and effective than that in the UK. (The country with the most reported cases, the US, has excellent campaigns from local and private groups, but still has no national government campaign.) There is a striking similarity in the ads in the European press, except that the source of infection is displaced to other countries, as syphilis once was. (UK ads in airline terminals warn travellers abroad to take condoms; an ad in the SAS flight magazine, in English, warns Danish businessmen visiting London.) But it is worth comparing the ads in a country like Uganda, which not only has a high incidence of HIV, but is immeasurably poorer than the UK, and must face this public health problem in the aftermath of a civil war. Gill Seidel, who has an important article on the Uganda AIDS campaigns, points out that there were two campaigns, somewhat different in focus, as suggested by their slogans.

> Love Carefully
> Love Faithfully

The secular authorities produced a campaign based on 'Love carefully', emphasising the condom. The religious groups, who provide most of the health care in Uganda, produced a campaign treating AIDS as a moral issue of faithfulness in marriage. The two campaigns were based on different definitions of the disease, but they were able to work together. Seidel points out that a later campaign for World AIDS Day

> 'Thank God I said No to AIDS'

seemed to stress moral aspects. At this point her article takes an interesting turn. She says it is not enough for European analysts to bring their own frameworks to Uganda – they should look at local interpretations of the ads. And she quotes a Uganda newspaper article that criticises the ads for failing to recognise the brutal social and economic facts that led to people 'choosing' behaviours that spread AIDS.

The differences in perspective on the disease in different countries was brought home to me by a 6 shilling stamp on a package sent to me from Kenya. It says

AIDS has no cure.

Below a picture of a man in a bubble, there are pictures of pills, capsules, syringes, and sachets crossed out. People in the UK to whom I showed it thought it was discouraging intravenous drug use. But a moment's thought will tell you that there isn't much of that in a country as poor as Kenya. I asked about this when I went to Kenya and was told it is aimed at the many locally marketed products that claim to cure AIDS. Many Kenyans believe the cure has been discovered but is being withheld from Africans by powerful western drug companies. The public health authorities, it seems, are worried that people might engage in unsafe sexual behaviour, hoping to be cured later, just as nineteenth century men contracted syphilis casually thinking that mercury treatments would cure them. The stamp illustrates how we need social as well as linguistic analysis to understand a text; this stamp changed its apparent meaning as it went from the country in which it was mailed to the country in which it was delivered.

AIDS in discourse

Just as military and vampire metaphors, drawn from other discourses, shape our sense of AIDS, AIDS becomes a metaphor used in discourses besides that of public health. The most famous example is the notorious Benetton poster that showed a man dying of AIDS, with the only text being

United Colours of Benetton.

This controversial ad appeared before the duck ad discussed in Chapters 1 and 11. Whatever else you think about the use of that image of suffering for commercial purposes, it is a striking example the omnivorousness of advertising discourse – anything can become material for an ad.

Those who were so appalled about Benetton – including the editor of *Campaign* – may not have noticed how many other ads joke about AIDS – or more accurately, about AIDS ads. A poster in the Netherlands for Love Jeans says

Love Safely

and shows a couple in a sexual embrace – but still prudently wearing their jeans. Posters for Piz Buin sun cream were the subject of controversy recently because of the nudity in them, but I have heard no criticism of their parody of the public health slogan:

Practice safe sun.

A Seat car ad with the headline

Safe Sex

was withdrawn in Northern Ireland when criticised as sexist and crude, but again it was not criticised for playing with a disease. The creative director of the ad agency, Steve Grimes, said in *Campaign* that it could be taken literally: 'The Ibiza is one of the safest cars in its class and when you see it in the flesh one of the most sexy' (29 October 1993).

Some ads for products play on the vagueness and euphemism that characterises some AIDS ads. A computer firm, Total Control Ltd., plays on the ambiguity of *virus*:

Before you put it in . . . make sure you know where it's been!
Protect yourself now with VIS anti-virus facilities

The language of computer viruses carried over from public health to information technology long before this ad, but computer users may hardly remember the origin of the term. This ad for Confident tampons uses the advice about safer sex to sell another product, a tampon with a cover:

These days shouldn't anything that goes inside you be wearing a sheath?

The key of course is the vagueness of the 'anything that goes inside you'. The ad can work, linking the two discourses, because of the vagueness of both AIDS ads and tampon ads.

Ourselves and other bodies

Struggles over how to respond to AIDS are in part struggles over what can be said in public, what cannot be said, and what can go without saying. These struggles did not begin in 1981, and they will not end when, as we hope, better treatments for AIDS or preventives for HIV are found. I will end with a story from an earlier epidemic, the Victorian writer Thomas Carlyle writing in *Past and Present* (1843).

A poor Irish widow, her husband having died in one of the lanes of Edinburgh, went forth with her three children, bare of all resource, to solicit help from the Charitable Establishments of that City. At this Charitable Establishment and then at that she was refused; referred from one to the other, helped by none; – till she had exhausted them all; till her strength and heart failed her: she sank down in typhus fever; died, and infected her Lane with fever, so that 'seventeen other persons' died of fever there in consequence . . . Very curious. The forlorn Irish Widow applies to her fellow creatures, as if saying, 'Behold I am sinking, bare of help: ye must help me! I am your sister, bone of your bone; one God made us: ye must help me!' They answer, 'No; impossible; thou art no sister of ours.' But she proves her sisterhood; her typhus fever kills them: they actually were her brothers, though denying it!'

As in earlier epidemics, AIDS is seen in terms of existing social boundaries, and public health measures reinforce these boundaries. In Carlyle's example the boundaries are Irish/Scottish, male/female, rich/poor. Then as now people who suffered from a disease could be treated as the cause of that disease, and one response was to try to keep barriers, physical and psychological, between the sufferers and one's own group. The people who turn her away see her as part of a foreign and threatening group. But the typhus has its own networks (we now know it is spread through body lice). Similarly the HIV virus makes its own links, through sex, needles, or blood supplies. One response is to try to strengthen the boundaries between gay / straight, men / women, natives / foreigners. But the maintenance of social boundaries can have public health consequences for everyone. Some of the beliefs people hold that make them feel safe ('I'm in the general population; they are in a risk group') lead to dangerous behaviour. Besides, these boundaries can victimise those who fall on the wrong side, not just those who are HIV positive, but those deemed to be 'at risk', or those who can become symbols of the danger. And such boundary drawing also has consequences for the way anyone, gay or straight, thinks of themselves, their bodies, pleasure, and fear.

I have argued that close attention to the texts of ads, the words and the pictures, can help us see how AIDS ads represent society, and in particular, how they categorise people:

- Choices of terms suggest blame and fear.
- Metaphors of invasion or carrier/vampires reflect hostility to people with AIDS, and to stigmatised groups.
- Taboos keep the focus of campaigns on people, rather than practices.
- Some campaigns in the gay community and for HIV positive people attempt to redraw the social boundaries.
- Ads in other countries may require a different sense of the issues to be comprehended.
- AIDS itself becomes a metaphor to be used in ads for other products.

All this analysis of language should not make us forget that AIDS is, among other things, a disease with a concrete cause that causes terrible suffering, nor to forget those who carry the burdens of caring for this suffering. But we cannot understand HIV and AIDS just by studying the virus and its effects. We must trace how its signs and meanings are used in culture, to reinforce social boundaries, draw new ones, or perhaps someday, to break them down.

Further reading
AIDS and culture

This chapter draws largely from articles in Douglas Crimp. ed., *AIDS: Cultural Analysis, Cultural Activism* , especially the essays by Jan Zita Grover, Paula Treichler, and Simon Watney. This is a special issue of a magazine of art theory; it is high-flying critical stuff, but passionate and readable, and well-illustrated. There is another excellent collection, rather more popular in its style, edited by Erica Carter and Simon Watney, *Taking Liberties: AIDS and Cultural Politics*; see especially the pieces by Erica Carter, Judith Williamson, Lynne Segal, Keith Alcorn, and Simon Watney again. Other recent collections include Peter Aggleton and Hilary Homans, eds., *The Social Aspects of AIDS* , especially the pieces by Alcorn, Wellings, Aggleton and Homans, and Watney yet again, and a whole issue of *Social Research* with rather scholarly pieces, of which the most relevant is Allan M. Brandt, 'AIDS and Metaphor: Toward the Social Meaning of Epidemic Disease'. Gill Seidel's article, discussed here, is "Thank God I Said No to AIDS': On the Changing Discourse of AIDS in Uganda'. It has fascinating illustrations of leaflets that are worth further discussion. If you can't find the Crimp collection, Jan Zita Grover also has a piece called 'AIDS, Keywords, and Cultural Work', in Lawrence Grossberg, Cary Nelson, and Paula Treichler, *Cultural Studies.*

Despite this flood of material, one of the most powerful studies of these issues was written before the first diagnoses of AIDS, Susan Sontag's 1978 essay *Illness as Metaphor*, which is mostly about tuberculosis and cancer. It appeared first in sections in the *New York Review of Books* – that is, it's the sort of thing non-academics might sit down to read. Sontag wrote the book after her treatment for cancer, and she is ferocious in her attack on the ways the popular metaphors of illness heap blame and suffering on patients already in physical pain. If you do read it, don't be put off by the casual literary allusions; you don't need to have read as much as Sontag has to understand her argument. She later wrote a later essay called *AIDS and Its Metaphors*, but most of the ideas in that were already there in the earlier book.

The creative response to AIDS is a different story from that of the construction of AIDS in ads, but it is important. Two particularly moving accounts that raise issues of language are Thom Gunn's collection of poems, *The Man with the Night Sweats*, and Derek Jarman's movie, *Blue*. A benefit video, *Red, Hot, and Blue* showed how the romantic lyrics of Cole Porter could take on new meanings in the age of AIDS.

13

Audiences, Effects and Reg

Only the very brave or the very ignorant (preferably both) can say exactly what it is that advertising does in the market place.

Martin Mayer, *Madison Avenue USA* (1958).

One of the main assumptions of this book has been that audiences are active interpreters of ads. I have left it to this last chapter to spell out some of the implications of this view for those of us who study texts. To do this will require some excursions into fairly abstract theory. But I can start with just one ad to raise the issues.

If you were in Northern England in 1993 you could hardly have missed the posters for Regal cigarettes featuring Reg, a middle-aged, chubby-faced and smirking man, whose head is seen cut out, as if pasted on, in the style of ads of the 1950s. 'A bald beer-drinking bloke from the North cut out of an old *Daily Mirror*' was how one of my colleagues described him. Sometimes there is also a hand holding a cigarette, and there is always a medallion in the lower right with a picture showing a hand holding the packet – another 1950s touch. They all have blue backgrounds, the colour of the stripe on the cigarette pack, and large black print across the top saying something like:

Reg on party politics.

Across the poster, in smaller white type, in quotation marks, is Reg's comment, always a comic or banal misinterpretation of the words suggested by the headline, so that an important issue is reduced to triviality. In this particular ad, it was:

'If you drop ash on the carpet you won't get invited again.'

Reg on party politics.

"If you drop ash on the carpet you won't get invited again."

"I smoke 'em because my name's on 'em."

REGAL KING SIZE
13mg TAR 1.1mg NICOTINE

REGAL FILTER
11mg TAR 1.0mg NICOTINE

SMOKING CAUSES FATAL DISEASES
Health Departments' Chief Medical Officers

The only other text is the statement of tar and nicotine content, and the required health warning, in this case:

SMOKING CAUSES FATAL DISEASES
Health Departments' Chief Medical Officers

Other versions of this ad say things like:

Reg on the beginning of civilisation.
'c.'

Reg on race relations.
'I had an uncle who owned a bookie's.'

Reg on MI5.
'Great for flat pack tables and kitchen units.'

(The confusion of MI5, the counter-intelligence agency, and MFI, the furniture retailer, involves a particularly witty rearrangement of sounds.) As the campaign continued, there were more and more elaborate plays on this format, counting on your familiarity with the previous ads in the series.

Reg on industrial action. [a blank blue poster]

These ads seemed to mark a radical change of strategy from the elegant wordless pairs of pictures of the previous Regal campaign (see Chapter 5), both in the self-mocking visual style and in the use of a humorously unappealing spokesperson. They required a fair amount of verbal wit to make sense of them, and yet they invited us to mock this figure, or perhaps to mock the pretensions of people who discuss these issues seriously. They won a number of awards from advertising professionals. But who were they aimed at? How did they sell cigarettes? It was surely not by the methods usually used in cigarette ads of the past, the claims for filters or the image of the cowboy or the Salem couple or the elegant puzzles of Benson and Hedges or Silk Cut.

These questions of audience and effect are particularly important in the case of Reg, because this ad campaign was accused of encouraging children to smoke. A report in *Campaign* (5 February 1993, p. 15) quoted a Salford City Councillor who claimed that Reg had become 'a cult figure among children'. Clearly, that such an unlikely character could become a 'cult figure' is a rather complex effect. The same report said that Kirklees Education Authority (around Wakefield, in Yorkshire) conducted research showing:

- 85% of a sample of 113 children between 11 and 15 recognised Reg
- 49% 'liked the campaign and would have liked Reg as a friend'

- Of those who has seen the ads, a percentage 'in the low 40s thought they would influence young people and make them more likely to smoke.'

On the other hand, research by the advertising agency Lowe Howard-Spink 'backs its claim that the ads do not target or attract children'. The Advertising Standards Authority rejected the complaints, saying, 'We have no reason to assume that the approach used in these posters has or will acquire a cult following, nor that they will appeal more to those who are under 18 than to the population at large.' But a later report from the Health Education Authority led the Advertising Standards Authority to reconsider (the first time this had ever happened to an ad, once it was cleared). Imperial Tobacco did not accept the charges or the research on which they were based, but withdrew the ads in deference to the ASA (*Campaign*, 17 December 1993).

These conflicting claims show some of the difficulties of finding anything definite linking any ads to behaviour. The Philadelphia department store magnate John Wanamaker pointed this out a hundred years ago: 'I know that half the money I spend on advertising is wasted, but I can never find out which half' (quoted by Martin Mayer, p. 267). Despite the enormous amounts of money spent on effects research, it is still impossible to give a definite answer to Mr. Wanamaker. So much money is spent because these effects are crucial to the whole advertising business: the companies advertising want to know if they are getting their money's worth, the agencies want to know which approaches work better than others, the broadcasters and publishers want to be able to demonstrate the effectiveness of their particular medium or title.

Research departments use the questionnaires that most of us have seen; they also use depth interviews, focus-group discussions, and cleverly split runs of print ads. They work from elaborately developed samples and a fine-grained scale of social groups. In any case, despite this methodological sophistication, there is still a great deal of scepticism about any finding of effects research, and the scepticism is not just from academics, or from the people paying for ads, like Mr. Wanamaker, but from the ad agencies themselves. Histories of advertising are full of stories of creative directors over-riding research findings to go on a hunch, and *Campaign* is full of comments from creative people dismissing research-led advertising as dull, formulaic, and oddly ineffective.

Part of the problem with any audience research is that there is not one audience, there are many audiences. And it is very hard to tell beforehand which audience one is addressing in a poster that, like those with Reg, is seen by a wide range of people. Another problem is that the research often addresses quite different effects, so that one can have apparently conflicting results. Let's look again at the bits of research mentioned by the opposing sides in the *Campaign* article. In fact they need not conflict at all. These Kirklees Education Authority studies show:

- that kids are aware of the ads (showing their recall)
- that a figure shown in them is appealing (attitudes towards the character)
- that the kids say that behaviour may be affected (attributing behaviour to others)

Any advertising researcher would warn us against confusing recall with effects, against thinking that enjoyment of a character leads to identification with the product, and against believing people when they *say* they or others do one thing or another. Plenty of ad campaigns have failed on such confusions.

The ad agency says (and the ASA agrees) that it did not target children; this is a statement not about the effects at all, but about the intention of the producers. But critics could argue that producers' intentions aren't the same as audience effects; plenty of ad campaigns, successful or unsuccessful, have had quite unpredictable and unintended effects. In its initial ruling, the Advertising Standards Authority did not appeal to research; it just said there was no reason to assume such effects. It made its decision on the basis of an implied comparison, saying that the ads had wide appeal across age groups but did not appeal *more* to those under 18 than to anyone else. This shifts the issue from effects on kids to the differential effects on kids and on adults. The Advertising Standards Authority seems to have looked for a direct and demonstrated connection between text and behaviour. But there are far too many factors to show such a connection; each side in the debate points out the correlation or lack of correlation that suits its case.

This is an apparently simple and practical issue (the effect of a single ad campaign on a single audience) with important potential consequences (kids smoke). It shows we get tangled up in conflicting claims if we do not examine the theories we have about audiences. We can see three different theories at work in arguments like this one (see Table opposite). They parallel the three periods of ads discussed in Chapter 2.

I think we tend to take for granted, as common sense, a very simple idea of what ads do and what they shouldn't do. In this, which could be called for convenience a 'humanist' view, we are all free individuals, who can be persuaded to do this or that. So the only bad ads are those that try to violate this free individuality – ads that lie or mislead or use subliminal messages. In this view, the most important part of an ad is its explicit statement: 'Truth in Advertising'. One could attack cigarette ads like that for a US brand in 1946, that said

More Doctors Smoke [brand name] than any other cigarette

because this implies what is now known to be false, that smoking this brand is more healthy than smoking other cigarettes. This view of the audience, as rational agents to be protected from brainwashing, was assumed by most critics of advertising up to the 1960s. And it was useful to advertisers too, for it presents them as responsible professionals communicating product information. If you take this view of the audience, all you need to do is have an Advertising Standards Authority, like that to which the Reg ad was taken, and perhaps educate children to be sceptical of ads. The Advertising Code, which says that ads should be 'Legal, Clean, Honest, and Truthful', bears more than a passing resemblance to the Boy Scout Promise, and is based on the same model of ethical activity.

Three views of audience

View	Individual is	Control by	Critical focus	Example	Reference
Humanist	a free individual	persuasive text	advertisers, ad agencies	more doctors smoke…	Vance Packard
Structuralist Marxist	an effect of ideological structures	dominant class	texts	cowboy, perfume ads	Judith Williamson
Cultural studies	active, social interpreters	consumers	reception by audiences	Reg, Benetton, ads on ads	Paul Willis

But this view will not enable us to discuss the effects of the Reg ad, because they do not arise from any false or misleading statements. The explicit content of cigarette ads is now strictly regulated in most developed countries, so the sort of misleading statement in the 'More Doctors Smoke…' ad is impossible. Reg explicitly mocks any rational product claims, and Unique Selling Proposition, with a stupid reason for choosing one brand over another:

Reg on cigarette advertising.

'I smoke 'em because my name's on 'em.' [His finger on the pack covers the last two letters of the name Regal]

The only information the Reg ad gives us literally is that

SMOKING CAUSES FATAL DISEASES

which is true and which would not, in itself, seem to encourage children to smoke. Yet despite this warning, some people somewhere must think this ad helps sales (whether to minors or to others), or at least defends Regal's market share, or Imperial Tobacco would not pay for it.

In the 1970s some critics challenged the humanist view of audiences and effects, and developed an alternative I have called 'structuralist-marxist'. It provides the basis for many complex, insightful, and influential analyses of ads, such as those of Judith Williamson, though no one I know of still holds it entirely. People who take this approach usually cite the French philosopher Louis Althusser, and especially one very influential essay on Ideological State Apparatuses, his term for institutions like schools, the church, and the media. They use the term *ideology*, not as it is popularly used to mean a political bias, but to mean the taken for granted sense we have of what is real and natural, and they say this sense is determined by our place in a social system. They often have puns on *production* and *reproduction*. Production is the economic system of capital that defines our class and work, while reproduction is the cultural system, constantly supporting the way things are.

Althusser's key idea is that we see ourselves as individuals because structures like the police, education, the church – and advertising – address us this way. He uses the term *interpellation* for the way ideology positions us. He says to think of the way a police officer might say, 'Hey you!' If you turn around you have defined yourself as subject to the officer's authority, and as a subject who can act (that pun on *subject* is very common in this sort of writing). The idea of interpellation is very much counter to our common sense view of ourselves. It says we are not naturally free individuals – in fact the idea that we are free individuals is created by ideology. Ads position us in this way; to make sense of them we have to take on a position in terms of class, gender, race. For instance, to make sense of the famous cowboy used in ads for a cigarette (I am not allowed to quote the slogan), we have to draw on ideas of rugged Western independence, and compare our own confined daily lives to his. The cigarette can then serve as a link between our lived experience of work and routine and an imaginary life, an escape. The cigarette need not make explicit claims at all, but need only establish an image in terms of signs that will link to desires of consumers, the way we saw in Chapter 10. We consume, or wish we could consume, instead of changing things.

Ads are just one aspect of ideology. But they offer a useful insight, in this view, into how women are made into women, workers made into workers, consumers into consumers. So this approach was taken by both Marxists, trying to figure out why workers went along with their oppression, and feminists trying to show the pervasiveness of male domination, patriarchy. Note that this structuralist view is not saying that ideology imposes bad roles and bad images on us, when it should show good roles and images; that very common political complaint is a humanist view. In the structuralist-marxist view, all ads, not just misleading ones, are complicit in oppression, by the nature of the commodity system. The critic then analyses the text to reconstruct the position hidden by the ad.

Williamson and others show that this approach is very revealing with the powerful sexual and social imagery of 1970s tobacco ads. But it does not give us a clear basis for interpreting the Reg ad (or many other more recent tobacco ads). One reason this it doesn't is that the critique focuses on revealing a single implicit content, the real and hidden meaning of the ad. With the gradually tightening regulation of tobacco advertising in countries like the UK, not only explicit appeals but also the more familiar implicit appeals are ruled out. Advertisers can not use images of people to associate smoking with sex appeal or sports or success or pleasure. (Compare UK ads to those in countries that do not have such tight regulation, where they still have sexy couples in exciting locales.) Yet instead of stopping advertising, UK tobacco companies explored very indirect ads that could have multiple interpretations for fragmented audiences.

What sort of position are we being offered here in the Reg ad? It is not as if anyone aspires to be like Reg, and therefore buys the cigarettes. Nor can we be entirely comfortable making fun of him, and feeling superior. His mockery of all that is serious, and his defiance of our expectations about ads, open up all sorts of possible responses, even that of children who say they would like him as a friend. The structuralist approach also makes it hard to explain why some ads do not work as they should. Advertising writers know that some ads fail, or have unpredictable readings. Ironically, structuralist critics attributed too much power, not to the advertising writers, but to the advertising system.

In this book, I have been drawing on a third view of audience, one that is now current in cultural studies, assuming that ads and other institutions do not just impose ideology on a passive audience. Cultures and subcultures transform texts and practices, often making them serve their own needs. Green wellies can mean environmental awareness or upper-class land-owning; Levi's can symbolise youthful rebellion or blind consumerism; condoms can mean sexual promiscuousness or moral responsibility. As we saw in Chapter 12, there has been a massive attempt to change the meanings of condoms in various sub-cultures, not just by advertising, but by understanding the changing sexual practices in these cultures. Understanding and changing smoking behaviour requires a similar effort.

Consider the brand of cigarettes that is marketed with the word 'Death' in large letters, and a skull and crossbones. They have been accused of appealing to young people with ads showing a lung X-ray, headed, 'The Shadow of Death'. How could this appeal? The explicit message is that they kill you. The implicit message carries no pleasant associations of escape or solidarity. It is argued that they appeal to the oppositional culture of teenagers. An advertising campaign that set out to appeal directly to such an audience (as did the campaign 'You're never alone with a Strand' 30 years ago) might flop disastrously. And in surveys, 16 –19 year olds say they are very suspicious of ads that seem designed to appeal to their specific interests and identities. So if these cigarettes have an appeal, it can only be because of active use by some young people as an emblem of rebellion.

It is inherently difficult to give you a text to illustrate how cultural studies analyses ads, as I gave the doctor or cowboy ads to illustrate earlier theories and critiques, because this view says texts are not meaningful only in themselves, out of context. The text might be conversations about the ads, not the ads themselves. But the Reg ad is a good example, because it was meant to be talked about. Neither the explicit content nor the implicit image could be understood apart from the ways people play with it, relate it to earlier ads and competing ads, juxtapose stereotypes, enjoy mockery. That is why I said in Chapter 1 that our enjoyment of some ads can be a serious place at which to begin our analysis. Anger is not the only guide to political analysis.

The implication of this view is that we can't tell what the ad means just by close analysis of the text; we have to look at different and contradictory ways people can use it. Here, we can't just survey schoolchildren to ask if this makes them smoke or not, as they did at Kirklees Education Authority. We would have to look at the situations in which they smoke, what the practice means in their lives, what messages they get from authorities, how they see the future, and how Reg might or might not fit with their culture. Is he seen as a troublemaker, ridiculing serious adults? Is he seen in opposition to the idealised images of youth and beauty in other ads, and thus as a criticism of conventional consumerism? Is he seen as a misbehaving uncle rather than a forbidding father? We are likely to find, not an audience, but many audiences that respond in different, often unpredictable ways. And the only way to find out is to go out and observe the way people talk about and use the ads they see and the things they buy.

Usually when an academic presents three views of the same phenomenon, the third one is right. Here I am not so sure; we may draw on all three theories at different times. Certainly advertising professionals do, sometimes presenting themselves as rational persuaders, sometimes as all-powerful image makers, sometimes talking about how ads relate to other cultural practices. But the theory we choose will have practical consequences, for instance, for what we do about children smoking. The first view would favour public health messages: we just have to tell them it's bad for them. The second would favour anti-commercials that used the insecurities of young people, fears about image or appearance, to get them to stop; that has been a strategy of many public health campaigns. The third view is taken in *Campaign* by Mark Flanagan, from Action on Smoking and Health. He says,

> Young people will smoke because it's an act of defiance and it's a snub at society. You can run anti-smoking commercials until you are blue in the face without any effect.
>
> (*Campaign* 10th September 1993, p. 30).

Flanagan argues tobacco ads should be banned because they develop the image of smoking. In this view, Reg is more dangerous than the traditional ads because he is available for an oppositional reading. But anti-smoking ads would also reinforce this opposition. Those advertising agencies that still make tobacco ads argue that they cannot be recruiting new smokers with texts like this; kids will smoke anyway, so let the agency make its 15%. The two conclusions are, not surprisingly, opposed in their recommendations, but they both argue that practices, and not just texts, are crucial.

Both the structuralist and the cultural studies view of ads require a change in our usual humanist thinking, a change I think people sometimes miss. First, we cannot talk about audience as something given, a group of people that is already in categories based on income, house ownership, gender, age. I know advertisers and politicians talk about As and Bs and C1s – classes from government surveys. But those groups are imaginary. The ads themselves are not addressed so crudely. Whatever the brief for the Reg ads – and I can't imagine what it was – it wasn't to appeal just to bald beer-drinking Northern working-class types. Also, the audience should not be confused with the concrete people who read it. Interpretation is not a matter of finding the person the ad was really intended for and asking them what they think. Audiences are formed over time as people encounter and transform the texts. So we are left saying that if you want to know whether the Reg ads get more kids to smoke, you have to go from the posters to the playground.

There is an academic tendency to treat anything we've just noticed as something unique to our period, usually by calling it 'post-modern'. But if the audience for ads is active now, it was probably always active, even with earlier ads, like those for Lucky Strike, or Strand, or Bachelors, or Virginia Slims. The difference now is that advertisers often write the ads with these active processes in mind, not just discovering them as accidental effects. I could have made the same points using the controversial ads for Benetton (mentioned in Chapter 1), or the Nescafé Gold Blend ad (Chapter 8), or the Diesel ad (Chapter 11), or the US commercials for Converse All-Stars that deny they are worn by people in commercials, or even the pop video 'Low-down on Lancaster' that my own university uses to recruit students. All would look strikingly different from the ads of ten years ago, and all would offer complex texts open to ambiguous, multiple interpretations from different social positions.

In some ways ads like those for Regal are atypical. UK cigarette ads are known for their ingenuity; they have to deal with astonishingly complex regulations and voluntary agreements, a declining market, limited media outlets, terrible public opinion, and the ever-present threat of a complete ban. The earlier views of the audience persist in other sectors; ads for detergent still plug a Unique Selling Proposition, and ads for perfume may offer nothing but an image into which to plug ourselves. But in other ways cigarette ads, Benetton ads, Converse, and the Lancaster University pop video are just further down a line of exploration that other products may follow.

I have said that to understand Reg and smoking we need to go from the poster to the playground. But I am not ruling textual studies out of cultural studies, or I would not have written this book. We still need a close look at words and pictures in ads if we are to understand why Reg is different from the doctors or the cowboy. We could go back to the description of the Reg ad at the beginning of this chapter. This text is an occasion for what people make of it, but it is also a text. Here is a scattered list of ways one might start looking at it as a text.

1. The cluttered pastiche of the illustration, with the cut-out photo, gives it a kind of home-made look, something like *Private Eye* or *Viz*, though not as crude.

2. The text sets up the bare bones of a social situation; the two bits of text come from two different discourses, one serious and one undercutting. The heading is unattributed, so that the two voices can be reinterpreted in terms of other pairs, such as teacher/pupil or parent/child.

3. One of the two parts, 'Reg on…' or his quotation, is always much longer than the other, contributing to the humorous sense of their not matching.

4. Like many cigarette posters now, the text presents a puzzle. If we think of people seeing this as they pass by, the puzzle is an occasion for a question, a bit of competition, an evaluation. The successful interpretation always puts us in a position of knowing more than Reg. Or is he outsmarting us? The fact that this text has many readings, some identifying, some mocking, some oppositional, is in part dependent on the complex kind of text it is. That is why we need to go back to the words in the ad, as well as out to the people looking at it.

I have presented three views of audience, underlying three periods of criticism of ads.

1. A humanist view, which assumed rational individuals who needed to be protected from powerful advertisers who explicitly made false claims

2. A structuralist-marxist view, which presented individuals as effects of ideological structures, and focused on how texts implicitly positioned readers.

3. A cultural studies view, which focuses on diverse responses to ambiguous texts by an active, social audience

In chapter 2, I presented three similar periods in the advertising industry. If we compare them, we see that at each stage the leading innovators of the advertising industry changed their practices long before the critics changed their theories. In the early years of the century, the advertising agents figured out the centrality of marketing before the critics, who still focused on production. In the 1920s advertising agents got to the uses of signs long before the academic semioticians, and discussed the positioning of readers before the structuralists. Advertisers in the 1960s were making ads that demanded an active audience before cultural studies researchers pointed out such audiences. Advertisers base their careers on a theory of textual practice in a social world. It is important that there also be critics of advertising like F. R. Leavis, Raymond Williams, Stuart Ewen, or Judith Williamson, who insist that we look at these ubiquitous texts in new ways. Academics like me follow in their footsteps in insisting that ads be taken seriously. It worries me, but also gives me some sneaking pleasure, to realise that the advertising writers are always one step ahead of us.

Further reading
Audiences and effects

For a humanist view of the audience, see Vance Packard's best-seller, *The Hidden Persuaders*, and the critique made at the time in Martin Mayer's *Madison Avenue USA*. But many critics on the left, such as Raymond Williams in 'The Magic System', took a more sophisticated version of a similar position. Michael Schudson reviews different kinds of criticism of advertising and consumer culture, with recent references, in his 1991 'Afterword' to *Advertising, The Uneasy Persuasion*.

The key work for the structuralist position is Judith Williamson's *Decoding Advertisements*, to which I have already referred a number of times. Similar readings can be found in Gillian Dyer and in Vestergaard and Schrøder; Robert Goldman follows Williamson with a more complex view of audience-making. For explications of the work of Louis Althusser, try Norman Fairclough, *Language and Power*, which has lots of examples and explanation, or Diane Macdonell, *Theories of Discourse*, which gives more background but is rather hard for those not used to social theory. For more social historical background to a structuralist critique, see Stuart Ewen, *Captains of Consciousness*, and Stuart Ewen and Elizabeth Ewen, *Channels of Desire*.

For cultural studies, Lawrence Grossberg, Cary Nelson, and Paula Treichler, eds., *Cultural Studies,* has a very wide range of short studies and statements. Paul Willis, *Common Culture*, outlines an influential position, and John Fiske, *Television Culture*, gives an introductory outline (though oddly he does not deal with ads). One way of seeing the changing points of view on audience is to read Angela McRobbie, *Feminism and Youth Culture*, in which her views change over the course of a decade, from her work on *Jackie* to her work on *Just Seventeen*. Martin Barker and Anne Beezer, eds., *Reading Into Cultural Studies,* is valuable for suggesting how some classics of this young field might be read now; see especially Liz Wells on Judith Williamson.

There is a vast literature on smoking, advertising, and behaviour. Arguments on the Reg case are summarised in short articles in *Campaign*, 5th February and 17th December 1993. Discussions of tobacco advertising appear almost weekly in *Campaign* ; see for example Michele Martin, 'Should Tobacco Advertising Be Banned?' *Campaign* (19th February 1993), pp. 24–25. One admirably passionate study that includes detailed analysis of ads, very much along the lines set out by Williamson, is Simon Chapman, *Great Expectorations: Advertising and the Tobacco Industry*. It is particularly good on ads in developing countries, which I have not considered.

On television advertising and children, an area of discussion which I have skirted here by using a poster example, see Brian Young, *Television Advertising and Children*, a readable and detailed if somewhat repetitive review of the psychological literature; Tom Engelhardt, 'Children's Television: The Shortcake Strategy'; Stephen Kline, 'Empires of Play', in Carol Bazalgette and David Buckingham, *In Front of the Children*; and the most relevant perspective for this chapter, David Buckingham, *Children Talking Television*, Chapter 10, 'Hidden Persuaders? Advertising, Resistance, and Pleasure'.

Bibliography

Advertising Age, Editors of: *Procter and Gamble: The House that Ivory Built* (Lincolnwood, ILL, NTC Business Books, 1989).

Aggleton, Peter, and Hilary Homans, ed., *The Social Aspects of AIDS* (Lewes, UK, Falmer Press, 1988).

Arlen, Michael J., *Thirty Seconds* (Harmondsworth, Penguin, 1981).

Atkinson, J. Max, and John Heritage, ed., *Structures of Social Action: Studies in Conversation Analysis* (Cambridge, Cambridge University Press, 1984).

Barker, Martin, and Anne Beezer, ed., *Reading Into Cultural Studies* (London, Routledge, 1992).

Barthes, Roland, *Mythologies* (London, Paladin, 1973 [1954–1956]).

Barthes, Roland, 'The Rhetoric of the Image', in Trans. Stephen Heath, *Image–Music–Text* (London, Fontana, 1977 [1964]), pp. 32–51.

Barthes, Roland, *Camera Lucida* (London, Flamingo, 1984)

Beattie, Geoffrey, *Talk: An Analysis of Speech and Non-verbal Behaviour in Conversation* (Milton Keynes, Open University Press, 1983).

Berger, John, *Ways of Seeing* (London, BBC, 1972).

Betterton, Rosemary, ed., *Looking On: Images of Femininity in the Visual Arts and the Media* (London, Pandora, 1987).

Boden, Deirdre, and Don Zimmerman, ed., *Talk and Social Structure* (Cambridge, Polity, 1991).

Bordo, Susan, 'Reading the Slender Body', in Mary Jacobus, Evelyn Fox Keller and Sally Shuttleworth, ed., *Body/Politics* (London, Routledge, 1990), pp. 83–112

Bordwell, David, and Kristin Thompson, *Film Art: An Introduction*, 3rd ed. (New York, McGraw-Hill, 1990).

Brandt, Allan M., 'AIDS and Metaphor: Toward the Social Meaning of Epidemic Disease', *Social Problems,* 55 (1988), pp. 413–432.

Brown, Penelope, and Stephen Levinson, *Politeness: Some Universals in Language Use*, revised edition (Cambridge, Cambridge University Press, 1987 [1978]).

Brown, Roger, and Albert Gilman, 'Pronouns of Power and Solidarity', in T. A. Sebeok, ed., *Style in Language*, [rpt. in P Giglioli, ed., pp. 252–282.] ed. (Cambridge, MA, MIT Press, 1960), pp. 253–76.

Buckingham, David, *Children Talking Television: The Making of Television Literacy* (Lewes, Falmer Press, 1993).

Burgess, Jacquelin, 'The Production and Consumption of Environmental Meanings in the Mass Media: A Research Agenda for the 1990s', *Transactions of the British Institute of Geography* 15 (1990), pp. 139–161.

Burgin, Victor, ed., *Thinking Photography* (London, Macmillan, 1982).

Carter, Erica, and Simon Watney, ed., *Taking Liberties: AIDS and Cultural Politics* (London, Serpent's Tail, 1989).

Carter, Ronald, *Vocabulary* (London, Allen and Unwin, 1987).

Channell, Joanna, *Vague Language* (Oxford, Oxford University Press, 1994)

Chapman, Simon, *Great Expectorations: Advertising and the Tobacco Industry* (London, Comedia, 1986).

Cheshire, Jenny, ed., *English Around the World: Sociolinguistic Perspectives* (Cambridge, Cambridge University Press, 1991).

Cook, Guy, *The Discourse of Advertising* (London, Routledge, 1992).

Crimp, Douglas, ed., *AIDS: Cultural Analysis, Cultural Activism* (Cambridge, MIT Press, 1988).

Culler, Jonathan, ed., *On Puns: The Foundation of Letters* (Oxford, Blackwell, 1988).

De Voe, Merrill, *Effective Advertising Copy* (New York, Macmillan, 1956).

Drew, Paul, and John Heritage, *Talk at Work: Interaction in Institutional Settings* (Cambridge, Cambridge University Press, 1992).

Durand, J., 'Rhetorical Figures in the Advertising Image', in J. Umiker-Sebeok, ed., *Marketing and Semiotics* (Amsterdam, de Gruyter, 1987), pp. 295–318

Dyer, Gillian, *Advertising as Communication* (London, Methuen, 1982).

Engelhardt, Tom, 'Children's Television: The Shortcake Strategy', in Todd Gitlin, ed., *Watching Television* (New York, Pantheon, 1986), pp. 68–110.

Ewen, Stuart, *Captains of Consciousness: Advertising and the Social Roots of the Consumer Culture* (New York, McGraw-Hill, 1976).

Ewen, Stuart, and Elizabeth Ewen, *Channels of Desire: Mass Images and the Shaping of American Consciousness* (New York, McGraw-Hill, 1982).

Fairclough, Norman, *Language and Power* (Harlow, Longman, 1989).

Fairclough, Norman, ed., *Critical Language Awareness* (Harlow, Longman, 1992).

Fairclough, Norman, *Discourse and Social Change* (Cambridge, Polity, 1992).

Farb, Peter, *Word Play: What Happens When People Talk* (London, Jonathan Cape, 1974).

Fiske, John, *Television Culture* (London, Methuen, 1987).

Fiske, John, *Reading the Popular* (London, Unwin Hyman, 1989).

Fiske, John, *Understanding Popular Culture* (London, Unwin Hyman, 1989).

Fowler, Roger, *Linguistic Criticism* (Oxford, Oxford University Press, 1986).

Fox, Stephen, *The Mirror Makers: A History of American Advertising* (London, Heinemann, 1989).

Friel, Brian, *Translations* (London, Faber, 1992)

Fyfe, Gordon, and John Law, ed., *Picturing Power: Visual Depiction and Social Relations*, Sociological Review Monograph 35. (London, Routledge, 1988).

Giglioli, Pier Paulo, ed., *Language and Social Context* (Harmondsworth, Penguin, 1972).

Goffman, Erving, *Gender Advertisements* (London, Macmillan, 1979) [UK edition; US edition 1976].

Goldman, Robert, *Reading Ads Socially* (London, Routledge, 1992).

Grossberg, Lawrence, Cary Nelson, and Paula Treichler (ed.), *Cultural Studies* (London, Routledge, 1993).

Gumperz, John, *Discourse Strategies* (Cambridge, Cambridge University Press, 1982).

Gunn, Thom, *The Man With the Night Sweats* (London, Faber and Faber, 1992).

Halliday, M. A. K. and Ruqaiya Hasan, *Language, Context, and Text: Aspects of Language in a Social Semiotic Perspective* (Victoria, Deakin University Press, 1986).

Haraway, Donna, *Primate Visions: Gender, Race, and Nature in the World of Modern Science* (London, Routledge, 1989).

Hawkes, Terence, *Metaphor* (London, Methuen, 1972).

Heller, Agnes, *Everyday Life*, Trans. G. L. Campbell (London, Routledge and Kegan Paul, 1984 [1970]).

Hudson, Richard, *Sociolinguistics* (Cambridge, Cambridge University Press, 1980).

Jakobson, Roman, 'Concluding Statement: Linguistics and Poetics', in Thomas Sebeok, ed., *Style in Language* (Cambridge, MA, MIT Press, 1960), pp.

Jakobson, Roman, *Language in Literature* (Cambridge, MA, Harvard University Press, 1987).

Keat, Russell, Nigel Whiteley, and Nicholas Abercrombie, *The Authority of the Consumer* (London, Routledge, 1994).

Kempson, Ruth, *Semantic Theory* (Cambridge, Cambridge University Press, 1977).

Kline, Stephen, 'Empires of Play', in Carol Bazalgette and David Buckingham, ed., *In Front of the Children* (London, BFI Books, 1994).

Knowles, Gerry, *Patterns of Spoken English* (Harlow, Longman, 1990).

Kress, Gunther, 'Educating Readers: Language in Advertising', in J. Hawthorn, ed., *Propaganda, Persuasion and Polemic* (London, Edward Arnold, 1987), pp. 123–139.

Kress, Gunther, *Linguistic Processes in Sociocultural Practice* (Oxford, Oxford University Press, 1990).

Kress, Gunther, and Theo van Leeuwen, *Reading Images* (Victoria, Australia, Deakin University Press, 1990).

Lakoff, George, *Metaphors We Live By* (Chicago, University of Chicago Press, 1980).

Leech, Geoffrey, *English in Advertising* (London, Longman, 1966).

Leech, Geoffrey, *Introducing English Grammar* (Harmondsworth, Penguin, 1992)

Leech, Geoffrey, *A Linguistic Guide to English Poetry* (London, Longman, 1969).

Leech, Geoffrey, *The Principles of Pragmatics* (Harlow, Longman, 1983).

Leech, Geoffrey, *Semantics*, 2nd ed. (Harmondsworth, Penguin, 1981).

Leech, Geoffrey, and Michael Short, *Style in Fiction* (Harlow, Longman, 1981).

Leith, Dick, *A Social History of English* (London, Routledge and Kegan Paul, 1983).

Levinson, Stephen, *Pragmatics* (Cambridge, Cambridge University Press, 1983).

Lodge, David, *Nice Work* (London, Secker and Warburg, 1988).

Luhmann, Nikolas, *Environmental Communication* (Cambridge, Polity, 1990).

Macdonell, Diane, *Theories of Discourse* (Oxford, Blackwell, 1986).

Marchand, Roland, *Advertising the American Dream: Making Way for Modernity 1920–1940* (Berkeley, University of California Press, 1985).

Marx, Karl, *Capital* Volume 1, transl. Ben Fowkes (New York, Vintage, 1977)

Mattelart, Armand, *Advertising International* (London, Routledge, 1991).

Mayer, Martin, *Madison Avenue: USA* (Harmondsworth, Penguin, 1961).

Mayle, Peter, *Up the Agency: The Snakes and Ladders of the Advertising Business* (London, Pan, 1990).

McCrum, Robert, William Cram, and Robert McNeill, *The Story of English* (London, Faber and Faber and BBC Books, 1986).

McLaughlin, Margaret, *Conversation: How Talk is Organized* (Beverly Hills, Sage, 1984).

McRobbie, Angela, *Feminism and Youth Culture* (London, Macmillan, 1991).

Milroy, John, and Lesley Milroy, *Authority in Language* (London, Routledge and Kegan Paul, 1985).

Monaco, James, *How to Read a Film: The Art, Technology, Language, History, and Theory of Film and Media* (New York, Oxford University Press, 1981).

Montgomery, Martin, *An Introduction to Language and Society* (London, Routledge, 1986).

Morley, David, *Television Audiences and Cultural Studies* (London, Routledge, 1992).

Muhlhausler, Peter, and Rom Harré, *Pronouns and People: The Linguistic Construction of Social and Personal Identity* (Oxford, Blackwell, 1990).

Myers, Greg, 'The Pragmatics of Politeness in Scientific Articles', *Applied Linguistics,* 10 (1989), pp. 1–35.

Myers, Greg, 'The Double Helix as an Icon', *Science as Culture,* 9 (1990), pp. 49–72.

Myers, Greg, '"The Power is Yours" Plot and Agency in Captain Planet', in Carol Bazalgette and David Buckingham, ed., *In Front of the Children* (London, BFI Books, 1994).

Myers, Kathy, *Understains . . . The Sense and Seduction of Advertising* (London, Comedia, 1986).

Nash, Walter, and Ronald Carter, *Seeing Through Language* (Oxford, Basil Blackwell, 1990).

O'Connor, J. D., *Phonetics* (Harmondsworth, Penguin, 1973).

Ogilvy, David, *Confessions of an Advertising Man* (London, Longmans, 1964).

Packard, Vance, *The Hidden Persuaders* (Harmondsworth, Penguin, 1956).

Pateman, Trevor, 'How Is Understanding an Advertisement Possible?' in H. Davis and P. Walton, eds., *Language, Image, Media* (Oxford, Basil Blackwell, 1983), pp. 187–204.

Phillipson, Robert, *Linguistic Imperialism* (Oxford, Oxford University Press, 1992).

Reader, W. J., *Fifty Years of Unilever* (London, Heinemann, 1980).

Rees, Nigel, *Slogans* (London, George Allen and Unwin, 1982).

Richards, I. A., *The Philosophy of Rhetoric* (Oxford, Oxford University Press, 1936).

Rösing, Helmut, 'Music in Advertising', in P. Tagg and D. Horn, ed., *Popular Music Perspectives* (Göteborg and Exeter, International Assocation for the Study of Popular Music, 1982), pp. 41–51

Sacks, Sheldon, ed., *On Metaphor* (Chicago, University of Chicago Press, 1979).

Sayers, Dorothy, *Murder Must Advertise*, [rpt. Coronet, 1992] (London, Gollancz, 1933).

Scannell, Paddy, ed., *Broadcast Talk* (London, Sage, 1991).

Schudson, Michael, *Advertising: The Uneasy Persuasion – Its Dubious Impact on American Society* (New York, Basic Books, 1984).

Seidel, Gill, ''Thank God I Said No to AIDS': On the Changing Discourse of AIDS in Uganda', *Discourse and Society,* 1 (1990), pp. 61–84.

Simpson, Paul, *Language, Ideology and Point of View* (London, Routledge, 1993).

Smith, Dorothy E., *The Everyday World as Problematic* (Milton Keynes, Open University Press, 1988).

Sontag, Susan, *Illness as Metaphor* (New York, Doubleday Anchor, 1978).

Sontag, Susan, *On Photography* (Harmondsworth, Penguin, 1979).

Sontag, Susan, *AIDS and Its Metaphors* (New York, Doubleday Anchor, 1989).

Spitzer, Leo, 'American Advertising Explained as Popular Art', in ed., *A Method of Interpreting Literature* (New York, Russell and Russell, 1949), pp. 102–149.

Stubbs, Michael, *Discourse Analysis* (Oxford, Blackwell, 1983).

Symons, Julian, *The Advertising Murders* (Originally published as *A Man Called Jones* (1947) and *The Thirty-first of February* (1950), London, Victor Gollancz Ltd.) ed. (London, Pan, 1992).

Tannen, Deborah, *Conversational Style: Analyzing Talk Among Friends* (Norwood, NJ, Ablex, 1984).

Tannen, Deborah, *That's Not What I Meant* (New York, Ballantine, 1986).

Tannen, Deborah, *Talking Voices* (Cambridge, Cambridge University Press, 1989).

Tannen, Deborah, *You Just Don't Understand,* 1989).

Taylor, Janelle Sue, 'The Public Foetus and the Family Car', *Science as Culture,* 17 (1993), pp. 601–618.

Thornbarrow, Joanna, 'The Woman, the Man, and the Filofax: Gender Positions in Advertising', in Sara Mills, ed. *Gendering the Reader* (Hemel Hempstead: Harvester Wheatsheaf, 1994), pp. 128–151.

Toolan, Michael, 'The Language of Press Advertising', in M. Ghadessy, ed., *The Registers of English* (London, Francis Pinter, 1988), pp. 52–64

Trudgill, Peter, and Jean Hannah, *International English: A Guide to Varieties of Standard English* (London, Edward Arnold, 1987).

Turner, Geoff, and John Pearson, *The Persuasion Industry* (London, Eyre and Spottiswoode, 1966).

van Leeuwen, Theo, 'Persuasive Speech: The Intonation of the Live Radio Commercial', *Australian Journal of Communication,* 7 (1985), pp. 25–34.

van Leeuwen, Theo, 'Music and Ideology: Notes Towards a Sociosemiotics of Mass Media Music', *Sydney Association for Studies in Society and Culture Working Papers,* 2,1 (1988), pp. 19–44.

Vestergaard, Torben, and Kim Schrøder, *The Language of Advertising* (Oxford, Basil Blackwell, 1985).

Wardhaugh, Ronald, *How Conversation Works* (Oxford, Blackwell, 1985).

Wardhaugh, Ronald, *Language in Society* (Oxford, Blackwell, 1987).

Wicke, Jennifer, *Advertising Fictions: Literature, Advertisement, and Social Reading* (New York, Columbia University Press, 1988).

Williams, Raymond, 'Advertising: The Magic System', in *Problems in Materialism and Culture*, [originally printed in New Left Review (1960)] (London, Verso, 1980), pp. 170–195.

Williamson, Judith, *Decoding Advertisements* (London, Marion Boyars, Ltd., 1978).

Willis, Paul, *Common Culture: Symbolic Work at Play in the Everyday Cultures of the Young* (Milton Keynes, Open University Press, 1990).

Winship, Janice, *Inside Women's Magazines* (London, Pandora, 1987).

Winship, Janice, 'Sexuality for Sale', in Stuart Hall, Dorothy Hobson, Andrew Lowe, and Paul Willis, ed., *Culture, Media, Language* (London: Unwin Hyman, 1980), pp. 217–223.

Yearley, Steven, *The Green Case* (London, HarperCollins, 1991).

Young, Brian, *Television Advertising and Children* (Oxford, Oxford University Press, 1990).

Glossary

Words in *Words in Ads*

These are working definitions, intended to help readers follow my use of key terms. Nearly all these terms can have more complex or contentious definitions; in some cases I have referred to fuller discussions. I have tried to avoid specialised terminology in the text wherever possible; for some words I give a more technical term here, to help make the link to more advanced books. General dictionaries can be misleading for specialised meanings of academic terms; readers may want to look instead at such specialised dictionaries as Katie Wales, *A Dictionary of Stylistics* (Harlow, Longman, 1989); Geoffrey Leech, *Introducing English Grammar,* (Harmondsworth, Penguin, 1992); Chris Baldick, *The Concise Oxford Dictionary of Literary Terms* (Oxford, Oxford University Press, 1990); Richard Lanham, *A Handlist of Rhetorical Terms* (Berkeley, University of California Press, 1968), or Nicholas Abercrombie, Stephen Hill, and Bryan S. Turner, *Dictionary of Sociology* Second Edition (Harmondsworth, Penguin, 1988).

accent – a systematic variant within a language in the way words are pronounced. Received Pronunciation is one accent; accents of Lancashire or East Anglia are others. See Milroy and Milroy (1985).

advertorial – an advertisement that looks like the editorial content of a publication.

agency – the property of being able to act.

alliteration – repetition of consonant sounds.

ambiguity – the phenomenon in which a word or sentence has two or more distinct interpretations. See Kempson (1977).

analogy – an extended comparison of two entities, events, or situations.

anchorage – Barthes' (1977) term for a relation in which a picture constrains the multiple meanings of words.

assonance – repetition of vowel sounds.

attitude associations – my term for what Leech (1981) calls *affective meanings*.

code-switching – a general linguistic term for the way a speaker may move between two languages, or dialects, or accents, often within the same utterance. I have referred only to *language switching*. See Gumperz (1982).

cognate – one of a pair of words that are similar between two languages, and are ultimately derived from the same source, such as English and French *table*. A **false cognate** is a word that seems to be the same, where the meanings actually differ, as in English *library* and French *librarie* (bookstore).

collocation – two or more words that frequently go together. See Carter (1987).

command – the sentence type in which the speaker directs the hearer to do something; also called *imperative*. See Leech (1992).

commodities – things for sale in a system of exchange

consonant – a sound formed by blocking or restricting the airstream with, for instance, the tongue, palate, or lips; in English, those spelled with any letter except *a, e, i, o, u*, or *y*.

copywriters – the people who write the words in ads.

cultural studies – as I use the term here, an academic field that studies popular culture (such as popular music and literature and fashion) in a framework of critical social theory; for instance the work of Raymond Williams, and of researchers associated with the Centre for Contemporary Cultural Studies at the University of Birmingham (Willis, McRobbie, Winship). See Barker and Beezer (1992).

deviation – unexpected irregularity, a breaking of a norm or a pattern of sound or structure. See Leech (1969).

dialect – a systematic variant within a language in the words that are used and the ways sentences are typically structured; Standard English is one such dialect, Scouse and Geordie are others. See Milroy and Milroy (1985).

discourse – set of texts that is linked by subject matter, social group, or setting; for instance, football discourse, or political discourse, or the discourse of train spotters. See Kress (1990).

ellipsis – leaving out some words in a sentence which can be understood from the context. *It is. Are you?* See Halliday and Hasan (1985) and Leech (1992)..

euphemism – the use of some vague or indirect word instead of some unpleasant or taboo word, as in *passed away* for *died*. See Carter (1987).

everyday life – used here as a technical term to refer to the phenomena that give the impression of ordinariness, cyclical time, unmarked relationships. See Heller (1984).

exclamation – the sentence type that expresses surprise or strong emotion, marked with *!*. See Leech (1992).

figurative language – a general term for all uses of language that depart from literal meanings, including metaphor, simile, metonymy, and synechdoche.

foregrounding – a phenomenon in which one part of a text stands out for special attention. See Leech (1969).

gender – in feminist theory, the cultural construction of masculine and feminine, as opposed to **sex**, the biological differences between male and female.

genre – a stereotypical act of communication, such as a murder mystery, a riddle, a sonnet, a collections letter, or a demonstration ad. See Kress (1990).

graphology – the level of linguistic analysis that deals with the way letters and words look (as opposed to the way they sound), including spelling (and misspelling), line breaks, and layout on the page.

homophones – two or more words that are spelled differently but sound the same, such as *their* and *there*, *key* and *quay*. See Carter (1987).

homonymy – a kind of multiple meaning in which two or more unrelated words are spelled and sound the same, such as *light* as opposed to *darkness* and *light* as opposed to *heavy*. Compare *polysemy*. See Carter (1987).

iconic – the relation of resemblance between a signifier and a signified, for instance, the way a photograph resembles the thing of which it is a sign.

ideology – a taken for granted sense of what is real and natural, a systematic set of beliefs that supports the system of production. See Macdonnell (1986), Fairclough (1989).

indexical – a relationship of result or association between a signifier and a signified, for instance, the way droplets on a drinks can signify cold, or smoke can indicate fire.

interpellation – the term used by Louis Althusser for the way an ideological system positions subjects. See Williamson (1978), Macdonnell (1986).

intertextuality – the relationship between one text and others, for instance, interpreting an ad as a parody of *Robin Hood*. See Fairclough (1992).

intonation – the pattern of changes of pitch in a phrase or whole utterance, for instance, the fall and rise at the end of a question like "Are you ready?"

linguistics – the systematic study of language and languages.

metaphor – the figure of speech in which one thing (X) is spoken of in terms of another (Y), as in *You are my sunshine*.

metonymy – the figure of speech in which a thing is referred to by means of referring to something related to it, as when *the Queen* is called *the Crown*.

metre – a regular pattern of stressed syllables. See Leech (1969).

mutual knowledge – the set of knowledge shared by speaker and hearer that enables them to interpret each others' utterances.

myth – as used here, Roland Barthes' (1973) term for a second order system of signs in which we interpret some sign as having a given cultural meaning, the way a bottle of wine or a baguette can evoke France, or a cowboy can evoke America.

narrative – a story, events linked together into a sequence.

paralinguistic features – the aspects of language not described by linguistic analysis of sounds in sequence, such as emphasis, facial expression, speed, and gesture.

parallelism – unexpected pattern of similarity of sound or structure. See Leech (1969).

parody – an ironic imitation of the style and form of a text.

patriarchy – in feminist theory, a social and cultural system dominated by men, including economic institutions, the family, and conventional heterosexual relations.

phrase – a group of words that goes together as part of a sentence. See Leech (1992).

pitch – as in music, the change in sound frequency.

polysemy – a kind of multiple meaning in which the same word has two or more different but related meanings, as in *clear* meaning "unobstructed visually" or "obvious". Compare *homonymy*. See Carter (1987).

presupposition – a statement that is assumed to be true in producing or interpreting another statement. See Levinson (1983).

pronoun – one of a closed list of words that can be used to take the place of a noun or noun phrase, such as *I, me, we,* and *us* (first person), *you* (second person), and *he, him, she, her, it, they,* and *them* (third person). See Leech (1992).

pun – a play on words in which one word has two or more meanings, or one sentence structure can be interpreted in more than one way, such as, *Players please.*

question – the sentence type in which the speaker seeks information from the hearer; also called *interrogative.*

Received Pronunciation (RP) – a linguistic term, intended to be neutral, for the most socially prestigious accent of UK English, that popularly associated with the Queen, the older universities, and the BBC. See Leith (1983).

referent associations – my phrase for what Leech (1981) calls *connotative meanings.*

register – a specialised vocabulary of a field, for instance the register of sports or of law. See Carter (1987, Halliday and Hasan (1985).

relay – Barthes' (1977) term for the relationship of words and pictures in which the interpreter moves back and forth between the two, as in a comic strip.

rhetorical question – the device of asking a question for which both speaker and hearer already know the answer.

rhyme – repetition of the last sounds of words, as at the ends of lines of poetry.

rhythm - a pattern of stresses.

sentence fragment – a group of words that is punctuated as if it were a sentence, but that lacks a subject or a verb marked for time (the minimum requirements for a statement). Also called a *fragment* or a *minor sentence.*

semiotics – the academic field devoted to the study of a general system of signs.

sentence structure – usually called *syntax* in linguistics.

sign – as used here, a term in semiotics for the union of a *signifier* and a *signified*; it can include any carrier of meaning, not just words or conventional symbols.

signifier – in semiotics, the physical form of a sign, for instance the spoken or written word *cat* or an image of a cat, or a red traffic light, or a Rolls-Royce.

signified – in semiotics, the interpreted meaning of a sign, for instance, the meaning of *cat* as a animal, the meaning of a red light as "stop", or the meaning of a Rolls-Royce as wealth.

simile – a figure of speech in which one thing is compared to another, and it is marked by an explicit comparison word such as *like* or *as*.

sound – I use this common word where linguists might say *phonemes*, to refer to the set of the smallest units of sound used in a given language. So *thought* has seven letters but only three sounds. See O'Connor (1973).

speaker associations – my term for what Leech (1981) calls *social meanings*.

statement – the sentence type that makes true or false assertions about the world; also called *declarative*.

stress – a syllable spoken with more force, in a phrase or in a word with more than one syllable: *ZaNUSsi, the AppLIance of SCIence.*

subject position – marxist theory uses this as a pun, to refer both to the way individuals are constructed as subjects of their own actions, and the way they are subjected to a system. See Williamson (1978), Macdonnell (1986), or Fairclough (1992).

substitution – the use of a word like *do* to stand in place of a phrase understood from the previous text. In *If Thomson Don't Do It, Don't Do It.* the words *do it* substitute for such phrases as "take a room in a shady hotel" or "travel on a dilapidated bus". See Halliday and Hasan (1985).

syllable – a pronounceable unit, usually a vowel sound and the consonants pronounced with it; *France* is made up of one syllable, *England* is made up of two, and *Italy* is made up of three. See O'Connor (1973).

symbolic – an arbitrary or conventional relationship between signifier and signified, for instance, the way the written word *can* is related to the thing, a can.

synechdoche – the figure of speech in which a whole is referred to by naming a part, such as *a hand* to refer to a whole person in *Lend me a hand*, or, in a visual text, a button standing for a whole suit or a dashboard standing for a whole car.

tag question – a short question at the end of a statement, as in "He's coming, *isn't he?*"

tenor – in a metaphor, the thing that is talked about in terms of something else, such as *love* in "Love is a rose". See Richards (1936).

turn – in conversation analysis, the term for each complete utterance by a speaker, within an ongoing conversation, before another speaker takes over.

turn-taking – in conversation analysis, the phenomenon in which each participant talks, and then stops, and another participant talks, with few overlaps or gaps, and with a perceived relationship between one turn and the next. See Levinson (1983).

vagueness – a relationship of meanings in which a word or sentence has a range of possible interpretations that cannot be divided into separate and distinct meanings. See Kempson (1977).

vehicle – in a metaphor, the thing that is referred to to talk about something else, such as *rose* in "Love is a rose". See Richards (1936).

vowel – a sound formed by changing the shape of the moth and lips, without blocking or restricting the airstream; in English, those sounds spelled with *a, e, i, o, u,* or *y,* alone or in some combination.

word link associations – my term for what Leech (1981) calls *collocative meanings.*

Acknowledgements

I have made every effort to contact the holders of copyrights for those ads I have reproduced or quoted extensively. I have also acknowledged trademarks, where they were pointed out to me. If anyone knows of holders of copyright that I have not acknowledged, I would appreciate hearing from them, and will gladly make appropriate acknowledgement in any future editions.

Most advertisers contacted were prompt and helpful. But several asked for changes in my comments on the ads, or refused permission on the grounds of what I had to say. Readers should be aware that it may be difficult to quote examples of, for instance, sexism, or vagueness, or ambiguity if the advertiser has final approval. These occasional difficulties make me all the more appreciative that most advertisers allow free comment. I am personally grateful to advertising managers and account executives who took time from more important matters to respond to my queries; I give the names of contact people in brackets. I am happy to acknowledge the creative work on these ads; I have reproduced credits as they were given to me, and I apologise if this means I miss acknowledging some individual contributions.

My thanks to:

David Higham Associates Ltd. [Kate Lyall Grant] for permission to quote from Dorothy L. Sayers, *Murder Must Advertise*, published by Hodder and Stoughton.

Societé des Produits Nestlé SA [D. G. Minto, Nestlé UK Ltd]. Aero advertising used by kind permission of Societé des Produits Nestlé SA, Trademark Owners.

Lever Brothers, for permission to reproduce advertisements for Persil produced by J. Walter Thompson Company Ltd. [Annie Parkinson]; 'Restore Your Clothes to their Former Glory', Jono Wardle (Art Director), Fiona O'Brien (Copywriter); and 'Persil Supports Trees,' Jono Wardle (Art Director), Paul Chown (Copywriter), and Robert Dowling (Photographer). The 1891, 1927 and 1947 ads for Lever Brothers products were reproduced from W. J. Reader, *Fifty Years of Unilever* (London, Heinemann, 1980).

Pilkington Glass Ltd. [Ray Jennings], for permission to reproduce a slogan from an advertisement written by The Progress Agency.

J. W. Spear & Sons plc [Candida Brown] for permission to use the brand name Scrabble®, which is a registered trademark of J. W. Spear & Sons plc in the UK, and **Hasbro (Inc.)** [Dawn Pawlitschek], owner of the Scrabble® trademark in the US.

Fuji Photo Film (UK) Ltd., for permission to reproduce 'You can Fudgi It or You Can Fuji It,' produced by Kelly Weedon Shute Partnership [Steve Smith], Gary Willis (senior art director) and Martin Hodges (Senior Copywriter).

Procter and Gamble Ltd. [L. J. Gibson], for permission to quote a television advertisement for Ariel.

PepsiCo, Inc. [Carol Cavallerano], for permission to use the slogan 'Get that Pepsi Feeling.' PEPSI and 'Get that Pepsi Feeling' are registered trademarks of PepsiCo, Inc. Purchase, NY, USA.

Kimberly-Clark Ltd. [John Waters], for permission to quote a Kleenex® advertisement. Copyright 1990 Kimberly-Clark Ltd. All Rights Reserved.

Nike (UK) Ltd. [Tony Hill], for permission to reproduce 'Baby', produced by Bartle Bogle Hegarty.

Sony Consumer Products UK [Michelle Whing], for permission to reproduce 'First shoot your dog, then freeze it.'

Imperial Tobacco Ltd. [P. M. Manzi], for permission to reproduce two advertisements for Regal cigarettes, both produced by Lowe Howard Spink, and for further information about the campaign.

McDonald's Corporation [Rhonda Urbik] for permission to quote a McDonald's slogan.

Highland Spring Ltd., [Jane Harkness] for permission to reproduce a press ad.

The Employment Department [Eric Davies], for permission to reproduce 'Just the Job', produced by DMB&B.

National & Provincial Building Society [Peter Shackleton], for permission to quote from an N&P television commercial.

Procter and Gamble (Health and Beauty Care) Ltd., for permission to quote from a television commercial produced by Saatchi and Saatchi. HEAD & SHOULDERS is a registered trademark of Procter and Gamble.

Carter Wallace, for permission to reproduce the ad for First Response, 'You heard it first from us', produced by Bainsfair Sharkey Trott, Ltd. [Simon Hunter], Paul Leeves (Creative Director), Nick O'Brien-Tear (Copywriter), Lee Goulding (Art Director), Branka Jukic (Photographer).

Berry Bros. and Rudd, Ltd. [S. A. Hazlehurst], for permission to quote from an advertisement for Cutty Sark.

Whitbread plc, for permission to reproduce a Boddington's press ad, produced by

Bartle Bogle Hegarty Ltd. [Erica Clark], Mike Wells and Tom Hudson (creative team); reproduced by kind permission of the photographer, Tif Hunter.

Watts Lord Ltd. [Ken Buckfield], for permission to reproduce 'Tina Shanur', a press ad for Trio-Kenwood (UK) Ltd., produced by Ian Cater (Art Director), Nick Swallow (Copywriter), Lawrence Everard (Typographer), and David Perry (Photographer).

Bombay Spirits Company Ltd. [Benedict Ely, of Dallas Brett, Solicitors and Attorneys], for permission to reproduce 'Pour something priceless', produced by TBWA.

Moschino [Gai Pearl Marshall] for permission to reproduce a print advertisement created by Moschino.

Volvo Car UK Ltd., [Graham Storey, Product Manager] for permission to reproduce 'Now this Volvo carries just as much as a Granada Estate', produced by Abbott Mead Vickers BBDO Ltd., Will Barnett (Copywriter) and Tony McTear (Copywriter).

The Spastics Society [James Rye] for permission to reproduce 'One has Cerebral Palsy. The other has full human rights', produced by DMB&B.

V. A. G. (United Kingdom) Ltd.[Nigel Brotherton] for permission to reproduce 'No Smoking', produced by BMP DDB Needham Worldwide Ltd. [Jorian Murray, Account Director], Jeremy Craigen (Writer), Jeremy Carr (Art Director), Mike Parsons (Photographer), Kevin Clarke (Typographer).

Lancashire County Council [Graham Pinfield] for permission to reproduce the leaflet 'Go green for good', produced by the Lancashire Environment Forum.

British Sugar plc [Geoff Lancaster] and **Tate and Lyle plc** for permission to reproduce 'If you thought sugar was made in manufacturing plants', produced by Collett, Dickenson, Pearce and Partners Ltd., Advertising.

The Co-operative Bank [Anne Manock], for permission to reproduce 'Wilkinson's Trees', produced by Butterfield, Day, Devito, Hockney Ltd..

The Terrence Higgins Trust [Ewan Armstrong], for permission to reproduce 'Safer sex, keep it up', which was originally produced by the Amsterdam Health Education Centre (buro gvo), with financial support from the Dutch Ministry of Welfare, Public Health and Cultural Affairs. The copyright of the image remains with the photographer, Martien Sleutjes, and the concept came from Menne Vellinga GVN.

Health Education Authority [Stephen Thorogood], for permission to reproduce 'They don't have safer sex just because it's safer', with kind permission of the photographer, Jean Baptiste Mondino.

London Lighthouse [Tara Treacy], for permission to reproduce 'How I Survived AIDS', produced by TBWA Holmes Knight Ritchie, David Woods (Copywriter), Peter Harle (Art Director) and Susanna Hailstone (Account Director).

Procter & Gamble [Dianna S. Icenhower] for permission to quote the trademarks 'it floats' and '99 44/100 percent pure'.

Mars Confectionery [Una Brown], for permission to quote the Mars® slogan. Mars® is a registered trademark symbol.

Coca-Cola Great Britain and Ireland [Kate Wilson] for permission to quote the brand names 'Coca-Cola' and 'diet Coke'.

Thomson Tour Operations Ltd. [Katy Vize], for permission to quote their advertising line.

Carlsberg-Tetley Brewing Ltd. [Janine Chandler], for permission to quote the slogan of Castlemaine XXXX.

Jersey Tourism [Douglas Creedon], for permission to quote copy from their 1991 ad campaign.

Van den Bergh Foods Ltd. [Anne Winterbone], for permission to quote from a television advertisement for Stork.

Nestlé UK Ltd. [M. Casey], copyright owner of the Nescafe Gold Blend television advertisement, for permission to quote. The ad was produced by McCann Erickson.

British Airways plc [Paul H. Jarvis], for permission to quote from a television ad. The slogan 'The World's Favourite Airline' is a protected trademark in certain countries.

Clarins Paris (Division Internationale) [Christian Courtin-Clarins], for permission to quote an advertisements for Clarins Ltd.

Index